Male and Female in the Epic of Gilgamesh

Male and Female in the Epic of Gilgamesh

Encounters, Literary History, and Interpretation

Tzvi Abusch

Winona Lake, Indiana
EISENBRAUNS
2015

www.eisenbrauns.com

Library of Congress Cataloging-in-Publication Data

Abusch, Tzvi.
Male and female in the epic of Gilgamesh : Encounters, literary history, and interpretation / Tzvi Abusch.
pages cm
Includes bibliographical references.
ISBN 978-1-57506-349-2 (pbk. : alk. paper)
1. Gilgamesh. 2. Epic poetry, Assyro-Babylonian—History and criticism. 3. Man-woman relationships in literature. I. Title.
PJ3771.G6A24 2015
892′.1—dc23

2014042513

The paper used in this publication meets the minimum requirements of the American National Standard for Information Sciences—Permanence of Paper for Printed Library Materials, ANSI Z39.48-1984. ♾™

For Martha, with love

Contents

Preface ix

Introduction 1

Sources 10

1. Ishtar's Proposal and Gilgamesh's Refusal: An Interpretation of *The Gilgamesh Epic*, Tablet VI, Lines 1–79 11

2. Gilgamesh's Request and Siduri's Denial, Part I: The Meaning of the Dialogue and Its Implications for the History of the Epic 58

3. Gilgamesh's Request and Siduri's Denial, Part II: An Analysis and Interpretation of an Old Babylonian Fragment about Mourning and Celebration 89

4. Mourning the Death of a Friend: Some Assyriological Notes 108

5. The *Epic of Gilgamesh* and the Homeric Epics 119

6. The Development and Meaning of the *Epic of Gilgamesh*: An Interpretive Essay 127

7. The Courtesan, the Wild Man, and the Hunter: Studies in the Literary History of the *Epic of Gilgamesh* 144

8. Hunting in the *Epic of Gilgamesh*: Speculations on the Education of a Prince 166

9. The Tale of the Wild Man and the Courtesan in India and Mesopotamia: The Seductions of Ṛśyaśṛṅga in the *Mahābhārata* and Enkidu in the *Epic of Gilgamesh* (coauthored with Emily West). 177

Abbreviations 219

Bibliography 221

Index of Citations 233

Preface

This book brings together my several studies of the *Epic of Gilgamesh* (including an article written jointly with Emily West) because I felt that as a body they make a contribution to the study of the epic. The chapters were written over a period of years and are presented here in the order in which they were published. However, for an overview, the reader may wish to begin with chapter 6, "The Development and Meaning of the Epic of Gilgamesh: An Interpretive Essay."

I have reissued these studies in their original published form, and inevitably there is some overlap and repetition between chapters. For this volume, I have corrected typographical errors, clarified the occasional phrase, provided cross-references between chapters, and introduced a uniform mode of bibliographical citation throughout. Also, I have changed references to the line numbers of the *Epic of Gilgamesh* to those of A. R. George's edition when they differed, though I have kept column numbers when these were cited in my original publication.

This volume comes at the urging of Jim Eisenbraun, and I thank him for his encouragement. I am grateful to Jim and his staff for the care with which they prepared the volume. I also thank the original publishers or editors for permission to reprint my studies here. I greatly appreciate Gene McGarry's valuable assistance; he unified bibliographical citations, prepared the general bibliography and index, and suggested a number of corrections. I thank my student Lenin Prado for reading through the volume in search of errors.

Introduction

The *Epic of Gilgamesh* is an ancient Mesopotamian account of the deeds and struggles of Gilgamesh, a king of the city-state Uruk in the land of Sumer. Its study draws us into an orbit that is engaging and thrilling, for it is a literary work of fantasy and history that centers on some of the very existential issues with which we ourselves grapple. We experience the excitement of trying to penetrate the mind-set of another civilization, an ancient one—in this instance, a civilization that gave rise to our own.

The purpose of this introduction is to orient the reader both to the epic and to my approach to it. The studies in this volume are not of a piece, except of course that they are written by one scholar and deal with one text. I did not take up these studies with an agenda in mind other than to understand the individual episodes that interested me at the moment of study and to determine general issues of literary history and meaning. I first took up episodes that deal primarily with male-female relations; only later did I take up the larger questions of prehistory, changes in the meaning of the epic as it evolved, and its influence on later works. Accordingly, this work is not exhaustive in any way. Many other episodes could be studied, other aspects or levels examined, and other methods employed.

Many approaches to the study of Gilgamesh may be cited (historical, literary, psychological, etc.). But rather than present a broad sweep of Gilgamesh research, I will comment simply upon approaches of philologically based scholars. Of these, most presentations of the epic are retellings of the story. But there are also allegorical interpretations that treat the text not as a story of an individual but as if it were primarily a representation of cosmological/theological truths in a symbolic mode reminiscent of esotericism, Gnosticism, and/or mysticism.[1] Between these two modes are situated various studies that try to understand the meaning of the text on its own terms. It is in this middle position that I imagine myself. For I try to treat the text as a literary work that presents with depth and sensitivity the story of an individual whose life is rooted

1. See, e.g., M.-A. Ataç, "'Angelology' in *The Epic of Gilgamesh*," *Journal of Ancient Near Eastern Religions* 4 (2004) 3–27; S. Parpola, "The Assyrian Tree of Life: Tracing the Origins of Jewish Monotheism and Greek Philosophy," *JNES* 52 (1993) 161–208, esp. 192–95.

in a sphere of Mesopotamian culture and whose story explores several of its cultural and existential dimensions. If I were to characterize this approach, I would say that it is rooted in a close reading of the text and represents an exegesis that makes use of the tools of literary, structural, and critical analysis[2] but is attuned primarily to personal and psychological levels of the narration, while trying to remain rooted in the cultural ambience of its composer. I should probably note here that I count myself among those who "value coherence so highly that they are willing to tolerate more disparity between fact and hypothesis than others, for whom such discrepancies loom so large that they cannot share the pleasure that such 'explanations' might afford."[3]

The Text

The epic was composed in Akkadian, the main Semitic language of ancient Mesopotamia.[4] It is preserved on tablets written in the cuneiform system of writing. In its final and longest form, the text probably contained about 3,500 lines and was organized and set out in twelve tablets. This twelve-tablet version is referred to as the Standard Babylonian (SB)

2. Exegesis and interpretation, on the one hand, and critical textual and/or literary analysis and reconstruction, on the other, remain in my opinion crucial for the understanding of literary texts. Even more than the study of its individual words, the goal of a close reading of a text is the understanding of its structure, logic, and underlying meaning and of the intent and originality of its composer. It may well be true that some of our texts are rooted in oral performance and took form in an oral tradition, but we do not yet understand the oral milieu that might have shaped some of the early Akkadian literary texts, nor do we know the characteristics of the Akkadian oral formulary or the distinction between it and its mimicking in script in early written poetry (cf. W. J. Ong, *Orality and Literacy: The Technologizing of the Word* [London: Methuen, 1982; repr., London: Routledge, 2002] 26). Therefore, close reading, where the meaning of every word counts, should not be set aside on the grounds that literary texts might have been composed orally—composed, that is, by means of formulas, traditional phrases, and fixed units—rather than in writing. Thus, for heuristic purposes, if for no other reason, we should view most of our literary texts as having been composed by/in a system of written literature. I might add here that, given how little we know of Akkadian oral literature, I do not understand how at one and the same time one can regard an interpretation of the Gilgamesh text that is rooted in close and nuanced reading as speculative but claim an oral origin for the text without the existence of specific evidence.

3. R. Ackerman, *The Myth and Ritual School: J. G. Frazer and the Cambridge Ritualists* (London: Routledge, 2002) 170. I should add here my belief that "the true test of an hypothesis, if it cannot be shown to conflict with known truths, is the number of facts that it correlates and explains" (F. M. Cornford, *The Origin of Attic Comedy* [London: Arnold, 1914] 220; quoted by Ackerman, *Myth and Ritual School*, 144–45).

4. For a comprehensive edition of the epic, see A. R. George, *The Babylonian Gilgamesh Epic: Introduction, Critical Edition, and Cuneiform Texts* (2 vols.; Oxford: Oxford University Press, 2003).

version. The text of this version is known to us from the libraries of the first millennium B.C.E. The fullest text comes from the libraries of Nineveh. This is not surprising, for in Nineveh, Assurbanipal, the great Assyrian emperor of the seventh century, added to collections started by Sennacherib and Esarhaddon and created the first world-class library. Nineveh was among the first major excavated sites in Mesopotamia; excavations took place there starting in the 1840s. Using tablets from Nineveh, scholars began reconstructing the *Epic of Gilgamesh* already in 1870, and one recalls with both awe and amusement the story of George Smith's discovery of the Flood tablet. Though Nineveh provides the lion's share, many important first-millennium texts were also found in the libraries of Assur, Nimrud, and Sultantepe in the north, and Babylon, Sippar, Ur, and Uruk in the south.

The Epic:
The Story Contained in the Standard Babylonian Version

In gross terms, the story line of the final twelve-tablet version is as follows: Tablet I is introduced by a prologue and paean to Gilgamesh, king of Uruk. But the king exhausts his subjects by his unceasing demands on them to participate in his constant round of activities. The people complain to the gods, who realize that Gilgamesh's enormous energy must find a different channel. To relieve the people, the gods create Enkidu, a wild man whose strength is equal to that of the king, to serve as a companion who can be Gilgamesh's equal and partner in the various activities that he is driven to undertake. Enkidu is humanized by a prostitute, who then acculturates him and leads him to Uruk. There, Enkidu prevents Gilgamesh from participating in a wedding ritual. Gilgamesh and Enkidu do battle and, as a result, become fast friends.

In search of adventure and fame, Gilgamesh proposes, and the two friends undertake, a dangerous expedition against Huwawa, the powerful monster appointed by Enlil, leader of the pantheon, to guard the Cedar Forest. They reach the Cedar Forest, kill Huwawa, and return victoriously to Uruk. Ishtar, the goddess of Uruk, then proposes to Gilgamesh, who, however, spurns her proposal in insulting terms. Enraged, the goddess unleashes the great Bull of Heaven against Gilgamesh, but Gilgamesh and Enkidu slay the Bull and celebrate their victory.

The gods now decide that Enkidu must bear the punishment for the friends' acts of hubris. Enkidu dies, having first cursed those whom he held responsible for his death, but in the end he accepts his lot. Gilgamesh buries Enkidu but cannot accept the death of his companion. He is devastated by Enkidu's death, both because of the grievous loss of his dearest friend and because he now fears his own death mightily. He leaves Uruk and travels the world in search of immortality. He flees reality and enters into what might almost be called a psychotic state. First, he roams the steppe, where he strips off culture and acts as if he himself were a wild man. Then, he leaves the natural world, thereby attempting to strip off his own humanity. He traverses a world inhabited by animalistic, divine, and dead creatures.

In the twelve-tablet version, Gilgamesh's quest is defined as a search for the secret of immortality held by Utnapishtim, the hero who survived the Flood and was granted immortality by the gods. After a number of adventures, Gilgamesh reaches Utnapishtim. The latter disabuses him of his illusion, demonstrating by story (the account of the Flood) and by action (a test of Gilgamesh's ability to remain awake) that immortality is no longer attainable, even by Gilgamesh. The lesson is forced on him but is not yet internalized. He would have returned home in a depressed state but for the subsequent loss of the plant of youth, which was given to him as a farewell gift. On the way back to Uruk, Gilgamesh does something very human: he sets down the plant in order to bathe; but as he bathes, a snake steals off with the plant (thus explaining the snake's ability to slough off its old skin). Gilgamesh now realizes that his suffering and toil have resulted in nothing other than a benefaction for the snake; he laughs and sees himself for what he is—a human being. Tablet XI ends with Gilgamesh's return to Uruk, whereupon he signals his acceptance of reality by pointing out to the boatman the architectural wonders of the city that he had built.

Tablet XII contains the end of a different account of Enkidu's death. On an errand for Gilgamesh, Enkidu descends into the netherworld. He is seized by the netherworld and cannot escape death; he returns only as a shade in order to describe to Gilgamesh the state of the dead.

The Epic: A Historical Sketch

The Pre-epic Tradition

The twelve-tablet version is known to us primarily from tablets written in the first millennium, but the work is much older. The Gilgamesh tradition began sometime during the third millennium, and Sumerian tales about Gilgamesh were composed during the Neo-Sumerian renaissance of the Third Dynasty of Ur at the turn of the third millennium; the earliest version of the Akkadian epic itself first took form during the Old Babylonian period. By the first millennium, the epic had already undergone many changes and had assumed a number of different textual forms in the course of its development. Let us look back to the beginning of the tradition and sketch the emergence of the tradition and the growth of the various literary forms.

The Gilgamesh tradition seems to have originated in the Early Dynastic II period (ca. 2700 B.C.E.); the Akkadian epic and the various Sumerian tales are set in that time. To be sure, we possess no contemporary inscriptions that speak of Gilgamesh, and many of the stories are "fiction," but there are indications that Gilgamesh may well have been a king of Uruk in the aforementioned period and that some of the traditions preserved in later literary works go back to that period and to his person. But Gilgamesh was also a god. It is usually assumed that Gilgamesh the king was deified soon after his death because of his magical and martial qualities in life.[5] In any case, soon after his putative rule, we find indications that Gilgamesh was treated as a god. He is mentioned as a god in early administrative texts. Already in a literary work treating the death of Ur-Nammu, the founder of the Third Dynasty of Ur, Gilgamesh appears as an officer of the netherworld. He retained that role down to the first millennium when he is invoked as a divine administrator of the netherworld in incantations dealing with ghosts and witches.

The Sumerian tales of Gilgamesh probably drew upon oral traditions, but it seems to have been his role as the ancestor and brother of the king during the Ur III period that led court poets to compose and/or set down in writing the various Sumerian epic tales about Gilgamesh. The main tales are the following: *Gilgamesh and Agga*; *Gilgamesh and Huwawa*; *Gilgamesh, Inanna, and the Bull of Heaven*; *Gilgamesh, Enkidu, and the Netherworld*; and *The Death of Gilgamesh*. These texts entered the scribal curriculum. Although there are a few earlier attestations, the tales are known to us in the main from later Old Babylonian copies and were found in school buildings from around 1700 B.C.E.

These Sumerian works center on the themes of either martial prowess or death, or both. As Thorkild Jacobsen has noted, the Sumerian

5. One should not dismiss out of hand, however, the possibility that Gilgamesh, like Tammuz, might originally have been a god. (But see recently J. Klein, "The Assumed Human Origin of Divine Dumuzi: A Reconsideration," in *Language in the Ancient Near East*, vol. 1 of *Proceedings of the 53e Rencontre Assyriologique Internationale* [ed. L. Kogan et al.; Winona Lake, IN: Eisenbrauns, 2010], part 2, 1121–34; Klein reiterates and renews the argument for the human origin of Tammuz.)

tales show diametrically opposed attitudes toward death. In some, death is courted; in others it is the great enemy. "These contradictory attitudes united in the person of Gilgamesh prefigure, as it were, what was to become the theme of the later epic: the change from an earlier disdain for death to the obsessive fear of it which drives Gilgamesh on his quest after Enkidu's death."[6]

The Akkadian Epic of Gilgamesh

The Sumerian tales were individual stories and did not necessarily even form a cycle. But around 1700 B.C.E., a Babylonian author created a unified epic about the hero Gilgamesh. We call this the Old Babylonian (OB) version. The OB version has been preserved in two types of texts: student copies or exercises as well as good exemplars.

Although I once contemplated the possibility that the present epic was "the result not of a linear development but rather of the conflation of two independent parallel versions,"[7] I now think that it is far more likely that the text was composed by means of a supplementary method. But the composer of the original epic did not simply repeat and attach one episode to another; rather, he drew on an existing literary pattern—one that originally had little to do with Gilgamesh—and laid out the text in which it was expressed as the basis or matrix of his new epic. The kernel of the text was the expedition against Huwawa.[8] The composer then added several episodes to this core; for these he drew on some of the other Sumerian Gilgamesh tales as well as on folkloristic and mytho-

---

6. T. Jacobsen, *Treasures of Darkness: A History of Mesopotamian Religion* (New Haven, CT: Yale University Press, 1976) 213.

7. T. Abusch, "The Courtesan, the Wild Man, and the Hunter: Studies in the Literary History of the *Epic of Gilgamesh*," in *"An Experienced Scribe Who Neglects Nothing": Ancient Near Eastern Studies in Honor of Jacob Klein* (ed. Y. Sefati et al.; Bethesda, MD: CDL, 2005) 430 [here, p. 161]. For a discussion of the possibility of parallel versions, see ibid., 430–33 [here, pp. 161–64]; as noted above, I no longer think that this hypothesis is correct, but I would not alter my interpretation of the Enkidu-courtesan episode presented in the earlier part of the essay (pp. 413–29 [here, pp. 144–61]).

8. See now D. E. Fleming and S. J. Milstein, *The Buried Foundation of the Gilgamesh Epic: The Akkadian Huwawa Narrative* (CM 39; Leiden: Brill, 2010). I had earlier realized that the Huwawa episode was central to the origin of the epic because of its emphasis on hunting (see my "Hunting in the *Epic of Gilgamesh*: Speculations on the Education of a Prince," in *Treasures on Camels' Humps: Historical and Literary Studies from the Ancient Near East Presented to Israel Ephʿal* [ed. M. Cogan and D. Kahn; Jerusalem: Magnes, 2008] 11–20 [here, pp. 166–76) and even sensed some of the inner tensions in the work (see Abusch, "Courtesan," 430–33 [here, pp. 161–64), but I failed to see the full implications of these insights or to follow them up before the important discoveries made by Fleming and Milstein.

logical themes that were independent of the Gilgamesh tradition. But in addition to drawing on this older material, the composer reconfigured some of it and added much that was new.

In the OB version, the following tale is told: Gilgamesh is a powerful king of Uruk. Enkidu is created by the gods so that Gilgamesh may have a companion who is his equal. Enkidu is seduced and humanized by a prostitute, who then leads him to Uruk, where he encounters Gilgamesh. They forge a deep friendship. They undertake an expedition to the Cedar Forest, where they defeat and kill Huwawa. Enkidu is sentenced to death by the gods as a punishment for that killing. Gilgamesh is devastated by his loss and flees the city for the wild. In the course of his wanderings, he finally encounters Siduri, a divine tavernkeeper at the edge of the world. She tells him that he cannot attain immortality and advises him to resume normal life. In its early form, this Gilgamesh tale, in my judgment, did not include the Utnapishtim episode. Rather, Siduri was his final stop prior to returning to Uruk. But already, the OB tale hints at the presence of an embryonic form of the Utnapishtim episode.[9]

As can readily be seen from this retelling, the composer redesigned and developed the character and story of Enkidu (who was now Gilgamesh's dear friend and not the usual servant of the Sumerian tales),[10] developed the story of Enkidu's death in the context of this new tale, and presented Gilgamesh's reaction, flight, and wandering as part of a response to Enkidu's death that is far more anguished than his response in the Sumerian tale. It is these changes that characterize the new work.

9. Note that Gilgamesh's encounter with the Flood hero is already mentioned in the Sumerian tale *The Death of Gilgamesh* (lines 57 and 61 // 148 and 152); for text and translations, see A. Cavigneaux and F. N. H. Al-Rawi, *Gilgameš et la mort: Textes de Tell Haddad VI* (CM 19; Groningen: Styx, 2000) 15, 27, 56; and N. Veldhuis, "The Solution of the Dream: A New Interpretation of Bilgames' Death," *JCS* 53 (2001) 141, 143. But the occurrence of the motif in a Sumerian text does not vouch for its antiquity or for its occurrence in the earliest versions of the OB Akkadian Gilgamesh epic. While the date of composition of *The Death of Gilgamesh* is not certain, it is likely that the present version was a product of the Old Babylonian period; it is thus possible that *The Death of Gilgamesh* was even contemporaneous with the Akkadian Old Babylonian Gilgamesh epic (cf. W. Sallaberger, *Das Gilgamesch-Epos: Mythos, Werk und Tradition* [Munich: Beck, 2008] 49 and 69). The relationship of the Akkadian Gilgamesh epic and *The Death of Gilgamesh* might be comparable with that of the epic and *Gilgamesh and Huwawa A* (see Abusch, "Hunting," 11–20 [here, pp. 166–176]) and similar to that of *The Sumerian Flood Story* and *Atrahasis*.

10. But note that Gilgamesh occasionally refers to Enkidu as his friend in the Sumerian tale *Gilgamesh, Enkidu, and the Netherworld* (cf. J. H. Tigay, *The Evolution of the Gilgamesh Epic* [Philadelphia: University of Pennsylvania Press, 1982] 29 and n. 27).

The epic now comprises two different stories or *Bildungsromane* about the two main characters: a minor one about Enkidu and a major one about Gilgamesh.

The composer's act of genius was in creating a new and brilliant epic that was drawn together and given unity by a new focus on the friendship of Gilgamesh and Enkidu and on Gilgamesh's reaction to the death of Enkidu. Here, the two powerful emotions of loss and fear—that is, the loss of a friend and the fear of one's own death—take over and become the central themes of the work. It is deeply moving to hear Gilgamesh's words even today:

> [My friend, whom I love dearly,]
> Who with me underwent all hardships,
> Enkidu, whom I love dearly,
> Who with me underwent all hardships,
> Has gone to the fate of mankind.
> Day and night I wept over him,
> I would not give him up for burial—
> (saying) "My friend perhaps will rise up to me at my cry!"—
> Seven days and seven nights
> Until a maggot dropped out at me from his nose.
> Since his death, I have not found life.
> I keep roaming like a trapper in the open country.
> Now, alewife, that I have seen your face,
> The death that I constantly fear may I not see.
>
> (OB Sippar Tablet, ii 1′–13′)

The extant OB version of the *Epic of Gilgamesh* is among the earliest, although perhaps the most immediately felt and compelling, versions of the Akkadian epic. Subsequent to the OB period, the epic circulated throughout the ancient Near East. Second-millennium copies have been found, for example, at such Mesopotamian sites as Nippur and Ur as well as at Emar and Ugarit in Syria, Megiddo in Israel, and Bogazkoy in Turkey. As mentioned earlier, first-millennium copies of the epic were found in most of the major Mesopotamian cities.

Not suprisingly, the work underwent many changes and developments. The Babylonian tradition itself changed and evolved during the course of the second and early first millennium. A number of new recensions and versions took form. The eleven-tablet version, with an expanded prologue, probably assumed its present form during the latter part of the second millennium. Following the development of this version, the fuller though less coherent twelve-tablet version was created in the first millennium by the addition of a twelfth tablet to the eleven-tablet version. This last tablet is a translation of the second half of the Sumerian tale *Gilgamesh, Enkidu, and the Netherworld.* It tells how Enkidu descends to the netherworld in search of Gilgamesh's *pukku* and *mekku* but is seized by the netherworld and loses his life. Enkidu then returns to Gilgamesh in the form of a shade and describes the fate of the various classes of inhabitants of the netherworld. Although the twelfth tablet may have been added in a mechanical fashion, the twelve-tablet version is nonetheless meaningful, for this latest version has acquired a new thematic coherence by means of the addition.[11]

But not only did a number of new versions take form in Akkadian, versions were created as well in other languages. Thus, for example, Hurrian and Hittite versions were created during the second millennium. But the text extended its reach even outside the cuneiform world. It influenced other contemporary cultures, as well as later ones such as Israel, Greece, and even India.

11. See my "Ishtar's Proposal and Gilgamesh's Refusal: An Interpretation of *The Gilgamesh Epic*, Tablet 6, Lines 1–79," *History of Religions* 26 (1986) 179–87 [here, pp. 48–57]; and "The Development and Meaning of the *Epic of Gilgamesh*: An Interpretive Essay," *JAOS* 121 (2001) 620–21 [here, pp. 139–42]; cf. B. Sommer, "Reflecting on Moses: The Redaction of Numbers 11," *JBL* 118 (1999) 602 and n. 2.

Sources of Essays

Chapter 1: reprinted from *History of Religions* 26, no. 2 (1986) 143–87.

Chapter 2: reprinted from *The Tablet and the Scroll: Near Eastern Studies in Honor of William H. Hallo* (ed. Mark E. Cohen, D. Snell, and David Weisberg; Bethesda, MD: CDL, 1993) 1–14.

Chapter 3: reprinted from *Comparative Studies in Honor of Yohanan Muffs* = *Journal of the Ancient Near Eastern Society of Columbia University* 22 (1993) 3–17.

Chapter 4: reprinted from *The Frank Talmage Memorial Volume, Part I* (ed. Barry Walfish; Haifa: University of Haifa Press, 1993) 53–62.

Chapter 5: reprinted from *Mythology and Mythologies: Methodological Approaches to Intercultural Influences. Proceedings of the Second Annual Symposium of the Assyrian and Babylonian Intellectual Heritage Project Held in Paris, France, October 4–7, 1999* (ed. Robert M. Whiting; Melammu Symposia 2; Helsinki: Neo-Assyrian Text Corpus Project, 2001) 1–6.

Chapter 6: reprinted from *Journal of the American Oriental Society* 121, no. 4 (2001) 614–22.

Chapter 7: reprinted from *An Experienced Scribe Who Neglects Nothing: Ancient Near Eastern Studies in Honor of Jacob Klein* (ed. Y. Sefati et al.; Bethesda, MD: CDL, 2005) 413–33.

Chapter 8: reprinted from *Treasures on Camels' Humps: Historical and Literary Studies from the Ancient Near East Presented to Israel Ephʿal* (ed. M. Cogan and D. Kahn; Jerusalem: Magnes, 2008) 11–20.

Chapter 9: reprinted from *The Ancient World in an Age of Globalization* (Melammu Symposia 6; ed. M. J. Geller; Berlin: Max-Planck-Gesellschaft zur Förderung der Wissenschaften, 2014) 69–109.

Ishtar's Proposal and Gilgamesh's Refusal

An Interpretation of The Gilgamesh Epic, *Tablet VI, Lines 1–79*

—For Thorkild Jacobsen, beloved teacher and friend

Since its rediscovery in the nineteenth century, the Babylonian *Epic of Gilgamesh* has again captured the imagination of the literate public. The epic combines the power and tragedy of the *Iliad* with the wanderings and marvels of the *Odyssey*. The epic has reentered the mainstream of Western culture and now takes its place beside Homer and the books of Judges and Samuel. I can hardly do better than quote the words of a reviewer in a recent issue of the *New York Times Book Review*: "The Gilgamesh epic is a powerful tale in almost any telling. Rilke once called it the greatest thing one could experience, and many consider it the supreme literary achievement of the ancient world before Homer. It has something of the qualities Henry Moore once said he admired in Mesopotamian art—bigness and simplicity without decorative trimming. It is about nature and culture, the value of human achievements and their limitations, friendship and love, separation and sorrow, life and death."[1]

In the epic, man is addressed both as an individual and as a social being. The formulation is writ large, and the characters, feelings, and actions are exaggerated, for Gilgamesh is no mere man—he is Hero, King, God. The monumental form is an advantage, for by projecting human questions onto a colossus, the author is able to explore the human predicament more deeply and to formulate his answers with greater boldness and clarity. And indeed, the work does explore many issues; it provides

---

The substance of this paper was read before the 193rd meeting of the American Oriental Society, Baltimore, March 1983. I have enjoyed conversations with several friends here in Boston, notably Thorkild Jacobsen, William Moran, Piotr Steinkeller, and Irene Winter, about my interpretation of the text. I recall gratefully also the various scholars who reacted with questions and observations during the discussion following the presentation of my paper to the AOS. I should like to express my gratitude to Peter Stark for his generous assistance and to thank Kathryn Kravitz for her help.

1. W. L. Moran, "Ut-napishtim Revisited," *New York Times Book Review* (November 11, 1984) 14.

a Mesopotamian formulation of human predicaments and options. The work examines the possibility of life in nature; yet, while it is not blind to the costs of civilization, it finally comes down in favor of urban life. It allows for the possibility of natural disorder but then affirms the political restructuring of the cosmos. But most of all, the work grapples with issues of an existential nature. Gilgamesh must learn to live. He must find ways to express his tremendous personal energy but still act in a manner that accords with the limits and responsibilities imposed upon him by his society and universe. Yet in the final analysis, he must also come to terms with his own nature and learn to die, for Gilgamesh is both a man and a god, and as both he will experience loss and will die.

The *Epic of Gilgamesh* (GE) gives voice to many of our concerns and fantasies. The depth and immediacy of its effect are remarkable, even startling. And its impact grows stronger with each reading. Occasionally, though, familiarity has a lulling effect, and we come to accept Gilgamesh's behavior without really understanding why he acts as he does: why he chooses a certain course of action and then performs it in a particular manner. We acquiesce until our attention is arrested by something that interests us or perplexes us. Some years ago I noted that GE Tablet VI, line 16 was similar to a line in an incantation that I was then reconstructing; this observation suggested an explanation for some of Gilgamesh's actions in Tablet VI and set me thinking about the first part of the tablet. The main purpose of this paper, then, is to present a new reading of Ishtar's proposal and Gilgamesh's response in GE Tablet VI, lines 1–79.[2] I hope thereby to contribute to a better understanding of the episode as well as to a fuller appreciation of the character of the goddess and of Gilgamesh. In addition, I shall remark on one or two

2. For exemplars and composites of our text, see P. Haupt, *Das babylonische Nimrodepos* (Assyriologische Bibliothek 3; Leipzig: J. C. Hinrichs, 1884–91) 29ff.; R. Campbell Thompson, *The Epic of Gilgamesh* (Oxford: Clarendon Press, 1930) 38–39 and pls. 20ff.; R. Frankena, "Nouveaux fragments de la sixième tablette de l'épopée de Gilgameš," in *Gilgameš et sa légende* (ed. P. Garelli; Paris: C. Klincksieck, 1960) 113ff. For a partial layout, cf. K. Hecker, *Untersuchungen zur akkadischen Epik* (AOAT, Sonderreihe 8; Kevelaer: Butzon und Bercker; Neukirchen-Vluyn: Neukirchener Verlag, 1974) 181–83. There are many translations; I have repeatedly consulted E. A. Speiser, *ANET*, 83–84; R. Labat et al., *Les religions du Proche-Orient asiatique: Textes babyloniens, ougaritiques, hittites* (Paris: Fayard-Denoël, 1970) 181ff.; A. Schott and W. von Soden, *Das Gilgamesch Epos* (Stuttgart: Reclam, 1970) 50ff. There are many retellings of our episode; one of the most interesting and sensitive readings is T. Jacobsen, *The Treasures of Darkness* (New Haven, CT: Yale University Press, 1976) 201, 218–19. My reading differs from Jacobsen's, and it may well be that our interpretations are mutually exclusive. Still, I should like to think that they may be complementary, each seeing the scene from a different perspective and playing it out on a different plane.

points in the epic that seem to invite comment in light of the proposed interpretation: the place of the episode in the epic and the reason for the addition of Tablet XII.[3]

I

Although the episode is well known, it will facilitate our discussion if we first set out the verbal interchange between Ishtar and Gilgamesh in summary form. King Gilgamesh dons his royal raiment (lines 1–5). Spying the king, the goddess Ishtar is struck by his attractiveness and grows desirous of him (line 6). She proposes to him (lines 7–21): pronouncing a marriage formula of sorts, she asks him to bestow upon her his fruit. In return she offers him a marvelous chariot drawn by powerful steeds, the fragrance of cedar upon his entrance into their new home, the obeisance there of rulers, their delivery to him of tribute of the earth, and the enhancement of the numbers and powers of his animals. In response, Gilgamesh speaks up (lines 22–23) and delivers a long speech (lines 24–79) in which he spurns Ishtar's offer. The speech divides neatly into three sections: (1) lines 24–32, (2) lines 33–41,[4] (3) lines 42–79.

3. Elsewhere I hope to discuss the connections and common mythological background of such myths as the *Epic of Gilgamesh* (GE), Tablet VI; the *Descent of Inanna/Ishtar*, and *Nergal and Ereshkigal*.

4. E. A. Speiser began his study of GE Tablet VI, line 40 with the remark "the second stanza of Gilg. VI (22–44)—marked off as such by horizontal lines in the text . . ." ("Gilgamesh VI 40," *JCS* 12 [1958] 41). As noted above, I have divided Gilgamesh's speech differently. The separation of lines 24–32 from lines 33–41 is based, first of all, on the observation that each of these sections is characterized by thematic and formal features that unify it and set it off from the other. As for lines 42–44, I need only note that lines 42–43 look forward—they anticipate the accounts of the first two lovers in lines 45–50, and that line 44—following the opening questions in lines 42–43—contains Gilgamesh's own statement that he will now recount Ishtar's various amatory escapades and, so, introduces the recital itself. The horizontal dividing line after line 44 is in no way decisive; I suspect that it does not even exist. It is absent in E. Ebeling, *Keilschrifttexte aus Assur religiösen Inhalts* (Leipzig: J. C. Hinrichs, 1915–23) (hereafter *KAR*), no. 115+ (cf. Frankena, p. 120) as well as in Sm. 2112 (Haupt, p. 32) and K. 231 (Haupt, *Nimrodepos*, 38; cf. Thompson, *Epic of Gilgamesh*, pl. 21, nn. 3, 10). Outside of the Haupt and Thompson composites (Thompson, *Epic of Gilgamesh*, pl. 21; cf. Haupt, *Nimrodepos*, 43 n. 18: "Theilstrich."), I only find the dividing line in Haupt, *Nimrodepos*, 30 (= [?] K. 4579a; P. Jensen [*Assyrisch-babylonische Mythen und Epen* (Keilinschriftliche Bibliothek 6.1; Berlin: Reuther & Reichard, 1900) 166 n. 2] treats K. 4579a as unpublished, but it seems to be the unnumbered text in Haupt, *Nimrodepos*, 30–31), but in view of Haupt's procedure there (see p. 30, col. 2 after line 11), the horizontal lines seem to have been a modern copyist's device that was subsequently erroneously introduced into the edition. If so, there is probably no dividing line between lines 44 and 45; collation is required. Because of its fragmentary nature, I have not taken account of line 45 in the present essay.

1. Much of the first section is broken, and it is difficult to ascertain its purport. The section is framed by the verbal form *aḫḫazki*; it treats food, garments, and toiletries. Gilgamesh seems to be saying that he is unwilling to marry Ishtar; while it is possible that he declares his willingness to bestow gifts upon her,[5] it is more likely that he states that Ishtar has no need for the kinds of gifts that a bridegroom would normally bestow upon his bride.[6]

2. In the second section, Gilgamesh addresses Ishtar by nine kennings. One line is given over to each kenning. In each case, an object is first introduced and then defined by an epithet that describes or denotes a seemingly negative or destructive characteristic (e.g., *ekallu munappiṣat qarrādi*, "a palace that crushes the warrior" [line 35]).

3. The third section is devoted to a recital of Ishtar's dealings with six lovers. Gilgamesh recounts the story of each of the lovers and the destructive treatment that Ishtar has meted out to them. The section begins and ends with rhetorical statements (lines 42–43, 79). The final statement (line 79) refers to as many lovers as had been previously listed: "If you love me, will you not treat me as you treated them?" (*kī šâšunu*). Similarly, the opening two questions (lines 42–43) also refer to Ishtar's lovers: "Which spouse have you loved forever? Which shepherd bird kept pleasing you?" These two questions make actual reference only to the first two lovers in the subsequent recital. They serve as a stylized abbreviation and assume the full sequence of lovers.[7]

5. Compare the translation of lines 27–30 in I. M. Diakonoff, review of F. M. T. de Liagre Böhl, *Het Gilgamesj Epos*, and L. Matouš, *Epos o Gilgamešovi*, *Bibliotheca Orientalis* 18 (1961) 63.

6. Compare the translation of lines 27–28 in Labat, *Les religions*, 182.

7. Line 42 (*ayyû ḫāmiraki* . . .) anticipates the Tammuz story of lines 46–47, and line 43 (*ayyû allalki* . . .) anticipates the shepherd-bird story of lines 48–50. The fact that the opening questions refer only to the first two lovers may be interpreted in one of two ways. It may reflect an earlier form of the text in which Gilgamesh limited his recital to these two lovers. More probably, it serves as a stylized abbreviation, citing only the first two lovers, but assuming the full list. I prefer this second explanation. The use of the device is known elsewhere. Here I should note that the use of a similar form of abbreviation explains, I think, the mention of only the "eye" and the "tooth" in the unit dealing with slaves in Exod 21:26–27: instead of repeating the various parts of the body and types of wounds mentioned in verses 24–25, the writer cited only the first two. In providing only for the eye and tooth of the slave, he intended nothing more than to save himself the bother of running through the whole sequence. It has been noted that the "H[ittite] L[aws] 8, similar to Exodus, lists the blinding of a slave and the knocking out of his teeth" (S. M. Paul, *Studies in the Book of the Covenant* [Leiden: Brill, 1970] 78 n. 4); this may perhaps be a necessary condition, but it is not a sufficient explanation for the formation of these verses. The composer understood "eye" and "tooth"—the first two entries of the standard list—as standing for the full list and left

The entire episode is curious. Gilgamesh's refusal to wed Ishtar is strange. We tend to condone his refusal and to treat it as if it were a perfectly natural way to act. Perhaps we do so because we think of the goddess—especially when she is an initiator—as an aggressive and harmful woman; but on the face of it, at least, Gilgamesh has not convinced us of the necessity or even the desirability of refusing her. Gilgamesh concludes his speech by stating that Ishtar will treat him as she treated her previous lovers. But these earlier encounters are simply illustrative; by themselves they do not prove anything. They simply exemplify and assert a belief that Gilgamesh already holds. Why, then, did Gilgamesh arrive at this conviction and assume that his relationship with Ishtar would end like the others? The motivation for the refusal is not immediately apparent. Nor have we been prepared for a refusal. If anything, we have been led to expect a positive response on Gilgamesh's part. Gilgamesh has just overcome a male monster, a guardian of a treasure; even if we give credence to the possibility that Gilgamesh might have some ambivalent feelings about killing a male and taking a female, still he should now want and be able to claim his reward and take Ishtar. Furthermore, the Gilgamesh that we have met thus far in the epic is surely not the kind of man to fear a challenge or to imagine himself vulnerable to that which might harm a lesser being. If anything, Ishtar's destructive treatment of some of her previous lovers should spur him on. He should be tempted by the challenge that she poses and believe himself able to enjoy her without submitting to her powers. He can beat her at her own game. Moreover, the composer has not prepared us for knee-jerk misogynism; up to this point, at least, the relationship of Enkidu and Shamhat has led

---

it to the reader to supply the rest of the list. Certainly, later readers have extended the mention of "eye" and "tooth" in these verses to include additional parts of the body. However, this shortcut has occasioned some misundertanding, and to the writer's selection of "eye" and "tooth" has been imputed a significance that was probably not intended. So understandably the Babylonian Talmud (*Qiddushin* 24^{a-b}) and the Halakhic Midrashim (*Mekilta de-Rabbi Ishmael* [ed. J. Z. Lauterbach; 3 vols.; Philadelphia: Jewish Publication Society of America, 1933–35] 3:72–73; and *Mekhilta d'Rabbi Šimʿon b. Jochai* [ed. J. N. Epstein and E. Z. Melamed; Jerusalem: Meqitse Nirdamim, 1955] 177), followed by such medievals as Rashi ad Exod 21:26 and the East European Rabbinic scholar Baruch Epstein (*Torah Temimah*); but also more recently and less understandably, e.g., M. D. Cassuto, *A Commentary on the Book of Exodus* [Hebrew] (Jerusalem: Magnes, 1951) 193; and B. S. Childs, *The Book of Exodus* (Philadelphia: Westminster, 1974) 472–73: "A clear example of the new Hebrew stamp on old material emerges in the law which follows, vv. 26f. If a master injures his slave, *whether in a serious way with the loss of an eye, or with the insignificant loss of a tooth*, the slave is to be freed. Obviously the law is seeking to prevent any kind of mistreatment toward slaves by lumping all injuries together without distinction" (italics mine).

us in the opposite direction. Finally, Ishtar is a goddess, and on the face of it, her offer does indeed seem attractive: status, power, wealth, and the goddess herself are Gilgamesh's for the taking.

Turning to Gilgamesh's speech, we notice immediately that it is rather long. It fills close to sixty of the seventy-nine lines of the section; by contrast, Ishtar's speech takes up only fifteen lines. Moreover his speech does not ramble as might a violent emotional response;[8] for all its length and detail, it is organized in a clear and coherent fashion. Surely Gilgamesh's refusal could have been stated in a shorter and simpler form. The first section (nine lines), certainly the first two sections (two sections of nine lines each), should have sufficed to convey his refusal. And as regards the third section, what is achieved by listing more than, say, two lovers? To the extent that the opening rhetorical question could be limited to the first two lovers, so the recital could also be so limited. For that matter, the composer could have limited himself to the rhetorical frame of this third section; by itself, the frame manages to convey the unfaithfulness of Ishtar. Such observations indicate that we do not yet appreciate the full import of the individual sections of Gilgamesh's speech or the interconnection of the sections.

It is obvious, then, that we must provide an explanation for Gilgamesh's rejection of Ishtar as well as for the length, makeup, and purpose of his speech. The explanation lies—I submit—in the proposal itself. There must be something about Ishtar's offer that might disturb any man but would especially distress Gilgamesh, a being so very concerned about living and dying. There must be something about the offer that provokes the rejection, and Gilgamesh's speech must be a meaningful response, a response that takes off from the offer and returns to it. So in asking the question, Why did Gilgamesh refuse Ishtar's proposal and state his refusal in the form that he did? we are asking, What are the meaning and relation of her speech and his response?

II

We begin with the proposal. What did Gilgamesh see in Ishtar's offer that we have not seen? It is immediately evident that he is being offered something different from a normal marriage, for the animals that will draw his carriage are designated *ūmū* (line 12). They are supernatural beasts, animals that are not of this world. In fact, the marriage formula itself—*attā lū mutīma anāku lū aššatka*, "Be thou my husband, I will be

8. For a different opinion, see Jacobsen, *Treasures*, 201, 218–19.

thy wife"—points in the same direction and may well be a giveaway. Formulations of this sort in literary texts have served scholars as evidence for the existence and composition of the marriage formula.[9] It has also been argued, correctly, I believe, that apparently both groom and bride recited separate marriage formulas—he said, "You are my wife"; she said, "You are my husband."[10] The marriage formula was mutual; the divorce formula, on the other hand, was unilateral—for example, "You are not my wife, I am not your husband."[11] What seems to have been overlooked is that the marriage formula in the three literary passages that have been cited in support of the formula is also unilateral. Moreover, the identities of the speaker and addressee in these three texts must be noted and taken into account:

> *attā lū mutīma anāku lū aššatka,*

so Ereshkigal, queen of the netherworld, to her future and forever spouse Nergal;

> dam.mu hé.me.en g̃á.e dam.zu hé.a
> *attā lū aššatu anāku lū mutka,*[12]

so the demon Arad-Lilî to a human female;

> *attā lū mutīma anāku lū aššatka,*

so Ishtar to Gilgamesh in our text.

The unilateral formulation suggests finality and control. The use of this formulation rather than the mundane mutual and the contexts of these offers suggest that the proposal has its setting in the infernal regions, that Ishtar is inviting Gilgamesh to become her husband and thereby formally to join the denizens of the netherworld.

This interpretation finds confirmation in line 16. For in this line, Gilgamesh is addressed as an official of the netherworld. That he is being so addressed is strongly suggested by the occurrence of a similar line in an incantation directed to Gilgamesh. In this incantation, as elsewhere in Mesopotamian religious literature and ritual, Gilgamesh appears in

9. See S. Greengus, "The Old Babylonian Marriage Contract," *JAOS* 89 (1969) 514–20, esp. 516–17.

10. See ibid., 520–22; and M. A. Friedman, "Israel's Response in Hosea 2:17b: 'You are my husband,'" *JBL* 99 (1980) 202–3.

11. Ibid., 202.

12. For a recent edition, see S. Lackenbacher, "Note sur l'*ardat-lilî*," *RA* 65 (1971) 126, lines 13–14. *attā* = *attī*; . . . *-ka* = . . . *-ki*; cf. Greengus, "Old Babylonian Marriage Contract," 516 n. 51.

his accustomed role as an important official of the netherworld.[13] This Gilgamesh incantation is part of a well-known ritual.[14] This ritual gives

13. For the netherworld role of Gilgamesh, see, e.g., W. G. Lambert, "Gilgameš in Religious, Historical and Omen Texts and the Historicity of Gilgameš," in *Gilgameš et sa légende* (ed. P. Garelli; Paris: C. Klincksieck, 1960) 39ff.; T. Abusch, "Mesopotamian Anti-Witchcraft Literature: Texts and Studies, Part I: The Nature of *Maqlû*: Its Character, Divisions, and Calendrical Setting," *JNES* 33 (1974) 259–61; and Jacobsen, *Treasures*, 209–12. The Gilgamesh incantation was edited by E. Ebeling, *Tod und Leben nach den Vorstellungen der Babylonier* (Berlin: Walter de Gruyter, 1931), p. 127, line 7–p. 130, line 9. (Contrary to Ebeling's description of these lines as forming three incantations: "*Gebet an Gilgameš . . . Beschwörung gegen Zauberer und Zauberin . . . Rest einer Beschwörung an Gilgameš*" [*Tod und Leben*, 122], all portions are part of one incantation.) For a partial translation, see M.-J. Seux, *Hymnes et prières aux dieux de Babylonie et d'Assyrie* (Paris: Éditions du Cerg, 1976) 428–29. As a result of the identification of new fragments and further joins (see next note), I have been able to put together a text of some eighty lines. Although there are now no gaps, every line of the incantation being extant wholly or in part, and we have a much fuller text of the incantation than that provided by Ebeling, some portions of the incantation are still fragmentary. This does not affect our use of the Gilgamesh incantation to elucidate GE Tablet VI, line 16; the relevant line is set in a clear context and is well known: see Haupt, *Nimrodepos*, no. 53, line 9 = Ebeling, *Tod und Leben*, 127, line 15 = Lambert, "Gilgamesh," 40, line 9. (The ten lines quoted by Lambert are also duplicated by E. Ebeling et al., *Literarische Keilschrifttexte aus Assur* [Berlin: Akademie-Verlag, 1953] [hereafter *LKA*] no. 89, obverse right col., lines 14–22.)

14. This ritual was edited by Ebeling, *Tod und Leben*, 124–33. I am preparing a new edition of the ritual as part of my reconstruction and edition of the Mesopotamian witchcraft corpus. To facilitate study until such time as the edition appears, I note the following "bibliographical" information based on work done on this text up to 1975. Ebeling's edition is based almost exclusively on the Assur pieces (*a*) *KAR*, no. 227 and (*b*) *LKA*, nos. 89 (VAT 13656) + 90 (13657). The **Assur** tablets were or should have been used as follows: (*a*) *KAR* 227: obv. col. I = Ebeling, p. 124, line 1–p. 127, line 50; obv. col. II = p. 127, lines 1–12, p. 128, line 5*–p. 129, line 10*; rev. col. III = p. 130, line 27–p. 133, line 75. (*b*) *LKA* 89 + 90 (89 forms the upper portion of the tablet; 90, the lower portion): *Obverse*: 89 obv. left col. (poor photo) = Ebeling, p. 124, lines 3/4–ca. p. 125, line 25; 90 obv. left col. = p. 126, line 41–p. 127, line 65; 89 obv. right col., lines 1–7 (the section of *KAR* 227 obv. col. I that would have contained these lines is not preserved) were omitted by Ebeling—they are to be placed between p. 127, line 65 and p. 127, line 1 (2. Kol.); 89 obv. right col., lines 8ff. = p. 127, line 1–p. 127, line 16; 90 obv. right col. (poor photo) = p. 128, line 1*–p. 129, line 23*. *Reverse*: 90 rev. right col. = p. 129, line 1–p. 131, line 33; 89 rev. right col. = p. 131, line 33–p. 133, line 70; 90 rev. left col., lines 1–4 = p. 133, lines 72–75; 90 rev. left col., lines 5ff. and 89 rev. left col.: these lines were not included in *KAR* 227. 90 rev. left col., lines 5ff. were omitted by Ebeling (but see W. von Soden, "Bemerkungen zu den von Ebeling in *Tod und Leben* Band I bearbeiteten Texten," *ZA* 43 [1936] 267), but Ebeling did include 89 rev. left col. on p. 133 immediately after line 75. For the catchline, cf. O. R. Gurney and P. Hulin, eds., *The Sultantepe Tablets*, vol. 2 (London: British Institute of Archaeology at Ankara, 1964) no. 254 rev.(!) 22. **Nineveh**: (My identifications and joins of unpublished fragments were made on the basis of F. W. Geers's copies; all joins are confirmed.) The Kuyunjik copy of the ritual contained at least three tablets. They are (*A*) K. 9860 + 13272 + 13796: K. 9860+ duplicates and restores Ebeling, p. 125, line 21–p. 126, line 34. (*B*) K. 6793 + Sm. 41 + 617 + 717 + Haupt, *Nimrodepos*, no. 53 (Sm. 1371 + 1877) (R. Borger and I independently joined Sm. 41 + Haupt, *Nimrodepos*, no. 53; cf. Borger, "Das Tempelbau-Ritual K 48+," *ZA* 61 [1971] 80): K. 6793+ duplicates and restores Ebeling, p. 127,

the impression of being far more complicated than it really is, in part because its purpose has not been adequately clarified. Therefore, while this is not the place to present a detailed treatment of the ritual, we should at least state succinctly our provisional understanding of its purpose before drawing the Gilgamesh incantation into our discussion of GE Tablet VI. The goal of the ritual is to free the patient of witches (*kaššāpu u kaššaptu*) and of the evil (*mimma lemnu*) that they had brought upon the patient. This riddance is accomplished by having them conveyed to the netherworld by means of an *eṭem lā mammānama*, a ghost that had previously been deprived of the rites of the dead. Accordingly, (1) the approval and support of Shamash, Gilgamesh, the Anunnaki, and the family ghosts are secured; (2) the ghost is accorded the rites of the dead and adjured to carry off the witches and the *mimma lemnu* to the netherworld; (3) and, finally, the witches and the evil are themselves adjured to depart.

In the incantation, Gilgamesh is addressed in his role of judge of the netherworld. He is invoked by such epithets as *šarru gitmālu dayyān Anunnaki*, "perfect king, judge of the Anunnaki" (line 1)[15] and *šatam erṣeti bēl šaplâti*, "administrator of the netherworld, lord of the dwellers-below" (line 3),[16] and is said to render judgment in the netherworld (e.g., *tazzaz ina erṣeti tagammar dīna*, "you stand in the netherworld and pronounce final judgment" [line 5]). The hymnic introduction of this incantation concludes with the statement:

> *šarrū šakkanakkū u rubû maḫarka kamsū*
> *tabarri têrētīšunu purussâšunu taparras*
>
> [Lines 9–10]

To paraphrase the text: In the netherworld, Gilgamesh, you render judgment, and there kings, governors, and princes bow down before you in order to receive your pronouncements.

line 7–p. 130, line 10 (Haupt, *Nimrodepos*, no. 53 obv. 1–24 = Ebeling, p. 127, line 7–p. 128, line 30). (*C*) Sm. 38: Sm. 38 duplicates and restores Ebeling, p. 130, line 11–p. 131, line 28. *B* and *C* are definitely part of the same ancient copy of the text; probably also *A*. **Sippar**: Si. 747 duplicates and restores Ebeling, p. 131, line 38–p. 132, line 50. According to R. Borger, *Handbuch der Keilschriftliteratur* (3 vols.; Berlin: De Gruyter, 1975) 2:57, ad E. Ebeling, *KAR* 227, Bm. 98638 is also a duplicate of our ritual (identification: W. G. Lambert). Important parallel texts include F. Köcher, *Die babylonisch-assyrische Medizin in Texten und Untersuchungen* (Berlin and New York, 1963–), vol. 3, no. 231 // vol. 4, no. 332 and Si. 908.

15. For ease of reference, I follow the line count of the Kuyunjik text K. 6793+; simply see Haupt, *Nimrodepos*, no. 53, and cf. Lambert, "Gilgamesh," 40.

16. *Ḫā'it kibrāti* appears at the beginning of line 3 in K. 6793+ immediately before *šatam erṣeti* and joined to the preceding line (*rubû muštālu rappu ša nišī ḫā'it kibrāti*). This division is supported by Assur MSS (*KAR*, no. 227 and *LKA*, no. 89 set *šatam erṣeti* at the beginning of a new line).

The line *šarrū šakkanakkū u rubû maḫarka kamsū*, "Kings, governors, and princes bow down before you," recalls GE Tablet VI, line 16. This is precisely the form of homage that Ishtar promises to Gilgamesh should he marry her, and she uses almost exactly the same words: *lū kamsū ina šaplika šarrū kabtūtu u rubû*, "Kings, nobles, and princes shall bow down before you." In all probability, the composer of GE Tablet VI drew the line from the incantation tradition. But even in the unlikely event that the opposite is the case and the epic is the source from which the incantation derived the line, the use of the line in the incantation would indicate that also the composer of the incantation presumably understood the line in the epic to refer to Gilgamesh's place in the netherworld and would thus lend the support of an ancient Mesopotamian reader to our interpretation. In any case, the line has the same force in the epic as in the incantation. Of course, Ishtar intended Gilgamesh to think that the power and status she was offering him were to be his in this world; in reality, she was offering him the obeisance of dead rulers in the netherworld. She seems to be offering him, in fact, the very role in the netherworld that was accorded to him by the Mesopotamian religious tradition.

We would now read Ishtar's address in the light of the following thesis: Ishtar's marriage proposal constitutes an offer to Gilgamesh to become a functionary of the netherworld. The details of her offer may be understood as referring to funeral rites and to activities that Gilgamesh will perform in the netherworld. The order in which the items are cited may even represent a continuous progression: Gilgamesh the king will wed Ishtar and go to his new home, the tomb, the netherworld; there he will be accorded the rites of the dead and exercise his infernal powers. Our text describes a funeral ritual. Obviously our text makes use of figures and forms drawn from the realms and rituals of marriage, food and fertility, sexuality, and perhaps even political activity. But the unifying and dominant image remains that of the grave and Ishtar as its symbolic representation.[17] We may now review the proposal section by section.[18]

17. To view the text as a funeral ritual is not to deny that the text can be read on other levels as well: as a marriage ritual, as a fertility ritual involving the giving of food, as a sexual ritual involving intercourse. But since the funereal dimension of our text seems not to have been noticed and remains unexplored, and explains, moreover, many features of the text that have gone unexplained, I shall focus on this dimension and attend to the others as they serve the image of death. Love and death are closely associated—be the relationship one of identification, opposition, or ambivalence—and the text takes this association for granted; it is Gilgamesh who must decide how and where he will situate himself between the two.

18. I am not unaware that I cite evidence from different periods in support of my interpretation of the text. In itself, this does not invalidate the interpretation. The uneven

a) Lines 7–9: Come, Gilgamesh, be thou (my) lover!
Do but grant me of thy fruit.
Thou shalt be my husband and I will be thy wife.[19]

Ishtar invites Gilgamesh to become her husband and therewith to depart this world and take up permanent residence in the netherworld. The formula spoken by Ishtar is the formula used to introduce a mate to the netherworld. It is one-sided and implies a lack of mutuality. Whether it will take effect depends on whether Gilgamesh provides some sign of acquiescence and places himself under Ishtar's control. A relationship will be established and Gilgamesh's status will be transformed, then, if he satisfies Ishtar's requests of lines 8–21 and voluntarily gives over for consummation the food—vigor—of the living (line 8)[20] and travels to (lines 10–12) and enters into (lines 13ff.) his new home. Note that only in regard to these three actions is a second-person verb form of request or command used: *qīšamma*, "grant" (line 8), *lū ṣamdāta*, "drive" (line 12), *erba*, "enter" (line 13).

b) Lines 10–12: I will harness for thee a chariot of lapis and gold,
Whose wheels are gold and whose horns are brass.
Thou shalt have storm-demons to latch on for mighty mules.

Gilgamesh will be transported to the tomb by means of a chariot drawn by asses. The ceremonial and even supernal character of the transport is

distribution of data aside, I recall an observation of M. P. Nilsson, *The Mycenaean Origin of Greek Mythology* (Berkeley: University of California Press, 1932; repr., New York: Norton, 1963) 13–14: "In regard to these elements in Homer, derived from widely differing times and civilizations, scholars have divided themselves into two parties engaging in a tug of war. One party tries to put as much as possible in a time as late as possible; namely, into the developed Geometric and the Orientalizing periods, and to treat the elements which it is impossible to fit into this scheme as irrelevant survivals. The other party treats the elements which undoubtedly belong to a late age as irrelevant additions and takes Homer on the whole to be Mycenaean. It appears that neither of these two methods is the right one. We have to concede without circumlocutions that Homer contains elements from very differing periods and to try to comprehend and explain this state of things, not to obliterate it and get rid of it through artificial interpretations."

19. With the exception of lines 15–16, the translation of lines 7ff. at the head of each section is that of Speiser, *ANET*, 83–84.

20. The giving of food here has a twofold immediate connotation: the settling of a marriage gift by the groom and the surrender of the stuff of life. Food is both the source as well as the force of life. To give food is to give up one's life when the giver and the food are identified; to give is to spend oneself or to be consumed. Additionally, here, food and sexual force are fused, as are eating and sexual intercourse. The combination allows one to stand for the other or the two to be joined in mixed figures. In any case, to give food over to Ishtar effectively means to surrender the food that humans grow and eat in this world in exchange for the food that they are given once they are dead.

indicated by the description of the chariot—a chariot of lapis and gold, whose wheels are gold and whose horns are amber—and the demonic nature of the animals that draw it: *ūmī kūdanī*[21] *rabûti*, "wind demons, the great mules." The transport is part of the funeral and will convey Gilgamesh to his new abode. In this way, then, Gilgamesh was to travel to the netherworld.[22] Note Urnammu's association with a chariot on his arrival in the netherworld (*The Death of Urnammu*, lines 74–75),[23] the chariots or wagons in the Early Dynastic tombs at Ur, Kish, and Susa,[24] the association therewith of asses at Kish,[25] and the mention of chariots

---

21. For *kūdanu*, see *CAD*, vol. K, pp. 491–92, and J. Zarins, "The Domesticated Equidae of Third Millennium B.C. Mesopotamia," *JCS* 30 (1978) 14–15, and note the description of Enkidu: *ibrī kūdanu ṭardu akkannu ša šadî nimru ša ṣēri / Enkidu ibrī kūdanu ṭardu akkannu ša šadî nimru ša ṣēri* (O. R. Gurney, "Two Fragments of the Epic of Gilgamesh from Sultantepe," *JCS* 8 [1954] 93, lines 7–8 // Thompson, *Epic of Gilgamesh*, Tablet VIII, col. 2, lines 8–9 [= VIII 50–51]).

22. As with many burial offerings, the offer of a chariot may also have been intended to provide Gilgamesh with equipment that he had used during his lifetime and would need in the netherworld itself.

23. S. Kramer, "The Death of Ur-Nammu and His Descent to the Netherworld," *JCS* 21 (1967 [1969]) 114, line 75.

24. For Ur, see simply C. L. Woolley et al., *The Royal Cemetery* (Ur Excavations 2; London: Trustees of the British Museum and the University of Pennsylvania, 1934) (hereafter UE 2) 64–65, 74, 78–80. For Kish, see P. R. S. Moorey, "A Re-consideration of the Excavations on Tell Ingharra (East Kish), 1923–33," *Iraq* 28 (1966) 41–43; and "Cemetery A at Kish: Grave Groups and Chronology," *Iraq* 32 (1970) 104 n. 96, and, esp., *Kish Excavations, 1923–1933* (Oxford: Clarendon Press, 1978) 103–10 and references there. P. Steinkeller informs me that G. Algazi has reexamined the chariot burials at Kish ("Private Houses and Burials in the 'Y' Trench Area of Ingharra: Kish" [M.A. thesis, University of Chicago, 1980] 27–35). For Susa, see L. Le Breton, "The Early Periods at Susa, Mesopotamian Relations," *Iraq* 19 (1957) 122 and n. 2; and M. E. L. Mallowan, "The Early Dynastic Period in Mesopotamia," in *The Cambridge Ancient History*, vol. 1, pt. 2 (3rd ed.; Cambridge and New York, 1971) 274 and n. 2.

25. See Moorey, *Kish Excavations*, 106–10 and references there. While donkeys (in this note I use this term without prejudice as to whether the equid is a donkey or hybrid) are shown drawing chariots on the Standard of Ur (UE 2:266–73) and a donkey mascot occurs on the rein ring in Grave 800 at Ur (UE 2:78; pl. 166; cf. the onager rein ring also associated with a chariot in a burial at Kish [Moorey, *Kish Excavations*, 106–7]), the animals attached to the wagons in the royal tombs of Ur seem to have been oxen (see, simply, P. R. S. Moorey, *Ur 'of the Chaldees': A Revised and Updated Edition of Sir Leonard Woolley's "Excavations at Ur"* [Ithaca, NY: Cornell University Press; London: The Herbert Press, 1982] 61–76). Note that the animals found in Grave 800 that were originally thought to be donkeys (UE 2:74, 78, 272) were later identified as oxen (R. H. Dyson, Jr., "A Note on Queen Shub-Ad's 'Onagers,'" *Iraq* 22 [1960] 102–4). The significance of the use of oxen rather than donkeys in the burials has been discussed. Moorey suggests a practical reason for the preference for bovids at Kish (*Kish Excavations*, 107). There is evidence of equid burials without chariots; P. Steinkeller draws my attention to the recent finds at Tell Madhhur (J. N. Postgate and P. J. Watson, "Excavations in Iraq,

and asses among burial offerings in presargonic texts.[26]

c) Line 13: In the fragrance of cedars thou shalt enter our house.

Gilgamesh will enter the tomb to the accompaniment of the fragrance of cedar (*ana bītini ina sammāti erēni erba*). Incense forms part of a funeral ritual.[27] Thus in a Neo-Assyrian funeral ritual (K. 164),[28] the corpse is laid out on a bed (*eršu*), a torch containing aromatic reeds is held (*ziqtu ša qanê ṭābi tanašši* [obv. lines 3, 19–20]), the corpse's feet are kissed (*šēpē tanaššiq* [obv. lines 6, 21]), and cedar is burnt (*erēnu tašarrap* [obv. lines 7, 21]). Note, further, the description of funerary rites in the inscription of Adad-Guppi. Regarding several Neo-Babylonian kings, she states, "I have been making funerary offerings for them, performing and instituting for them permanent incense offerings, abundant (and) of sweet smell."[29]

d) Lines 14–17: When our house thou enterest,
Noble purificant priests shall kiss thy feet!
Kings, nobles, and princes shall bow down before thee!
The yield of hills and plain they shall bring thee as tribute.

As he enters his new residence (*ana bītini ina erēbika*), Gilgamesh will be greeted and receive the homage of priests and rulers. They will submit to him and present him with offerings or tribute, gifts that the living give to the dead and that the dead offer up in the netherworld. Here in the netherworld, Gilgamesh will rule over the rulers. As noted earlier, the similar line in the Gilgamesh incantation establishes this setting for

1977–78," *Iraq* 41 [1979] 176) and Tell Razuk (Mc. Gibson et al., *Uch Tepe 1* [Chicago: Oriental Institute of the University of Chicago, 1981] 73–74).

26. See D. A. Foxvog, "Funerary Furnishings in an Early Sumerian Text from Adab," in *Death in Mesopotamia: Papers Read at the XXVIe Rencontre assyriologique internationale* (ed. B. Alster; Mesopotamia 8; Copenhagen: Akademisk Forlag, 1980) 67ff. After hearing my paper at the AOS in 1983, P. Steinkeller informed me of his AOS (1980) presentation, "Early Dynastic Burial Offerings in Light of the Textual Evidence," and generously placed a copy at my disposal. Steinkeller discusses the Foxvog text and F.-M. Allotte de la Fuÿe, *Documents présargoniques* (Paris: E. Leroux, 1909) no. 75. In both texts, equids and chariots are listed among the funerary furnishings.

27. Is there any connection between this use of incense and its use in Adonis rituals? For its use in the latter and the Near Eastern connections thereof, cf. W. Burkert, *Structure and History in Greek Mythology and Ritual* (Berkeley: University of California Press, 1979) 106, and reference in 192 n. 7.

28. See W. von Soden, "Aus einen Ersatzopferritual für den assyrischen Hof," *ZA* 45 (1939) 42ff.; cf. E. Dhorme, "Rituel funéraire assyrien," *RA* 38 (1941) 57–66.

29. C. J. Gadd, "The Harran Inscriptions of Nabonidus," *Anatolian Studies* 8 (1958) 50, col. 3, lines 1–4; translation of A. L. Oppenheim, *ANET*, 561.

our line 16: "Kings, nobles, and princes shall bow down before you."[30] This same netherworld setting applies equally well to line 15. This line is difficult, and the text should probably be emended. A plausible reading is *išippū* (⟨*i*⟩-*šip-pu*)[31] *arattû linaššiqū šēpēka*, "May the noble purificant priests kiss your feet."[32] The *išippu*-priests of line 15 certainly provide an apt parallel to the rulers of line 16; one notes the several priests and rulers that Enkidu encountered in the netherworld in Tablet VII, column 4, lines 193ff. and the appearance among them of the same *išippu*-priests (line 200). The kissing of the feet of line 15 takes place after death. The mention of the rite of kissing the feet of the corpse (*šēpē tanaššiq*) alongside incense in the epic and in the aforementioned Neo-Assyrian funeral ritual indicates that line 15 is set in a funeral context.[33] This is confirmed by the description of the funeral rites for Enkidu in Tablet VII, column 3, lines 139ff., and Tablet VIII, column 3, lines 85ff.; there in addresses to Enkidu by Shamash (Tablet VII) and Gilgamesh (Tablet VIII), we learn that Gilgamesh lays out the dead Enkidu on a litter (*mayyālu*) comparable, I should think, to the bed (*eršu*) of the Neo-Assyrian ritual, and that *malkū ša qaqqari unaššaqū šēpēka*, "Princes of the earth kiss your feet" (Tablet VII, col. 3, line 143; Tablet VIII, col. 3, line 87). Kissing the feet in Tablet VI, line 15, the bowing down in line 16, and the

30. We interpret the line as referring to the homage by dead rulers. It may allude also to acts of homage accorded the dead Gilgamesh by living rulers; cf. Gadd, "Harran Inscriptions," 52, lines 20–21.

31. *CAD*, vol. A/2, p. 239; cf. Labat, *Les religions*, 182.

32. The emended reading—however attractive—is not absolutely certain. It is possible that our interpretation of Ishtar's speech provides an explanation for *sippu*. Lines 13–14 treat the act of entering into a chamber (*ana bitīni ina erēbika* . . .). The entranceway is "the boundary. . . . Therefore to cross the threshold is to unite oneself with a new world . . . [and] the rites carried out on the threshold itself are transition rites" (A. van Gennep, *The Rites of Passage* [Chicago: University of Chicago Press, 1960] 20). Since entering the chamber here in GE Tablet VI is the central act of the passing from the world of the living to that of the dead, one might well expect the very act of passing over to be concretized. The unemended form of line 15 can fulfill the terms of this requirement. Perhaps, then, we should retain *sippu* and view the door frame's kissing of Gilgamesh's feet as a rite of transition: the tomb is animated, and the dying Gilgamesh is greeted and drawn into his new home by its entranceway. Additionally, submission and acceptance of his rule by his new domain—a theme further developed by *lū kamsū*—could thus be symbolized. For the present, however, I think it wiser to follow the emended reading.

33. Perhaps we should connect the kissing of the feet with the holding of the aromatic torch rather than with the burning of cedar, yielding the order: aromatics, greeting and submission, offering (GE Tablet VI, lines 13, 15–16, 17 // K. 164: 3a = 19b–20a, 6a = 21a, 7a = 21b). Note that the burning of cedar in the funeral ritual may represent the beginning of a meal: "Elle procède maintenant à une série d'actions destinées à procurer au mort sa subsistance, jusqu'à la mise au tombeau: 'Elle brûle du cèdre, dans du vin elle l'éteint; . . .' Le cèdre est brûlé pour renforcer l'arome et la force du vin" (Dhorme, "Rituel funéraire," 61).

offerings of tribute in line 17 combine—individually or in combination—the meanings of acts performed at funerals and acts of obeisance accorded a ruler, here a master of the netherworld who receives the homage of his infernal subjects.

e) Lines 18–21: Thy goats shall cast triplets, thy sheep twins, etc.

With his settlement in the netherworld, Gilgamesh will become the possessor of vigorous herds, and they will become his embodiment. Perhaps this power is activated by the offerings of tribute (line 17). In any case, Gilgamesh will serve as a source of fertility, a power not unusual in one who resides in the earth.

Ishtar offers token and substance: honor, power, wealth. Here she intended to deceive Gilgamesh; she presented their marriage as if it were this-worldly whereas actually it would lead directly to his transferral to the netherworld. Such a stratagem requires that her words admit of more than one meaning. She takes advantage of the similarities of the behavior of, and the treatment accorded to, rulers of the living and rulers of the dead.[34] Even more important—perhaps central to the deception—are the similarities of a psychological, procedural, and symbolic nature between a wedding and a funeral.[35] One need only recall that just as divorce may serve as a metaphor for ridding oneself of a demon and resuming a healthy state, so marriage may serve as a metaphor for demonic

34. For example, such acts of submission to an overlord as kissing the feet and bowing; see *CAD*, vol. N/2, pp. 58–59; cf. M. Liverani, "The Ideology of the Assyrian Empire," in *Power and Propaganda: A Symposium on Ancient Empires* (ed. M. T. Larsen; Mesopotamia 7; Copenhagen: Akademisk Forlag, 1979) 311; and R. Firth, *Symbols: Public and Private* (Ithaca, NY: Cornell University Press, 1973) 308: "Bodily posture is important in many greeting conventions. One mode of showing respect is by sinking to the ground, conveying a depreciation of the self and symbolizing humility and recognition of superior status."

35. Underlying this aspect of the deception may also be the fact that death was the original outcome of the marriage of priest-king and goddess. But for the present, this possibility is best ignored. While it would be a mistake to dissociate our text completely from the sacred marriage, we should also not overestimate the latter's importance. Of course, in the composition of the early part of GE Tablet VI, the author may well have drawn on texts or traditions describing the sacred marriage. (See, most recently, J. H. Tigay, *The Evolution of the Gilgamesh Epic* [Philadelphia: University of Pennsylvania Press, 1982] 174–76.) I find it hard to believe that our composer was reacting to the actual religious institution. The ceremony provided him with the motif with which to operate. See below, nn. 71 and 68. My reluctance to treat the text as a response to an actual ceremony is not dependent on the dating of the text. But the reader will certainly sympathize with my reluctance if my late dating of GE Tablet VI is correct (see below, Sec. V) and we proceed on the assumption that already the kings of the first dynasty of Babylon did not practice the rite of the sacred marriage (see recently J. Klein, *Three Šulgi Hymns* [Ramat-Gan: Bar-Ilan University Press, 1981] 33 n. 48).

possession and entering into a deadly state. And the epic itself is aware of the association, as we learn from Gilgamesh's treatment of Enkidu at the latter's death:

> *iktumma ibrī kīma kallati pānuš*
> He covered the face of his friend as if he were a bride.[36]

In large measure these similarities derive from the fact that both marriage and death involve leaving one state and group and entering another, with the wedding and funeral facilitating the transition. Thus wedding and funeral ceremonies have ritual elements and structures in common;[37] in addition, each may contain rites and symbols normally associated with the other.[38] And in regard to funerals, we find not only that marriage rites may be used to represent separation from kin, the living, and joining a new family, the dead, but also that sexuality and fertility may form part of, or even dominate, the symbolism of funerals.[39]

So the emphasis on marriage and fertility does not contradict our reading of Ishtar's speech as a description of a funeral; it is precisely what we would expect to find. Perhaps it is the purposeful ambiguity of Ishtar's proposal that has prevented the modern reader from discerning its meaning. But Gilgamesh was not deceived; he remarked the allusions to the netherworld and responded in kind. Our interpretation draws support, then, not only from the specific allusions that we have isolated and the coherence that our reading imparts to Ishtar's speech but also from Gilgamesh's response; his speech contains allusions to the grave to the extent even of identifying Ishtar with a tomb[40] and makes sense only if he is responding to an offer of death.

Furthermore, it is reassuring to notice that Ishtar's speech conforms to the scheme of a rite of passage: acts of separation, transition, and in-

36. Tablet VIII, line 59. For the text, see Gurney, "Two Fragments," 93, line 13 (= Thompson, *Epic of Gilgamesh*, Tablet VIII, col. 2, line 17). Our translation follows Jacobsen, *Treasures*, 203; so, too, Schott and von Soden, *Gilgamesch Epos*, 67, and Labat, *Les religions*, 196. For a different translation, see Gurney, "Two Fragments," 95, followed by *CAD*, vol. K, p. 299.

37. See van Gennep, *Rites of Passage*, and cf. the references on p. 190.

38. For weddings, see, e.g., H. Schauss, *The Lifetime of a Jew throughout the Ages of Jewish History* (New York: Union of American Hebrew Congregations, 1950) 171–72, 212ff.; and I. Abrahams, *Jewish Life in the Middle Ages* (New York: Macmillan, 1896; repr., New York: Meridian; Philadelphia: Jewish Publication Society, 1958) 187, 204–5. For funerals, see, e.g., van Gennep, *Rites of Passage*, 152; and M. Pope, *Song of Songs* (AB 7C; Garden City, NY: Doubleday, 1977) 210–29.

39. See R. Huntington and P. Metcalf, *Celebrations of Death: The Anthropology of Mortuary Ritual* (Cambridge: Cambridge University Press, 1979) 12, 93–118; and Pope, *Song of Songs*, 210–29.

40. See below, Sec. III.

corporation;[41] this should be the case if a funeral—a rite of passage—is being described. Gilgamesh is asked to depart his present state, to cross a threshold, and to enter a new group: Gilgamesh is to leave the living (lines 7–9); the transition (lines 10–17) begins with the hitching up of the animals and ends with the entrance into the tomb, the crucial or pivotal acts being the entering (*erēbu*) and the attendant greeting; the journey will be completed when he is integrated into his new domicile and assumes his new role (lines 18–21).

The journey belongs to Gilgamesh alone. No one moves toward him; only he is seen moving. Everyone else remains stationary. They are already in the netherworld. The rulers—his future subjects—await him; they will kiss his feet and sink down before him in submission when he joins them. He enters and they greet him; through their greeting a new relationship is established.[42] Even Ishtar is there; she beckons him from the place whither he is asked to journey:

> *ana bītini . . . erba* (ventive)
> Enter here . . . into our home.[43]
> [Line 13]

She speaks from the tomb. Gilgamesh is asked to pass alone through the stages leading to death, to give up old relations and forge new ones. To join Ishtar is to die and become part of a new community. This separation and reincorporation find their most concrete expression in the giving and receiving of symbols of fertility. Gilgamesh's separation will take the form of the surrender of his cultivated fruit (*inbīka*) as a grant

41. For these rites, see van Gennep, *Rites of Passage*; and V. Turner, *The Forest of Symbols: Aspects of Ndembu Ritual* (Ithaca, NY: Cornell University Press, 1967) 93–111.

42. For greetings generally, cf. van Gennep, *Rites of Passage*, 32–33; and Firth, *Symbols*, 299–327, esp. 301: "In general, greeting and parting conventions may be regarded as a mild variety of Van Gennep's *rites de passage*—what Elsie Clews Parsons characterized as *crisis ceremonialism*, 'ceremonial to signalize or allow of the passing from one stage of life to another.' . . . Following her lead, one might coin the term *teletic rites*, from the Greek concept of *telesis*, putting off the old and putting on the new. One can apply this term to greeting and parting behaviour, where the major stimulation is provided by the arrival or departure of a person from the social scene."

43. A further indication of the fact that she is in the grave and beckons him there is the difference between her address to Gilgamesh and the account of her behavior with Ishullanu. Below, we shall indicate that the Gilgamesh and Ishullanu episodes parallel each other; here, let it be noted, therefore, that, whereas Ishtar desires Ishullanu and comes toward him (*īnā tattaššīšumma tatalkiššu*), she desires Gilgamesh and asks him to come toward her (*īnā ittašši rubūtu* ^{d}*Ištar: alkamma* ^{d}*Gilgameš* . . .): in the account of her behavior with Ishullanu, she is the subject of both *našû* and *alāku*; in the speech to Gilgamesh, she is the subject of *našû* while Gilgamesh is the subject of *alāku*.

to Ishtar; his integration in the netherworld is represented by the grant to him of prolific and vigorous animals (*enzātīka* . . . *-ka* . . . *-ka* . . .).[44]

Here Ishtar is the tomb. Her nature and behavior in our text are characteristic of a type of early earth goddess who is both the source of fertility and life as well as the cause of death and the receiver of the dead. Ishtar gives and takes power. It may even be that the juxtaposition of Gilgamesh's entry into Ishtar's underground home (lines 13–17) and the granting of animals (lines 18–21) is due to the double role of the goddess as receiver of the dead and mother or mistress of animals and/or to the identity or conflation of cavern and animal birth hut.

Gilgamesh understood the nature of Ishtar's proposal. She invited him to assume the role that would eventually be his, to become a ruler of the netherworld. He could have viewed his washing and ceremonial dressing (lines 1–5) as a preparation of his body for burial. But he would not do so. In our epic, Gilgamesh appears sometimes as a character of unified will, sometimes as one whose will is divided between life and the absolute. One suspects that the Gilgamesh of Tablet VI would have seconded Achilles' response when he and Odysseus met in Hades in book 11 of the *Odyssey*:

> "The soul of swift-footed Achilleus, scion of Aiakos, knew me,
> and full of lamentation he spoke to me in winged words:
> 'Son of Laertes and seed of Zeus, resourceful Odysseus,
> hard man, what made you think of this bigger endeavor, how could you
> endure to come down here to Hades' place, where the senseless
> dead men dwell, mere imitations of perished mortals?'
> "So he spoke, and I again said to him in answer:
> 'Son of Peleus, far the greatest of the Achaians, Achilleus,
> I came for the need to consult Teiresias, if he might tell me
> some plan by which I might come back to rocky Ithaka;
> for I have not yet been near Achaian country, nor ever
> set foot on my land, but always I have troubles. Achilleus,
> no man before has been more blessed than you, nor ever
> will be. Before, when you were alive, we Argives honored you
> as we did the gods, and now in this place you have great authority
> over the dead. Do not grieve, even in death, Achilleus.'
> "So I spoke, and he in turn said to me in answer:
> 'O shining Odysseus, never try to console me for dying.
> I would rather follow the plow as thrall to another

44. The significance of the sequence: fruit-animals and its relationship to Gilgamesh's response will be discussed below in Sec. IV.

man, one with no land allotted him and not much to live on,
than be a king over all the perished dead.' "[45]

But there is another side to Achilles, and he may actually believe that in death he finds greatness.[46] Gilgamesh, in any case, moves between the realism, adaptability, and wholehearted commitment to life of Odysseus and the idealism, inflexibility, and inner conflict yet final embrace of divinity and death of Achilles. In Tablet VI, however, Gilgamesh is like that side of Achilles that wishes for life; he is also like Odysseus, who cannot abide a permanent relationship with a goddess of death. And further support for seeing in GE Tablet VI an invitation to a human male by a lonely and sexually needy goddess of the underworld—the home of the dead—to enter her abode and cohabit with her, thus attaining ageless immortality but losing human life, may perhaps be provided by the parallel accounts of Calypso and Circe in the *Odyssey*; on the Mesopotamian side, we note also the story of *Nergal and Ereshkigal.* Like Calypso, Circe,[47] and Ereshkigal, Ishtar is a death goddess. And Ishtar appears again in this guise in our own text when she involves the Bull of Heaven in her conflict with Gilgamesh. In the present context her association with the Bull takes on added significance. For, if we are not mistaken, the Bull of Heaven is none other than Ereshkigal's spouse Gugalanna; and the death goddess Ishtar not only makes her home—like Ereshkigal—under the ground,[48] but even seizes Ereshkigal's husband. For when Gilgamesh refuses to join her, Ishtar takes the Bull both as a

45. Homer, *Odyssey*, 11.471–91 (trans. R. Lattimore; New York: Harper & Row, 1965).

46. C. H. Whitman thinks that neither Achilles nor Odysseus is speaking a literal truth in the passage just quoted. Achilles, for his part, "is emphasizing the cost of his greatness, the incurable sorrow of being Achilles. He is saying, I have suffered the worst, and identified myself with it; you have merely survived. And Odysseus, for his part, says: you are very honored indeed, but you are dead; I am doing the really difficult and great thing" (*Homer and the Heroic Tradition* [Cambridge, MA: Harvard University Press, 1958] 180). For the characters of Odysseus and Achilles, see ibid., 175–220 and 296ff.

47. Regarding Circe and Calypso, see, e.g., R. Graves, *The Greek Myths* (2 vols.; Baltimore: Penguin, 1955), secs. 170.3 and 170.8 (2:367ff.); and G. R. Levy, *The Sword from the Rock: An Investigation into the Origins of Epic Literature and the Development of the Hero* (London: Faber and Faber, 1953) 149 and 152.

48. Having mentioned Ereshkigal, I would note that several further indications—perhaps vestiges—of Ishtar's chthonic character are the very act of descent to the netherworld in the *Descent of Inanna/Ishtar*, the subsequent loss of human and animal fertility, and Ishtar's threat in both GE Tablet VI and the *Descent of Ishtar* to raise the dead. By calling Ishtar a death goddess, I do not mean to deny her other aspects. (For presentations of Inanna/Ishtar, see, e.g., D. O. Edzard, "Mesopotamien: Die Mythologie der Sumerer und Akkader," in *Wörterbuch der Mythologie* [ed. H. W. Haussig; Stuttgart: E. Klett, 1962] 1:81–89; and Jacobsen, *Treasures*, 135–43.) Rather, I simply focus on an aspect that has

replacement for Gilgamesh and as a tool with which to destroy him; finally Ishtar succeeds only in depriving Ereshkigal of a spouse and driving even this male partner to death and destruction.

Thus while Gilgamesh could have viewed his washing and ceremonial dressing as the preparation of his body for burial, he chose instead to regard them as life-affirming acts. He believes with the writer of Proverbs that "her house is the entrance to Sheol, which leads down to the halls of death" (7:27), and he is not yet ready to make the journey. We begin to understand why Gilgamesh viewed Ishtar's provocative offer with something less than equanimity. She threatens to deprive him of that which he most values—life—and offers him the very thing he most fears—death.

III

With the insertion of the Gilgamesh-Ishtar episode into the epic, the original Old Babylonian epic was transformed. But before discussing the transformation, we must make sense of Gilgamesh's answer. We turn directly to Gilgamesh's recital of Ishtar's previous affairs and of the harm she brought her lovers (later we shall deal briefly with the first two sections of his speech). The primary purpose of recounting these incidents is not simply that of pointing up her unfaithfulness or of rebuking her for treating her lovers in an unbecoming and even cruel manner. The recital is made up of six units; each tells the story of one lover: Tammuz, the *allallu*-bird, the lion, the horse, the shepherd, and Ishullanu the gardener. It may well be that individual stories go back to independent traditions.[49] But however anecdotal the recital may appear, it comprises more than just a simple or random series of unconnected encounters. Rather, as presently formulated and ordered, the six units form a scheme.

To understand the scheme, we must subject the recital to a detailed examination. The formation of the scheme depends in no small measure on the way the composer selected and set out his material. Accordingly, we may best begin our discussion by first isolating several features of the presentation; we organize our observations under the headings of style, order of lovers, and grammar.

---

not been sufficiently noted and developed; note, moreover, that many if not all of her aspects (e.g., sexuality and aggression, war) relate directly or indirectly to death.

49. In addition to Tammuz-Ishtar compositions, note, e.g., the passage alluding to Ishtar's affair with the horse cited by M. Civil, "Notes on Sumerian Lexicography, I," *JCS* 20 (1966) 122.

Style: The first episode is short and lacks detail. Then, with one exception, the episodes become successively longer. In order of appearance, the number of lines devoted to each lover is two, three, (two), five, six, fifteen. The exception is the third unit, the account of the lion; this unit has two lines instead of the expected four. This deviation is due to an error of either textual omission or artistic commission, a conclusion substantiated also by the fact that the lion is the only lover of whom it is said neither that Ishtar established wailing for him nor that she struck him and changed his identity. Each story is less schematic and more detailed than the preceding one, with successive episodes providing increasing information on the interaction of Ishtar with her lovers. Moreover, whereas the first five stories are presented in simple narrative form, the style changes with the last lover; here dialogue is introduced into the narrative.[50]

Order: There is a pattern in the order of appearance of the lovers. We move from the nonhuman to the human and from a setting of nature to one of settlement.[51] The first lover is Tammuz, the personification of new life in nature. The next three lovers are animals: bird, lion, horse. Each animal is closer to the human, has more in common with or greater contact with human beings than the preceding one. This is true as regards geographical location, economic function, and physiology or, at least, human perception of animal anatomy and personality. In any case, settled society comes into contact more with horses than with lions, and more with lions than with birds off in the forest. Even when we reach the human lovers, the shepherd and Ishullanu the gardener, we are still progressing along the same axis. The shepherd is on a line toward the

50. After observing and working out the stylistic features, I noted the following remark by C. J. Gadd: "In the celebrated speech of Gilgamesh rejecting with contumely the advances of Ishtar (Tablet VI, 24ff.) the tale of her ill-fated lovers (45ff.) is evidently rich in allusions to stories which would have been largely familiar to the ancient audiences. As the line of six victims of her love and her caprice goes on, the stories tend to increase in detail, and the sixth, Ishullanu, has a veritable 'idyll' of his own, embellished with narrative, conversation, intimate detail, proverbial allusions, and even a moral, each, no doubt, with a background in folklore" ("Some Contributions to the Gilgamesh Epic," *Iraq* 28 [1966] 117).

51. In the discussion following my paper at the AOS, Ann Guinan noted the possibility that the text may also be organized along a vertical axis and move from above to below (bird—*dallalu*). Additionally there may also be a movement from the world of the dead to that of the living: Tammuz in the netherworld; the bird in the grove—a secluded place between the world of the living and the world of the dead; etc. Is this a vertical upward movement from the netherworld to the normal habitations of human beings?

settlement but not yet there. His camp represents an outpost of the settled community, a way station between nature and culture. We need only remember the role of the shepherds' camp earlier in the epic: to such a camp Shamhat brought Enkidu to familiarize him with civilized life and thence he took the road to Uruk. The shepherd stands, moreover, between the earlier animals and the later humans as suggested by the place of animals in his story: he cares for sheep, offers lambs to Ishtar, is turned into a wolf, and is attacked by his own dogs. With the gardener, we move into the settled human community and learn of human familial relations; in part, Ishullanu is presented in terms of his relationship with a father (Ishtar's) and a mother (his own). The next lover is Gilgamesh. He represents one further step in the progression; with him we have moved on to a city dweller with a well-defined social role. It is no accident that at the beginning of his episode, immediately prior to Ishtar's proposal, Gilgamesh is depicted donning royal attire, and that, immediately after his refusal, the first reference to him by a third party—Anu—is as *šarru*, "king" (line 89).[52]

Grammar: Shifts in style and progression from one lover to the next give the impression of movement and change; at the same time, the episodes seem to be intertwined with one flowing into the next, and so the recital also has the appearance of sameness and constancy. This appearance is due, of course, to the occurrence of common elements in the several episodes and the recurrence throughout of the same dominant theme. It is due no less to the composer's manipulation of the resources of lexicon and grammar: through the use of language, he conveys the notion that acts and effects of the past are carried over and forward into the present, that events continue from their point of origin to the point where Gilgamesh and the audience are located. This sense of repetition and persistence is effected (1) by the repeated use of such verbs as *râmu*, "love" (lines 42, 48, 51, 53, 58, 64, 79), and *maḫāṣu*, "smite" (lines 49, 61, 76); (2) by the use of adverbs of time (*šatta ana šatti* [line 47]) and distributive nouns (*7 u 7 šuttāti* [line 52]; *7 bēru* [line 55]); (3) by the use of durative and permansive verb forms in the description of the final state of several lovers: *izzaz*, variant *ašib*,[53] *išassi* (line 50), *uṭarradūšu*, *unaššakū* (lines 62–63), *elû*, *arid* (line 78); and, most of all, (4) by the systematic use of iterative /*tan*/ forms[54] throughout the section: *bitakkâ*

52. See Frankena, "Nouveaux fragments," 121, line 24.

53. See n. 56 below.

54. I note in nn. 55–59 below those instances where my grammatical analysis differs from that of W. von Soden, *Akkadisches Handwörterbuch* (Wiesbaden: Harrassowitz, 1959–81) (hereafter *AHw*).

(lines 47, 57)—*bakû* G-stem, *tan* form, infinitive; *taltīmiššu* / *taltīmī* (*taltimmiššu* / *taltimmī*) (lines 47, 54, 55, 56, 57)—*šâmu* G-stem, *tan* form, preterite;[55] *taltebbera*⟨*ī*⟩[56] (line 49)—*šebēru* G-stem, *tan* form, preterite;[57] *tuḫtarrîššu* (line 52)—*ḫerû* D-stem, *tan* form, preterite; *tuttirriššu* (lines 61, 76)—*târu* D-stem, *tan* form, preterite;[58] *tattaššîšumma* (line 67)—*našû* G-stem, *tan* form, preterite.[59]

Our interpretation can be more easily followed if we preface our detailed presentation with a succinct statement of the manner and purpose of the scheme. The recital recounts a series of events each more finite in time and space than the preceding one and sets them out in a progression along past-present, nature-culture axes, each successive event beginning at a point closer to the time and place of the speaker. The purpose of the recital is to join Gilgamesh to the sequence but to place him at the very end, right at a point where something new may happen. Gilgamesh is set there so that he may be identified with and yet separated from those who precede him, so that his encounter with Ishtar may be located in the familiar context of enhancement, transformation, and loss but be so placed as to suggest that his encounter will end differently from the encounters of all previous lovers. The familiarity tells us that Ishtar's offer amounts to an offer of death; Gilgamesh's appearance at the pinnacle tells us not only that he does not need or want her love, and the death that is attendant upon its acceptance, and that he will reject her offer, but also that he can withstand her anger and vindictive attack and emerge victorious.

This is only a summary and follows from our construction of the details that make up Gilgamesh's speech. With this summary in mind, we should therefore focus again on the features of style, order, and language and try to draw out the meaning and effect of these features: a natural backdrop is laid out, and a series of ever-recurring events is set in motion. The events start one after the other; as each succeeding event occurs for the first time, it joins a growing body of recurrent events that repeat throughout time until the present. (Suffice it to note the repeated use of the /*tan*/ iterative forms and the fact that the various episodes

55. *AHw*: Gt.

56. *Taltebber*⟨*ī*⟩ (line 49) is followed directly by the alternate readings *izzaz* and *ašib* (line 50). The /*ī*/ 2 f.s. afformative of **taltebberī* was lost because of the /*ī*/ prefix of *izzaz*; hence *izzaz* is probably an earlier reading than *ašib*.

57. *AHw*: G; the variant spelling *tal-te-eb-ber* excludes the analysis of the verb as a simple G.

58. *AHw*: D.

59. *AHw*: G; the variant spelling [*ta-at*]-*taš-ši-šu-ma* (Frankena, "Nouveaux fragments," 120, line 33 = Tablet VI, line 67) excludes the analysis of the verb as a simple G.

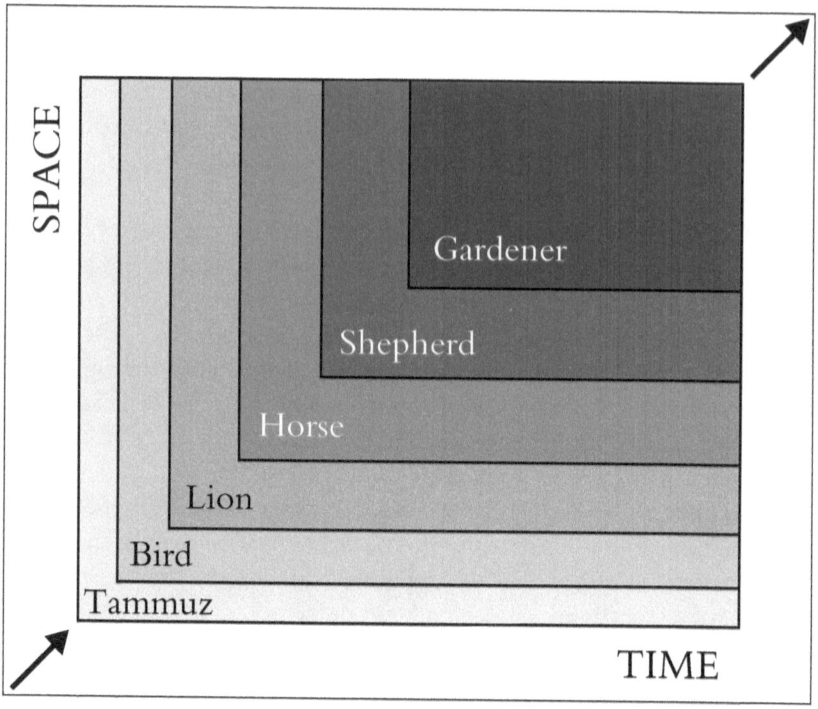

Fig. 1.

provide etiologies of recurring natural events.) Thus the wolf was not simply cut off from the sheepfold once upon a time in the distant past. Rather, once the shepherd is transformed into a wolf, he repeatedly and constantly tries to reenter, only to be expelled again and again. Obviously, succeeding events cover less time than preceding ones, so that, the earlier the event, the broader its duration; the later the event, the narrower its time span. Moreover, earlier events seem to range over more terrain than successive ones. I have tried to convey this sense by means of a graphic illustration (see fig. 1).

There is a steady decrease in the temporal duration and natural space covered by each successive event, and attention shifts increasingly away from animals and the wild and toward humans and civilized life. Successive episodes appear closer in time to the present and in location to the civilized. As spheres become narrower, our focus becomes sharper; as the action comes closer to and operates more in the mode of the punctual now and the civilized here, the episodes become familiar and are presented in greater detail. Without giving up that which is common to the whole, we move from the universal to the particular, the particular being both an extension as well as the opposite of the universal; we move from the animal to the human, the country to the city, the mythological to the historical, the durative to the punctual.

The text creates the impression of duration or constancy by repetition, by the use of iteratives, and so forth. It also creates the illusion of movement from the past to the present. The characterization of Tammuz as the lover of Ishtar's youth (line 46) and the seriatim listing of lovers contribute to this impression but do not suffice to create it. Although we are never told explicitly that Tammuz was the first and the others were later, that the account is progressing from the past to the present, the text makes it clear that the events happen in the order in which they are mentioned: by starting with a schematic presentation, the text creates a sense of distance; then, by moving from the alien to the familiar and presenting each successive episode in greater detail, the text brings the story closer and closer to us. And as the story progresses, there is a growing awareness of change and sense of psychic involvement.

A circle is created with Gilgamesh touching his most distant predecessor, Tammuz, and his most immediate one, Ishullanu. We move from Gilgamesh to Tammuz to Ishullanu and back to Gilgamesh. But the text does more than just create a circle. Having created the circle, the text moves forcibly to break out of it, to move away from Tammuz, to build up to the story of Ishullanu, and then to use his story not only as a way of focusing again on Ishtar's original proposal to Gilgamesh and its meaning but also as a way of preparing the ground for Gilgamesh's eventual refusal and successful stand against attack. The story of Ishullanu and Ishtar leads us back into the larger story of Gilgamesh and Ishtar. In effect we have a story within a story.

The text moves from the mythological to the actual. Tammuz is Gilgamesh's mythic counterpart, but Ishullanu is his actual counterpart. The story of Tammuz is paradigmatic. The story of Ishullanu introduces a new aspect into the interaction of Ishtar and her lovers, thus transforming the paradigm. For Ishullanu is the first to whom Ishtar is said to speak and the first to refuse her advances. The story of Ishullanu constitutes the first major break with the past. By presenting Ishtar's offer and Ishullanu's refusal and by the use of dialogue as a centerpiece to convey proposal and rejection, the story of Ishullanu and Ishtar becomes thematically and formally the direct literary precursor to the expanded account of Gilgamesh and Ishtar and to the extensive use of dialogue in that account.

Reading the recital of lovers is like traveling a road on which each way station is similar to and yet slightly different from the preceding one. Features are carried over from one story to the next; but the growing detail brings with it more and more change till finally we encounter in the Ishullanu story something really new and different. Here for the first time the text states that Ishtar raised her eyes and looked at the object of her desire (line 67) and recounts a verbal interchange between the goddess and the lover; inviting Ishullanu to make love to her, she suggests that they consume his vitality (lines 68–69); Ishullanu refuses, articulating his refusal in the form of two rhetorical questions (lines 71–74).[60]

It is important to notice that the very features that set the Ishullanu scene off from those that precede it correspond to major features of the larger Gilgamesh-Ishtar episode:

1. Thus Ishtar's gaze of line 67 (*īnā tattaššīšumma*) corresponds to her gaze of line 6 (*ana dumqi ša* ᵈ*Gilgameš īnā ittašši rubūtu* ᵈ*Ištar*).

2. Her desire to consume Ishullanu's strength in line 68 (*kiššūtaki*[61] *ī nīkul*) corresponds to her request for Gilgamesh's vigor in line 8 (*inbīka yâši qâšu qīšamma*).[62]

3. Ishullanu's first question (lines 71–73): *yâši mīnâ terrešinni / ummī lā tēpâ anāku lā ākul / ša akkalu akali pīšāti u errēti*) seems to correspond to the first section of Gilgamesh's speech (lines 24–32). In his question, Ishullanu picks up on the theme of eating introduced by Ishtar in line 68 and asks whether he should take up food that will spoil when he has already been fed; the food to which he refers is food that is offered to the dead and turns rotten. He does not want to eat the food of the dead. The text of the first section of Gilgamesh's speech (lines 24–32) is preserved in a fragmentary form; still it is at least possible that in these lines Gilgamesh picks up on Ishtar's request for a gift of food in line 8 and asks her whether it is not true that she has no need for the gifts—including food (lines 26–27)—that a bridegroom would bestow upon his bride and that by proposing to him she is in fact inviting him to lay out the offerings—including food—and appurtenances for his own funeral and burial.

---

60. Although I do not agree with R. Labat's assessment of Ishullanu's response (*Les religions*, 183 n. 7: "Ishoullanou feint de ne pas comprendre"), I have no doubt of the correctness of his observation there that *ākul*—*akkalu* and *elpetu* in Ishullanu's response play, respectively, on *ī nī/ākul* and *luput* of Ishtar's offer.

61. For *-ki* understand *-ka*; the *i* is due to the following /ī/.

62. Note the sound play between words in the corresponding lines 8 and 68: *qâšu qīšamma* (line 8) . . . *kiššūtaki* (line 68).

4. Ishullanu's second and final question (line 74: *ša kuṣṣi elpetu kutummūʾa*, "should reeds be my covering against the cold?") seems to correspond to the second section of Gilgamesh's speech (lines 33–41). Like lines 24–32, lines 33–41 are somewhat damaged and obscure; but even just *kutummīša* in line 36 and the mention of cold in line 33 suffice to indicate the existence of the connection with line 74. Ishullanu's remark in line 74 refers, I think, to grass as a covering of the grave or reed matting as a wrapping of the corpse; he does not want to be buried. In lines 33–41, Ishtar is addressed by nine destructive kennings. These nine entries refer similarly, I think, to the grave, its opening and lining, the covering of the dead, and funerary appurtenances. Even those entries that refer to parts of the burial also convey the notion of the grave as a whole. The individual parts adversely affect the corpse; in addition they also share in and add to the destructive force of the whole. In sum, the total grave described in these lines—the whole as well as the parts—does not preserve and house its inhabitant; rather it shrinks, squashes, and obliterates the dead body so that the corpse loses its form and is finally ground up into dust. Ishtar is a grave that may even betray the dead. Certainty is out of the question; but the interpretation here suggested at least makes some sense of most of the entries in lines 33–41 and lends a measure of coherence and unity to the list as a whole.[63]

These correspondences highlight the importance of dialogue in the Ishullanu and Gilgamesh episodes. It is the dialogue between Ishullanu and Ishtar that is responsible for the length of the Ishullanu episode and for its increase in length over the preceding episode (6 → 15 lines); similarly the dialogue between Gilgamesh and Ishtar is responsible for the length of the Gilgamesh-Ishtar interlude and for the creation of an epic segment wherein a dramatic verbal contest takes over and pushes the straight narration of events into the background. Ishullanu and Ishtar acted and spoke like Gilgamesh and Ishtar. By reminding the goddess of the events that transpired between her and Ishullanu, Gilgamesh links the present with the past and recalls speeches from the past that prefigure

63. *daltu*, line 34, opening of grave, the door that holds back or imprisons ([*ša i*]*kallû*) ghosts (*šāra u zīqa*) or the door that does not keep out ([*ša lā i*]*kallû*) the cold wind (cf. *šu-ri-pu*, line 33)—the dead are naked. *ekallu*, line 35, grave, netherworld. *pīru . . . kutummu*, line 36, cover of grave (cf. [?] *epera katāmu*, said of burying the dead) or of corpse. *ittu*, line 37, coating of grave. *nādu*, line 38, waterskin, travel provision for the dead. *pīlu*, line 39, lining of grave (cf. D. D. Luckenbill, *The Annals of Sennacherib* [OIP 2; Chicago: University of Chicago Press, 1924] 136, lines 18–19). *māt nukurti*, line 40, grave, netherworld. *šēnu*, line 41, footwear for the dead traveler.

and capture the meaning of the speeches presently being declaimed by Ishtar and Gilgamesh.

A systematic, line-by-line comparison of the two stories is instructive. All parts of the Ishullanu account seem to correspond to sections of the larger Gilgamesh account. The correlation between the two accounts is sufficiently high that we may even set out the shared elements in the form of an outline of the two stories (see table below).

OUTLINE OF SHARED ELEMENTS

	Tablet VI (Lines)		
Plot Elements	Ishullanu Story		Gilgamesh Story
a) The hero is presented playing his traditional role: Ishullanu, Gardener; Gilgamesh, King.[64]	64–66	:	1–5
b) The goddess sees and desires the hero.	67	:	6
c) She requests his vigor, using the language of food.	68	:	8
d) In return, she offers him a reward: the opportunity to enter her and dwell among the dead.[65]	69	:	9–21
e) The hero speaks.	70	:	22–23
f) He refuses the goddess. He states that he has no need for the materials—especially food—meant for those who die.	71–73	:	24–32
g) He calls Ishtar a grave.	74	:	33–41
h) The goddess hears the speech.	75	:	80
i) She reacts to the rejection.	76–78	:	81ff.

64. Gardeners and kings are associated; cf. W. W. Hallo and J. J. A. van Dijk, *The Exaltation of Inanna* (Yale Near Eastern Researches 3; New Haven, CT: Yale University Press, 1968) 6. If some form of *dalû* is read in GE Tablet VI, line 78 (see A. L. Oppenheim, "Mesopotamian Mythology II," *Orientalia*, n.s., 17 [1948] 37 and n. 4, and reference there; cf. *CAD*, vol. D, p. 56, and vol. M/2, p. 58; and *AHw*, p. 1550), we note also the association of garden work (*nukaribbu*) and water drawing (*dalû*) in both the Ishullanu episode and *The Sargon Legend* (B. Lewis, *The Sargon Legend* [ASOR Dissertation Series 4; Cambridge, MA: American Schools of Oriental Research, 1980] 25, lines 8–12).

65. Vagina (*ḫurdatni*, line 69) = house (*bītini*, lines 13–14) = tomb. Here *ḫurdatu* and *bītu* are recesses in the ground and represent the place of burial. The linking of *ḫurdatu and bītu* explains the otherwise inexplicable /*-ni*/, 'our', of *ḫurdatni*: *bītu* and, by analogy, *ḫurdatu* are treated as "our"—our chamber, our vagina. [But see now J. G. Westenholz, "A Forgotten Love Song," in *Language, Literature, and History: Philological and Historical Studies Presented to Erica Reiner* (ed. F. Rochberg-Halton; AOS 67; New Haven, CT: American Oriental Society, 1987), col. 1, line 13′, p. 422, and discussion on p. 417.]

The stories are modeled on each other. Each story elucidates the other even if some details still elude our understanding and others have been grasped with only a minimum of assurance. The story of Ishullanu and Ishtar is a miniature; in it are condensed most of the important events and speeches of the story of Gilgamesh and Ishtar.[66] The Ishullanu-Ishtar episode is set into the Gilgamesh-Ishtar episode as a small room with a window is set into and looks out on a larger room that is similar to but not quite identical with it.

For much of their course the two stories correspond and run parallel to each other. But we must now note that, for all the similarities, there are also some important differences. Ishullanu's speech corresponds only to the first two sections of Gilgamesh's speech (lines 24–32, 33–41); the third section, the recital of stories of Ishtar's previous lovers (lines 42–79), finds no echo in Ishullanu's speech.

The third section seems to be a purposeful addition to a more basic bipartite rhetorical form. This recounting of Ishtar's previous lovers looks to the past and tries thereby to point up the significance of Gilgamesh's present encounter with Ishtar. The very act of reciting these stories, the similarity of Gilgamesh's story to these others but especially

66. Even granting that Ishullanu and Šukalletuda may be parallel or related personages (cf., e.g., Gadd, "Some Contributions," 117–18; J.-M. Durand, "Un commentaire à *TDP* I, AO 17661," *RA* 73 [1979] 164–65, esp. p. 165 n. 45; W. W. Hallo, "Šullanu," *RA* 74 [1980] 94), for purposes of this essay, I did not find it particularly useful to draw upon the tale *Inanna and Šukalletuda* (for this composition, see simply S. N. Kramer, *History Begins at Sumer* [3rd rev. ed.; Philadelphia: University of Pennsylvania Press, 1981] 70–74 and 353). Instead, I have explored the relationship of the Ishullanu-Ishtar and Gilgamesh-Ishtar stories and tried to understand the place of the Ishullanu story in the larger Gilgamesh one. In retrospect, I can say that this approach has yielded good results. I should also note that I have not invoked the Sumerian *Gilgamesh and the Bull of Heaven* (MSS listed by C. Wilcke, "Politische Opposition nach sumerischen Quellen: Der Konflict zwischen Königtum und Ratsversammlung: Literaturwerke als politische Tendenzschriften," in *La voix de l'opposition en Mesopotamie: Colloque organisé par l'Institut des Hautes Études de Belgique, 19 et 20 mars 1973* [ed. A. Finet; Brussels: Institut des Hautes Études, 1975] 58 n. 69), partly because I have followed A. Falkenstein's ("Gilgameš. Nach sumerischen Texten," *RlA* 3:361) interpretation of the text. (So, too, e.g., Wilcke, "Politische Opposition," 58; and Tigay, *Evolution*, 174–75; contrast S. N. Kramer, *History Begins at Sumer*, 189, and *From the Poetry of Sumer* [Berkeley: University of California Press, 1979] 74–75.) In any case, my intention has been to explore certain aspects of the dialogue between Ishtar and Gilgamesh in the Akkadian epic and to provide an internally coherent interpretation thereof. If anything, C. J. Gadd's remark regarding a comparison of the Šukalletuda and Inanna and Ishullanu and Ishtar stories ("Some Contributions," 118: "If the comparison has any point it lies perhaps in the opposite conduct of the characters, especially of the goddess") seems to apply equally well to the relation of *Gilgamesh and the Bull of Heaven* to GE Tablet VI. Thus, where Ishtar offers dominion to Gilgamesh in the Akkadian version, she denies him dominion in the Sumerian version.

to Ishullanu's, and Gilgamesh's own assertion that Ishtar will treat him as she has treated the others (line 79) all link Gilgamesh with the others and set out the background against which and the terms in which Ishtar's original proposal is to be viewed. The Ishullanu episode forms the culmination of Gilgamesh's speech. This episode directs attention back to Ishtar's original proposal to Gilgamesh and holds the proposal up to full view; it then recalls and recapitulates Gilgamesh's lengthy response and leads up to and asserts the final contention that everything—her offer, the gift she requests, her nature, her past history—indicates that, should he accept her offer, she will treat him as she has treated the others and deprive him of that which he values above all else. Here perhaps for the first time Gilgamesh speaks clearly and unambiguously and tells Ishtar—and the text tells us—that he understands the meaning of her proposal and that, for the time being, he has decided that he must refuse her.

What I find so remarkable about Gilgamesh's recital of lovers is how the "already" and the "not yet" come together; how retrospect and anticipation combine to create meaning and emotional effect.[67] In what purports to be a mythological context, we witness an awareness of dynamic time, of past and future, and an understanding of history and change. Having been forced back into the past by the recital of lovers, a sense of identification is created; as we move forward a sense of familiarity grows, but with it comes the expectation that also change is built into reality and that in the future something new will happen. The recital thus also directs our gaze to the future, and here we learn how different Gilgamesh is. The very fact that Gilgamesh is the only lover to show awareness of the existence and experience of preceding lovers and to recount their story, and the gradual but increasing emergence and accumulation of change in the successive stories of the lovers prepare the way for something new. As we come to the end of Gilgamesh's speech, we begin to realize that the encounter is not over; the speech will be followed by a confrontation, and the conflict between Ishtar and Gilgamesh will be carried well beyond the Ishtar-Ishullanu one.

Gilgamesh ends his account of Ishtar's treatment of her lovers, and his speech as a whole, with the sentence: *u yâši taramminnima kī šâšunu*

67. Compare D. Daiches, *A Study of Literature: For Readers and Critics* (Ithaca, NY: Cornell University Press, 1948) 83: "Literature, like music and unlike painting and sculpture, is dependent for its effect on the time dimension: a literary work of art expresses its meaning over a period of time, and at each moment—William James's 'specious present' where the 'already' continuously merges into the 'not yet'—retrospect and anticipation combine to set up the required richness of meaning."

tu[. . .] (line 79). Alluding to the consequences of not refusing her offer, he makes a negative assertion in the form of what is either a question or perhaps, rather, a positive hypothetical statement of a condition unacceptable to him. He intends to say that they will not be lovers and Ishtar will not control his being. Here Gilgamesh anticipates the future by relating the past to the present; he intends his remark to conclude the episode. This last statement does indeed close the discussion, but, far from ending the encounter, it carries it into a wider arena. For while there is nothing left to be said between them, a reaction on the part of Ishtar is still called for and anticipated. (Note that Ishtar's reaction to Gilgamesh is introduced by a line—80—similar to one—75—that introduces her reaction to Ishullanu.) And Ishtar takes her cue from Gilgamesh's account of her lovers and his final assertion. This assertion has an effect opposite from the one intended, for it suggests to Ishtar the very plan of action that it was meant to avoid. She will treat his last question as if it were a statement and thereby transform a negation into an affirmation of the hypothetical condition. Even though Gilgamesh made no concession to Ishtar and entered into no relationship with her, thus not permitting her to "love" him, she will treat him as she had treated the others. To be sure, she will not follow her original plan of just gaining control over him and determining his destiny; now she will try to attack and destroy him. She had offered him a home in the netherworld; with his refusal she will transform death into an act and state of destruction.

Having been told how Ishtar has treated her previous lovers, we now expect an account of how she will treat Gilgamesh. A new chapter is opened, and our gaze is directed beyond the speech. The meeting of Gilgamesh and Ishtar must now be abandoned. She must respond to his speech; but by the logic of the situation further talking as well as the kind of one-on-one action appropriate to the Ishullanu episode are now excluded. She must move away from Gilgamesh and from the speech situation that has prevailed until now. Her response must originate elsewhere and involve additional forces; the action moves forward. Gilgamesh's refusal will have enraged Ishtar even more than Ishullanu's, and she must initiate an even stronger reprisal. Yet we are led to anticipate and hope for a victory on Gilgamesh's part even though Ishtar will mount an attack greater than any she mounted previously. Such is our expectation for several reasons; if nothing else we expect Gilgamesh to be victorious because in the evolving scheme of interactions between Ishtar and her lovers, victory is the most obvious variation on the proposal-rejection-defeat pattern of the Ishullanu episode. But until the fight we cannot be certain of the outcome. The tension is further stretched and suspense heightened by the length of the subsequent dialogue between Ishtar and Anu and Anu's initial resistance.[68] Finally the fight takes place and Gilgamesh triumphs. This is what we have been led to believe will happen, and this constitutes one of the greatest differences between Gilgamesh and Ishullanu: whereas Ishullanu was the first to refuse Ishtar and Gilgamesh is now the second, Ishullanu was not able to withstand Ishtar's reprisal, but Gilgamesh is able to withstand the attack and emerge victorious.

IV

Although Gilgamesh has vanquished Ishtar, he will eventually learn that resistance is ultimately futile; death is part of life, though it may feel so very alien. In Tablet VI, he is not yet ready to accept a new identity and assume a role in the netherworld. He is dominated most of all by the fear of loss. By modeling the Ishullanu account on sections of the Gilgamesh account and highlighting the similarities in their encounters with Ishtar, the composer has indicated that, like Ishullanu, Gilgamesh understood that acceptance of Ishtar's offer would lead to loss. Gilgamesh could not accept Ishtar's offer of marriage because he understood that to accept was to die, that Ishtar wished to deprive him of his life. He realized that Ishtar intended to deceive him by presenting their marriage as if it were this-worldly, whereas it would in fact lead directly to his transferral to the netherworld.

Recognizing in her offer the hidden promise of becoming a lord of the dead, he refuses and recounts the story of her previous lovers; their story exemplifies the treatment he can expect: first *enhancement*, then

68. In view of my interpretation of Ishtar's proposal, Anu's statement that Ishtar provoked Gilgamesh and has only herself to blame for his response makes perfectly good sense; it is congruous to and follows from her proposal and Gilgamesh's refusal to accept his new role. Accordingly, I cannot agree with C. Wilcke's opinion that the Akkadian version does not recount Ishtar's act of instigation ("Politische Opposition," 58: "An aber verweist sie darauf, dass sie selbst die Antwort Gilgameš's herausgefordert habe, was aber in dieser akkadischen Version nirgends berichtet war"). In reaction to Wilcke's interpretation of *Gilgamesh and the Bull of Heaven*, J. S. Cooper argues that it is understandable that Inanna of the Sumerian text would refuse Gilgamesh the right to judge in Eanna: "If, as in the Akkadian version, Gilgamesh had refused to do *his* duty to Inanna, then she had every right to keep him out of her temple" (*The Curse of Agade* [Baltimore: Johns Hopkins University Press, 1983] 13 n. 41). I cannot agree with Cooper's interpretation of the Akkadian text if his remark is intended to say that GE Tablet VI is simply an account of nothing more than Gilgamesh's refusal to enter into the rite of the sacred marriage.

transformation, and finally, *a loss of self leading to frenzied but futile attempts to regain that which had been surrendered.* Ishtar is attainment but also attenuation; Ishtar is the opposite of what one values. To love her is to surrender one's identity. The free become domesticated; insiders are expelled; the settled are forced to wander; the living die; and humans are turned into animals. Stability and balance are lost and are replaced by discontent, distress, and agitation. In proposing marriage, Ishtar offers to enhance Gilgamesh's identity while at the same time depriving him of it. Her proposal to Gilgamesh is an offer of power; it is also an offer to transform his living self into his dead self.

In Tablet VI the new identity that Ishtar offers or tries to impose is still conflict-ridden and untenable. Were Gilgamesh to accept it here, it would remain alien, and he, like the previous lovers, would constantly seek to regain that which he had lost and to return whence he had come. Such futile attempts to escape their new identities underlie the behavior of the other lovers. This is most evident and touching in the account of the shepherd turned wolf, for he will always try to rejoin the sheepfold and will always be chased away by the shepherds with whom he had once been almost identical and by the dogs with whom he is now almost identical. The similarity of the adversaries brings home the realization that absolute separation from those with whom one was and is closest is often the most distressing part of stepping over boundaries that divide the world into realms that touch but may not mingle; once one has taken the step one cannot turn back, even though the distance seems so very small. The contrast provided by Enkidu is instructive. In Tablet I, Enkidu at first acted like Ishtar's lovers and tried to rejoin the animals; he quickly understood that he could not and with Shamhat's help, he accepted and played his new role. But Ishtar is not Shamhat. Ishtar's demands on her lovers, their sense of loss and of being used, and the alienness of their new roles render Ishtar's lovers unable to assume their new identities wholeheartedly. And Gilgamesh can only assume his new role when he is prepared to accept his new identity wholeheartedly, for otherwise he will not be able to fulfill the functions of initiator, counselor, and arbitrator of the dead.

For the composer of the epic, a limited, orderly, and, above all, civilized existence is the most that one can hope for. Only civilization provides accomplishments and forms that make life worthwhile; the building of cities, the transmission of culture, and the enjoyment of this life are the only values of normal human life. Yet precisely because he is civilized, Gilgamesh has the most to lose. The list of lovers makes us realize that Gilgamesh is civilized. His position at the very end of the list—and the image of Gilgamesh as king—place him at the very pinnacle of civilized life. The closer the lover is to culture, the greater the sense that a relationship with Ishtar leads to a loss of what one prizes and the greater the realization that one has very little to gain and much to lose from the relationship. Gilgamesh has the most to lose—certainly more than any of the other lovers—because he is the most civilized and for him it is life, humanity, and a civilized existence that are at stake. Ishtar wishes to kill Gilgamesh and he resists courageously. From lover to lover there has been an increase in foresight and self-awareness and a growing belief that one can control one's own life. And Gilgamesh will refuse Ishtar and resist her offer to enter the netherworld until he himself can define his new identity and grow into it.

Here I must emphasize that it would be an oversimplification to say that Gilgamesh refused Ishtar's proposal only because he recognized it to be an attempt to transform him into a lord of the netherworld. He also recognized therein a form of death that was repugnant to him. For Ishtar wished not only to kill him but also to turn him into an animal; she wished to change him from a live, civilized man into a dead, wild animal. The prospect of death is all the more frightening when it is seen to involve not only the loss of life but also the loss of human form. Death, then, is the complete antithesis to human life, for everything that is familiar—our identity, our physical and social forms, our relations, and so forth—is lost. Death is absolutely alien. Perhaps death is less dread and its acceptance easier for us when it is thought to share some similarity with the life we know in this world—when for Gilgamesh the king death is not the total destruction or reversal of the civilized community.

Underlying the interaction between Gilgamesh and Ishtar, then, are the issue of mortality and the question of the form and nature of death. In Tablet VI, life and death still stand in stark contrast to each other and have not yet joined to form a continuum. The sense of life and death as balanced but conflicting opposites finds expression in a structured thematic design that draws together Ishtar's proposal and Gilgamesh's account of the lovers, again demonstrating the close connection between the two and confirming our reading of the proposal and our construction of the account as an apposite and reasoned response.

The design centers on the themes of fruit and animals, and these elements are set out in an inverted order. The end of Gilgamesh's speech recalls the beginning of Ishtar's speech. Ishtar's proposal begins with the request for Gilgamesh's fruit (*inbu* [line 8]) and then progresses toward and ends with the offer of animals (lines 18–21). In the ensuing account of lovers, Gilgamesh first mentions the animals and then draws away from them and links up with Ishullanu the gardener; his recital progresses from animals (lines 48–63) to fruit (lines 64–66). The layout follows a chiastic arrangement, with Gilgamesh's recital reversing and offsetting Ishtar's offer:

A)	Fruit	
B)		Animals
B′)		Animals
A′)	Fruit	

In our text fruit and animals function as opposites, with fruit connoting the cultivation of crops, human society, and order, and animals connoting wild nature, the netherworld, and destruction. Were Gilgamesh to have accepted Ishtar's offer, he would have granted her his fruit, entered the netherworld, received the fertility of animals, and become the source of animal life. Thus he would have been transformed into an animal or an animal spirit and taken on an identity similar to that of the animal lovers who accepted Ishtar's advances. But Gilgamesh refuses to offer up his fruit and to assume an animal identity. Hence he first mentions the animals but then dissociates himself from them and draws abreast of Ishullanu, he of the date orchard. Ishullanu thought that he could bestow his fruit on Ishtar without becoming her lover and suffering transformation into an animal. But Ishullanu miscalculated and was turned into an animal, and Gilgamesh must now move even beyond him. He must not only not accept Ishtar's love but also not give her his fruit, for only thus can he save himself from being transformed into an animal. Gilgamesh has shifted the arena from the animal back to the human cultivator; in this way he has thus far successfully opposed Ishtar and her wish to possess him.

Gilgamesh believes that only by holding tight to this course will he succeed in frustrating Ishtar's design and saving himself. But if he will not die and become an animal, she will forcibly impose death and animals. She now reverses the direction of the movement that Gilgamesh had instituted and turns back to the animals. But this reversal in movement is headed not toward animal fertility but, rather, toward the destruction of both animals and nature as a whole. Her move signals the opening of a new chiasm that inverts the prior one.

The direction of the prior chiasm is reversed. But also the design is altered and expanded. Ishtar does more than just counter Gilgamesh by simply moving in a direction opposite to that of his last move; that is, she does more than just reintroduce animals (as she previously had done by transforming the shepherd into a wolf and the gardener into a *dallalu*). Her move shifts the conflict to another plane, with higher stakes. She moves beyond Gilgamesh and thus expands the conflict. Ishtar now treats Gilgamesh as an animal that is to die at the hands of another and larger animal. The regression and expansion are achieved by Ishtar's introduction of the Bull of Heaven—an animal[69]—as Gilgamesh's counterpart and substitute. We are shocked but not surprised to discover that Ishtar ends up turning even this divine creature into a dead animal.

The composer extends the chiastic design and the thematic treatment of fruit and animals and creates a new and larger structure. The themes of fruit and animals are translated to a broader—almost cosmic—sphere of activity. Properly speaking, the Bull may represent either fertility or sterility—at one time he spent, I suspect, half the year in this world and the other half in the netherworld; here, in the *Gilgamesh Epic*, he is the exemplar of destruction. With the appearance of the Bull, the story of Ishtar's proposal and Gilgamesh's rejection is expanded and made part of a larger conflict between death, disorder, and sterility represented by the Bull, and life, order, and fertility represented by the gardener-king Gilgamesh. Even if Ishtar's use and misuse of the Bull is a continuation of the scheme presented by Gilgamesh whereby Ishtar's lovers are either animals or are turned into animals, everything now takes place on a larger scale and in a broader arena. The protagonists now loom larger than life. The Bull is the reverse of life and the powerful extension of death; Gilgamesh is the opponent of death and the powerful assertion of life. The two stand in conflict, each invading the territory of the other in ways that are unacceptable if not impossible in an ordered nature.

The game is no longer played by the same rules as before. Once Gilgamesh threatens to destroy the natural order by refusing to die and take on an animal identity, Ishtar herself moves outside the normal pattern and makes use of an animal[70] in an attempt to destroy Gilgamesh

69. Given that the main opponent of Gilgamesh and Enkidu in Tablet VI is an animal, it is worth noting that their earlier opponent, Huwawa, seems to be a tree spirit. Elsewhere I hope to amplify my remarks about the Bull of Heaven. Here I should mention that I very much regret that I am unable to shed new light on the animal identity of Ishullanu.

70. Her use of the Bull deviates from the standard pattern. One can gain some appreciation of the difference simply by noting the different roles accorded the Bull here and the dogs in the account of the shepherd; the shepherd was turned into a wolf by Ishtar and the dogs simply reinforce that identity. Moreover, there the dogs represent the

and the civilized, human identity he is trying to retain. But now the natural order is no longer in the ascendancy; actions and their outcome will depend less on custom and brute force, on the predictable sequence of natural events, and more on the strength of personality of the protagonists. And Ishtar discovers that far from destroying Gilgamesh, she enhances his social status and reputation and contributes to the destruction of the Bull. The Bull represents the old order; and now it is the power of personal will, exemplified by Gilgamesh's refusal and even by Ishtar's subsequent coercion of Anu, that is decisive.

Gilgamesh's refusal and Ishtar's response result in and represent the destruction of the old order. At one time, for at least part of the year, Gilgamesh was the husband of Ishtar and the Bull was the husband of Ereshkigal. Ishtar's proposal to Gilgamesh is a reflex of an earlier *hieros gamos*; the mourning over the slain Bull (Tablet VI, lines 165–167) is a reflex of an earlier seasonal funeral rite. In Tablet VI the marriage of Ishtar and Gilgamesh is rejected,[71] and the Bull is killed with finality, never again to descend and rise with the seasons. Seasonal cycles give way to the assertions of will and decisions of divine and human individuals; in turn these must be integrated into a cosmic order defined and characterized by more complex human organizations. This world and the next will now be organized and ruled in accordance with the forms of civic and imperial order.[72]

---

civilized community, while here the Bull threatens to destroy it. Obviously the composer is not unaware that the several stories share but expand and alter the role of animals.

71. I do not wish to be misunderstood as saying that Tablet VI is a parody of the sacred marriage; contrast J. J. A van Dijk, "La fête du nouvel an dans une texte de Šulgi," *BO* 11 (1954) 88 and n. 46. Also see nn. 35 and 68 above. Nor is my interpretation to be compared with Böhl's position; for Böhl—in the words of Diakonoff—"The subject of the Akkadian epic is a conflict between the highly ethical religion of Šamaš and the immoral religion of Ištar. . . . The heroes reach the highest point of their ethical elevation when Gilgameš refuses the love of Ištar" (review of Böhl, *Het Gilgamesj Epos*, 65). See simply Diakonoff's sensible critique (ibid.) of this position.

72. Whatever else they represent, Gilgamesh's rebuff of Ishtar and the literary movement from nature to city in the order of the lovers also seem to represent a distancing (I hesitate to say divorce or alienation) from nature and a view of humanity as separate from nature. One detects a rejection of that self-definition that views the Human/King as being a part of nature and as doing no more than playing a role in the natural order. In its stead, there is a strong sense of human self-consciousness, a sense of self as a being distinct from nature. If we are dealing with the consequences of actual social change, it would be tempting to relate this stance to the growing rift between the urban center and its natural hinterland and to the emergence of a clear sense of separation. For the arbiters of Mesopotamian literary culture in the second and first millennia (and perhaps for the urban populace as a whole), this process of physical and psychological

Gilgamesh will accept death when the netherworld is made over into an organized city, when death has assumed a familiar and even comforting guise. It is true that the fear of dying is only a little less sharp when the best life and the best death are depicted as organized cities. But death, then, is not wholly alien, for civilization—paradoxically and ambivalently—is then a corridor to death, and the state of death is seen as both the attainment and the attenuation of civilized existence. Death has been civilized. We witness the transformation of the netherworld from a wilderness wherein the goddess dwells with male animals to an orderly society wherein men retain their human forms. Here Gilgamesh will function as a divine official of an infernal extension or replica of a civilized political organization. For Gilgamesh will accept death when he can carry over his civilized identity into the netherworld and need not enter it in the form of an animal,[73] when he is able to translate Ishtar's offer into an opportunity to transmute the kingship of Uruk into the kingship of the netherworld.

V

Gilgamesh must eventually die. But in Tablet VI, he is not yet ready to accept a new identity and assume a role in the netherworld. He has not yet accepted the limits on his person or realized that the loss of his mortal life is inevitable. Thus far, we have investigated some of the forms of expression and symbolism associated with Gilgamesh's refusal and even touched on the social and cultural dimensions thereof. In this section, we wish to look at Gilgamesh's dilemma from the perspective of living and dying and to use the refusal as a point of departure for the further clarification of some of the psychological struggles and metaphysical implications of the essential Gilgamesh, the man and the god.

Although Gilgamesh rejects Ishtar's offer, he already senses that he will eventually have to come to terms with death. For we are told that Gilgamesh knows things that Ishullanu did not know: by amplifying Ishullanu's laconic remarks in great detail in the first two parts of his speech and, most of all, by then presenting an account of Ishtar's lovers in the third part of the speech, Gilgamesh indicates that he—in contrast to Ishullanu—understands that his own encounter with Ishtar is not

---

distancing seems to have found expression in a concomitant decrease in importance of natural deities in general, and the mother-goddess in particular.

73. Compare the changing forms of Ereshkigal's husbands. The theriomorphic Gugalanna ("the Bull of Heaven") is replaced by the anthropomorphic Nergal.

an isolated event but part of the unfolding of the established order of things. What is at stake is more than just the loss of a mother's care for the sake of a sexual relationship; rather, it is the surrender of his human life in order to take up his permanent place in a divinely determined cosmic order. Ultimately, Gilgamesh will come to accept the existence and interconnection of the realms of the living and of the dead and will learn that, while immortality and human life cannot go together for him, he is partially divine and can hold onto eternal life by accepting death and becoming a god of the netherworld; his place as an immortal is among the dead and not among living humans or gods of the above.

In Tablet VI, then, the seeds of change have already been sown. To appreciate the dimensions of the transformation that is set in motion in Tablet VI, we must look beyond this tablet. But to properly understand the relation of the events of Tablet VI to those of the following tablets, we must first consider the place of Tablet VI in the epic, for not only does Tablet VI occupy an important place in the epic, but it also affects and changes the meaning of the work. The impress of this episode on the epic and the transformation it effects in the overall meaning are more readily perceived when it is noticed that the events recounted in Tablet VI—Ishtar's proposal, Gilgamesh's refusal, and the killing of the Bull—probably did not belong to the earliest Akkadian version of the epic.[74] The secondary nature of the episode is suggested, first of all, by the fact that the episode as a whole is functionally equivalent to the battle with Huwawa insofar as both describe a battle with and a victory over a supernatural and divinely mandated power and supply a rationale for the death of Enkidu. One of these two incidents is superfluous. Obviously we must give precedence to the expedition to the Cedar Forest, for it and not the Akkadian precursor of Tablet VI is a documented part of the Old Babylonian version; moreover Enkidu's part in the killing of Huwawa provides the more plausible reason for the divine decision to cut short his life.[75] The extraneous character of our episode is intimated furthermore by the dissonance of its tonal quality; for example, whereas elsewhere in the epic all significant female characters are depicted

74. Of course, many scholars are of the opinion that this episode is part of the Old Babylonian epic; so, e.g., Jacobsen, *Treasures*, 213–14. At least some of the text of Tablet VI seems to have been part of the Akkadian epic by the time of the writing of text no. 12 in E. Weidner, *Bilinguen, mythologische Texte, medizinische Texte, Omina* (Keilschrifturkunden aus Boghazköi 4; Berlin: Akademie-Verlag, 1922), and this latter tablet provides the *terminus ante quem* of the inclusion of our episode.

75. See also Tigay, *Evolution*, 48–49 and n. 36.

sympathetically and positively,[76] Ishtar's image, qualities, and behavior in Tablet VI are destructive and negative. Especially in view of our judgment that Tablet VI is a later addition to the epic, it is no wonder that our novel interpretation of the Ishtar-Gilgamesh interchange leads us to a somewhat different understanding of the relation of Tablet VI to the rest of the epic and of the meaning of the latest version thereof.

The original epic treats the perennial problem of death. When death is only vaguely sensed, Gilgamesh turns reality on its head and deceives himself: he imagines that he will die heroically, thereby assuring his own immortality, and his friend Enkidu will live and serve as a vehicle to transmit his fame (Old Babylonian Yale tablet [cf. Speiser, *ANET*, 78–81] col. 4, lines 5ff. [= iv 140ff.]). But reality requires that Enkidu die and that Gilgamesh remain alive—alone and afraid. Through the death of Enkidu, loss is experienced and death becomes actual. Gilgamesh, bereft, depressed, and fearful, seeks a way to remain alive forever. First he roams like a wild man, and then his journey takes on direction. Finally he resigns himself to death and regains a sense of the meaning of life.[77] From being a hero who thought he could escape death, he resumes the identity of a king, yet becomes Everyman: he accepts the inevitability of death and the satisfactions of a limited life; he learns to take pride in realistic if monumental creations, man-made structures whose extent may be limited by divine and natural spheres that surround and intersect the area of the city, but which manage, all the same, to draw together the human and the divine, the civilized and the natural (Tablet XI, lines 323–328; Tablet I, col. 1, lines 11–23).

---

76. I have in mind Shamhat, Ninsun, the Scorpion woman, Siduri, and Utnapishtim's wife. All are solicitous mother figures, but a mother need not be beneficent; note the goddess of death in Tablet XII, lines 27–30, 47–50, 51–54 // 59–62 // 67–70 (cf. Tablet VII, col. 4, lines 203ff.).

77. On Gilgamesh's approach to death, cf., e.g., Jacobsen, *Treasures*, 202–4, 217; G. S. Kirk, *Myth: Its Meaning and Functions in Ancient and Other Cultures* (Berkeley: University of California Press, 1970) 144–45. As regards Gilgamesh's reaction to Enkidu's death, his identification with his dead friend, and his flight from reality, compare the opening pages of Freud's "Mourning and Melancholia." When confronted with his own impending death, Enkidu reacts in much the manner that we would expect of him. I have found it useful to compare his reaction to the stages of reaction to death noted by E. Kübler-Ross in her various publications (see, e.g., the chart prepared by M. Imara in E. Kübler-Ross, ed., *Death: The Final Stage of Growth* [Englewood Cliffs, NJ: Prentice-Hall, 1975] 161). His reaction is not out of proportion and is readily understandable. Certainly, by comparison with Gilgamesh, he rapidly regains his equilibrium and accepts his death. In part, the difference between Enkidu and Gilgamesh is due to differences in range of emotion and relationship to reality: Enkidu's range is much narrower, and he is essentially a pragmatist; Gilgamesh's reaction to the inevitability of death is prodigious.

This form of the epic (without Tablets VI and XII) presents an account of the man Gilgamesh. Put somewhat differently, we may say that it is the story of a powerful human being and his struggles with and acceptance of the inevitability of death.[78] For Gilgamesh the hero cannot accept his limited existence; he tests and tries to overcome his human form by recourse first to the heroic mode and then to the fantastic-psychotic mode. Initially he substitutes fame for life in the hope that fame is larger and more enduring than life. Future glory, however, is not as powerful as present experience. With the death of Enkidu, he becomes a human again, but Enkidu's death also renders his human life intolerable. He strips himself of his human form and tries to take on the appearance of a god. In both attempts, Gilgamesh substitutes absolutes for the compromises and limits of human life; rather than accepting mortal-human reality, he seeks first the fantasy of the future and then that of immortality-divinity. The quest is possible because he is a hero and is part god. Even so, he fails, for there are limits to both his heroic nature and his divine nature, and he must surrender the absolutes of omnipotence and immortality. He accepts a limited existence as the king, builder, and custodian of his city and resigns himself to death.

The original epic deals with the human condition. Gilgamesh the man has learned to die; but this is not enough, for he is also a god and he must learn to die as a god: Gilgamesh the human must die and Gilgamesh the god must become a lord of the netherworld. With the addition of Tablet VI, the epic is transformed: from being a work that treats the problem of mortal aging and death—a fate that entered the world after the Flood—of a giant and thereby of Everyman, it becomes a work that additionally seeks to define the place of the god Gilgamesh in the cosmic order. In its new form, it prepares the god for his death and sets out his divine role in the netherworld.

Ishtar invites Gilgamesh to become her husband and to take his honored place in the netherworld. Gilgamesh refuses. Far from being a compensation for the loss of eternal life,[79] the offer of a position in the netherworld heightens the sense of loss and imbues the work more than ever before with a tragic vision. Truly, now Gilgamesh is a tragic figure: he possesses both the nature and powers of a god and might expect to remain in the land of the living; yet now he must also come to terms with the fact that, though he is a god, he cannot enjoy immortality

78. Some of my formulations in this paragraph have not been uninfluenced by Whitman's statements regarding Achilles (Whitman, *Homer*, 181–220).

79. Contrast Lambert, "Gilgamesh," 51; and Tigay, *Evolution*, 35.

among the gods of the living. He is an immortal, but he is both a man and a god and as such he is destined to die and assume his ordained place in the netherworld. His is the immortality of a god of the netherworld.

Gilgamesh's rejection of Ishtar constitutes an attempt to hold onto his humanity, for by refusing to marry her he tells us that he does not wish to substitute the role of a dead god for that of a live human being; he thinks that he can hold onto life and, at the very least, postpone his death and perhaps even push it off long enough so as to render it no longer inevitable. But his refusal—in this recension—has as one of its consequences the death of Enkidu, for now the gods decide to kill Enkidu "because the Bull of Heaven they have slain and Huwawa they have slain."[80] Gilgamesh's attempt to remain a man causes the death of Enkidu, which loss then forces Gilgamesh (Tablets VIII–XI) to shed his humanity and to try to take on the form of an undying god. But just as this form of delusion and apotheosis could not work for Gilgamesh the man, it cannot work for Gilgamesh the god. He returns to his human state and thence accepts the particular divine identity/destiny ordained for him. Gilgamesh the man must die, and Gilgamesh the deity must become a god of the netherworld.

Gilgamesh's fate is to die. He resists his fate in both versions and on both levels of his being: The man Gilgamesh of the earlier version thinks he can become a god and thereby escape death. The god Gilgamesh of the later version thinks he can remain a human and thereby escape death. The conflict has its roots in the notion that Gilgamesh is part god and part man. In the earlier version Gilgamesh cannot accept his humanity and thinks he can be a god—he learns that he cannot be a god and must die as a human being. In the later version, Gilgamesh cannot accept his divinity and thinks he can be a human; he must learn that he is neither a normal human being nor a god whose immortality can be enjoyed among the living. Rather, he is a god who must prepare for death and for his role in the netherworld.

But now the reader of the epic is left to wonder: if in any case Gilgamesh will eventually die, why in Tablet VI is he not allowed to accept Ishtar's offer and proceed to the netherworld, instead of being subjected to both the toil and suffering described in Tablets VII–XI and the detailed information about the netherworld in Tablet XII? Furthermore,

---

80. The mention of the slaying of the Bull before the killing of Huwawa may be due to the fact that Tablet VI is an interpolation. Possibly the order also suggests that the redactor considered the slaying of the Bull to carry an equal if not greater weight of responsibility for the gods' decision to kill Enkidu.

the reader asks, when Gilgamesh does eventually die, will he have forfeited his special place in the netherworld by his initial refusal of Ishtar's proposal, or will some form of the original offer remain in effect?

Obviously Gilgamesh must refuse Ishtar if Tablet VI is to be integrated into the epic and not impede the movement of the work. But this is not a sufficient explanation, for ancient redactors have been known to interpolate episodes that are literary blind alleys. Gilgamesh's refusal does more than just advance the action; as indicated earlier, Gilgamesh must redefine Ishtar's offer so that death takes on more familiar human and social forms. But the refusal serves yet another important purpose. We now recall that Ishtar's proposal to Gilgamesh was an invitation to Gilgamesh to abandon, to renounce, a familiar role and to assume a new role that carried with it new rights and obligations as well as a new relationship to the world and the community.

In order that the passage from one state to the other be successful and that Gilgamesh understand the new norms according to which he will have to live, *there must be both a change of being as well as the acquisition of new knowledge.*[81] Prior to the events precipitated by the death of Enkidu, Gilgamesh was neither prepared nor qualified to undertake his new office in the netherworld, the office of instructor and counselor of the dead and arbitrator and administrator of the netherworld.[82] He was not yet ready to make a wholehearted commitment to his new role. Death would have left him feeling constrained and distraught, and he would have sought ways to leave the netherworld; certainly if his own initiation were not complete he would not be able to initiate and guide the newly dead. First, Gilgamesh must undergo the series of experiences recounted in Tablets VII–XI in order to be able to accept his own death; only then can he help the dying accept their own deaths. Only after he has been transformed, has undergone a change of being, will Gilgamesh be prepared to accept the offer of a role in the netherworld.

Thus far we have witnessed a change of being in Gilgamesh, but we recall that a rite of passage possesses "in addition to the separation-transition-incorporation form . . . another formal property: a combination of instruction and executive command. The rite of passage includes

81. For this aspect of rites of passage, cf. Turner, *Forest of Symbols*, 93–111; and A. F. C. Wallace, *Religion: An Anthropological View* (New York: Random House, 1966) 127–30.

82. For Gilgamesh in this role, cf., e.g., Kramer, "Death of Ur-Nammu," 114–15, lines 94, 142–43; and M. E. Cohen, "Another Utu Hymn," *ZA* 67 (1977) 14, line 77. Also see n. 13 above.

both some statement, or reminder, of how to play the expected role, and then a directive to commence its performance."[83] This brings us to Tablet XII.

Gilgamesh's acceptance of a limited human life is suggested by his experiences in Tablet XI and is expressed clearly in his statement of pride in the construction and compass of Uruk (Tablet XI, lines 323ff.). Of course the acceptance of death is implied in Tablet XI. But the more overt acceptance of death and of the role of administrator of the netherworld finds expression only in Tablet XII. It is well known that Tablet XII is a late addition to the epic, and that the manner of its addition is mechanical. Here we must emphasize, therefore, that Tablet XII was not added simply because the epic dealt with death and a late editor wished to append and preserve one more Gilgamesh text regarding death. The addition is purposeful and speaks to the heart of the late recension; as such, an organic connection exists between Tablets I–XI and XII.[84] The addition of Tablet XII, while probably not coterminous with the insertion of Tablet VI, is bound up with and is a consequence of the new configuration created by the inclusion of Tablet VI.[85]

83. Wallace, *Religion*, 130.

84. For a similar opinion, see Tigay, *Evolution*, 106–7; and Levy, *Sword*, 141–42. After completing this paper, I was pleased to notice that A. Draffkorn Kilmer has also come to the conclusion that Tablet XII is not simply a mechanical addition, but serves a special function ("A Note on an Overlooked Word-Play in the Akkadian Gilgamesh," in *Zikir Šumim: Assyriological Studies Presented to F. R. Kraus on the Occasion of his Seventieth Birthday* [ed. G. van Driel et al.; Leiden: Brill, 1982] 130–31).

85. Tablet XII (for this designation, see the two colophons in Thompson, *Epic of Gilgamesh*, pl. 58) contains an Akkadian translation of the latter part of *Gilgamesh, Enkidu, and the Netherworld* (hereafter GEN) (see A. Shaffer, *Sumerian Sources of Tablet XII of the Epic of Gilgameš* [Ann Arbor, MI: University Microfilms, 1963]). This tablet begins in the middle of Gilgamesh's plaint over the loss of his *pukku* and *mekkû*. Beginning Tablet XII in the middle of this speech creates an impression of clumsy and insensitive redaction, an impression that may have to be modified somewhat in light of A. Draffkorn Kilmer's suggestion ("Overlooked Word-Play," 130) that "the redactor of the canonical version has pulled together the preceding eleven tablets by adding the *pukku/mekku* story, Tab. XII, as a kind of inclusio." Especially in view of the way Tablet XII begins, I find W. G. Lambert's suggestion (personal communication, 1984) that our Tablet XII might represent the second tablet of a two-tablet version of GEN not unattractive. However, this suggestion does not warrant the conclusion that the editor who added this second tablet did not possess the first tablet and simply wished to preserve the stray second tablet. I would argue, to the contrary, that the redactor chose to ignore the first tablet and to incorporate only the material of the second tablet. In view of the fact that Tablet XII parallels parts of Tablet VII, it is surely not a coincidence that Tablet XII derives from an account (GEN) that contains a preceding section that parallels parts of our Tablet VI. Both GEN and GE Tablets VI–VII have accounts of an interaction between Gilgamesh and Ishtar followed by Enkidu's rash behavior, his vision of the netherworld, and his death. But whereas animosity and conflict characterize the

Tablet XII presents a vision of the netherworld and of the shades of the dead. Instruction is one of the main functions of this vision. To be sure, it is true that a vision of the netherworld already appeared in Tablet VII, but the two are different and do not serve quite the same purposes.[86] In Tablet VII, column 4, 162ff., Enkidu's vision of the netherworld provides a clear indication (as do so many of Enkidu's dreams) of what is happening: for Enkidu and Gilgamesh, it announces the death of Enkidu. It also contains a further message for Gilgamesh. The vision in Tablet VII focuses on the presence in the netherworld of princes and priests. At this point in the work Gilgamesh has attained the heights of heroism, kingship, and public acclaim and defines his identity in social terms. The vision informs Gilgamesh that even those who exercise power and privilege must die. This is a message of supreme importance for Gilgamesh the man; it contains nothing for Gilgamesh the god. In Tablet XII, on the other hand, Enkidu's report of what he saw in the netherworld centers on the fate of ordinary men. And this difference is accentuated by the fact that Tablet XII occurs in a work that now includes and revolves around Tablet VI and the account of Gilgamesh's struggle to accept the cosmic role of lord of the dead. Tablet XII has much to say to and about Gilgamesh the god; for the sake of these messages Tablet XII was added to the epic.

Tablet XII gives the signal that Gilgamesh has accepted the inevitability of even his own death, for he insists on knowing the order of

relationship between Gilgamesh and Ishtar in Tablet VI, the relationship of Gilgamesh and the goddess in GEN is supportive and sympathetic. GE Tablet VI and the Inanna-Gilgamesh episode of GEN are mutually exclusive, and the redactor of the twelve-tablet version suppressed the beginning of GEN perhaps because it was superfluous, but mainly because it contained a positive rather than a negative account of the relationship of Gilgamesh and Ishtar. By adding Tablet XII, the redactor has superimposed the new configuration: Tablets VI + XII (which now supersedes Tablets VI + VII). In any case, the fact that the description in Tablet XII of Enkidu's descent to the netherworld and subsequent report to Gilgamesh is drawn verbatim from a composition in which these events follow upon an interaction between Gilgamesh and Ishtar tends to support my impression that the redactor intended the reader to associate the events of Tablets XII and VI (and surely, then, Enkidu's instruction of Gilgamesh about the netherworld in Tablet XII supports our interpretation of Tablet VI as a proposal that Gilgamesh enter the netherworld).

86. Here I would note that such visions serve various purposes. For one, they help the living to accept the death of those whom they love. They allow the mourner to recall the departed and to realize that the relationship with those who have died is not sundered so long as the survivor can conjure up images of the departed and the feelings associated therewith; at the same time, the vision informs the living that those who have died belong to an absolutely different realm and must be given up. For another, visualizing a concrete destination may help those in the process of dying to accept their end.

the netherworld (Tablet XII, lines 89ff.), and Enkidu tells of the death and afterlife of all who have lived. Moreover, by providing a description of the rules that obtain in the netherworld, the text indicates that Gilgamesh is readying himself to assume the divine infernal roles and responsibilities that had been offered him in Tablet VI and that, in spite of his earlier refusal, he has not lost the opportunity; Ishtar's offer stands, albeit in the new social form that Gilgamesh has imposed upon it: the office is reserved for Gilgamesh, and he may accept it whenever he goes to his own death. The recital confirms Gilgamesh in the role of administrator of the netherworld.

But most important of all is the instructional value of Enkidu's report. The essence of Enkidu's message is not a vision of glory or dread but, rather, a simple description of the norms and procedures that govern life in the netherworld. These are the rules that Gilgamesh will be obliged to administer; only when he has been initiated into and mastered the ways of the netherworld will he be able to initiate the dead in their new stations and guide them in the ways of the netherworld.

Tablet XII was added, then, to express the notion that all who live must die, to reinforce Gilgamesh's acceptance of death, to proclaim that he will serve as a lord of the netherworld, and to communicate to him the rules of the netherworld. Now we finally have renunciation and assumption. To become lord of the netherworld Gilgamesh must undergo a transformation: a change of being and the acquisition of knowledge. When Ishtar proposed to him in Tablet VI, he had not yet grown nor been initiated; he was not ready to pass from the living to the dead. Gilgamesh underwent the spiritual transformation in Tablets VII–XI; in Tablet XII he acquired knowledge.

In the earlier epic, it was sufficient for the man Gilgamesh to accept limited human life and the inevitability of human death. In the new recension and construction created by the addition of Tablet VI, the god Gilgamesh must undergo a transformation of state and incorporate the knowledge appropriate to his new state in order to become the ruler of the netherworld. Tablet XII informs us that his transformation and transition are complete.

* * *

There are many ironies in the epic. The final irony—and the message of the work—is implicit in the rules and the objects of the rules that dominate Enkidu's recitation in Tablet XII and form the core of knowledge that Gilgamesh must master. On the whole, the characters who dominate Enkidu's vision are not heroes but ordinary men, and it is their everyday deeds that determine their place in the netherworld. Gilgamesh's discovery that the treatment of men in the netherworld depends on ordinary deeds must surely remind the god Gilgamesh of Gilgamesh the man; it recalls Siduri's advice to Gilgamesh: joy and meaning are to be found in the simple pleasures of life. So Gilgamesh the god learns what Gilgamesh the man already knows: Gilgamesh must reconcile himself to and live with his basic humanity in order to be a man in this world and a god in the next.

Gilgamesh's Request and Siduri's Denial, Part I

The Meaning of the Dialogue and Its Implications for the History of the Epic

My purpose here is to offer some comments on an Old Babylonian text that deals with loss and recovery, death and life. I shall try to define and solve a problem that occurs in the justly famous exchange between Gilgamesh and the divine tavernkeeper Siduri in an Old Babylonian version of the *Epic of Gilgamesh* (= OB Gilg., Meissner, cols. ii–iii[1]) and, thereby, offer a new interpretation of the dialogue. I shall then explore some of the implications of my study for the history of the epic.

This essay and its companion study ("Gilgamesh's Request and Siduri's Denial, Part II: An Analysis and Interpretation of an Old Babylonian Fragment about Mourning and Celebration" [here, pp. 89–107]) have benefitted greatly from the comments of several scholars. Stephen A. Geller discussed the text with me in great detail, and both he and Kathryn Kravitz read the several drafts and made a number of valuable comments and suggestions. In addition, William L. Moran discussed the text with me, Mordechai Cogan critiqued an early draft, and Diane Feinman and Michael Rosenbaum suggested improvements in the final draft. I am grateful to all these friends for their interest and help.

1. The Meissner fragment was published by B. Meissner, *Ein altbabylonisches Fragment des Gilgamosepos* (MVAG 7.1; Berlin: Peiser, 1902). More recently, it has been joined to a fragment in the British Museum; see A. R. Millard, "Gilgamesh X: A New Fragment," *Iraq* 26 (1964) 99–105. For translations of both the Old Babylonian text and the later Standard Babylonian version of the epic, see, e.g., E. A. Speiser and A. K. Grayson, *ANET*, 72–99, 503–7; and S. Dalley, *Myths from Mesopotamia: Creation, The Flood, Gilgamesh and Others* (Oxford: Oxford University Press, 1989) 39–153. In this essay, translations of the Standard Babylonian version are usually drawn from the recent translations by Dalley, *Myths*, or M. G. Kovacs, *The Epic of Gilgamesh* (Stanford, CA: Stanford University Press, 1989). For studies of the epic, cf., e.g., T. Jacobsen, *Treasures of Darkness: A History of Mesopotamian Religion* (New Haven, CT: Yale University Press, 1976) 195–219; J. H. Tigay, *The Evolution of the Gilgamesh Epic* (Philadelphia: University of Pennsylvania Press, 1982); T. Abusch, "Ishtar's Proposal and Gilgamesh's Refusal: An Interpretation of *The Gilgamesh Epic*, Tablet 6, Lines 1–79," *History of Religions* 26 (1986) 143–87 [reprinted here, pp. 11–57] (an abbreviated version, together with a number of other essays on Gilgamesh, has been anthologized in *Classical and Medieval Literature Criticism* [ed. J. Krstovic et al.; Detroit: Gale, 1989] 3:365–74).

Professor William W. Hallo is a scholar of broad interests, who has made significant contributions to our understanding of Mesopotamian literary history. It is a pleasure to dedicate this study of an Akkadian literary text to Bill Hallo, colleague and friend.

The text of the first interchange between Gilgamesh and Siduri in the Old Babylonian version reads:

col. ii

[*ibrī ša arammušu danniš*]
1′. *ittiya ittallaku kalu marṣ*[*ātim*]
2′. *Enkidu ša arammušu danniš*
3′. *ittiya ittallaku kalu marṣātim*
4′. *illikma ana šīmātu awīlūtim*

5′. *urrī u mūšī elišu abki*
6′. *ul addiššu ana qebērim*
7′. *ibrīman itabbeʾam ana rigmiya*
8′. *sebet ūmī u sebe mušiātim*
9′. *adi tūltum imqutam ina appišu*

10′. *ištu warkišu ul ūta balāṭam*
11′. *attanaggiš kīma ḫābilim qabaltu ṣēri*
12′. *inanna sābītum ātamar pānīki*
13′. *mūtam ša ātanaddaru ayāmur*

14′. *sābītum ana šâšum izzakaram ana* ᵈ*Gilgameš*

col. iii

1. ᵈ*Gilgameš êš tadâl*
2. *balāṭam ša tasaḫḫuru lā tutta*
3. *inūma ilū ibnû awīlūtam*
4. *mūtam iškunū ana awīlūtim*
5. *balāṭam ina qātīšunu iṣṣabtū*

6. *attā* ᵈ*Gilgameš lū mali karaška*
7. *urrī u mūšī ḫitaddu attā*
8. *ūmišam šukun ḫidûtam*
9. *urrī u mūšī sūr u mēlil*

10. *lū ubbubū ṣubātūka*
11. *qaqqadka lū mese mê lū ramkāta*
12. *ṣubbi ṣeḫram ṣābitu qātika*
13. *marḫītum liḫtaddâm ina sūni*[*k*]*a*

col. ii

My friend, whom I love dearly,
1′. Who with me underwent all hardships,
2′. Enkidu, whom I love dearly,
3′. Who with me underwent all hardships,
4′. Has gone to the fate of mankind.

5′. Day and night I wept over him,
6′. I would not give him up for burial—
7′. (saying) "My friend perhaps will rise up to me at my cry!"—
8′. Seven days and seven nights
9′. Until a worm dropped out at me from his nose.

10′. Since his death, I have not found life.
11′. I keep roaming like a hunter in the open country.
12′. Now, alewife, that I have seen your face,
13′. The death that I constantly fear may I not see.

14′. The alewife spoke to him, to Gilgamesh:

col. iii

1. Gilgamesh, whither do you rove?
2. The life that you pursue you shall not find.
3. When the gods created mankind,
4. Death they appointed for mankind,
5. Life in their own hands they held.

6. You, Gilgamesh, let your stomach be full.
7. Day and night keep on being festive.
8. Daily make a festival.
9. Day and night dance and play.

10. Let your clothes be clean,
11. Let your head be washed, in water may you bathe.
12. Look down at the child who holds your hand,
13. Let a wife ever delight in your lap.

I. Problem and Interpretation

Introduction

This interchange or dialogue between Siduri and Gilgamesh comprises a speech and its response. After describing his anguish at the loss of

Enkidu, Gilgamesh expresses his hope that Siduri will provide a solution to his predicament. Siduri's speech provides her response and her advice. Each speech contains three stanzas. At the end of the third stanza of Siduri's speech, there are an additional three lines that are largely broken.[2] The first of the three lines and perhaps the two that follow seem to be a concluding summary construction of her message.

Prior to this summary is the text which is the initial focus of our essay, a four-line quatrain which forms the third and last stanza of Siduri's response:

lū ubbubū ṣubātūka
qaqqadka lū mese mê lū ramkāta
ṣubbi ṣeḫram ṣābitu qātika
marḫītum liḫtaddâm ina sūni[k]a

Wear fresh clothes,
and wash your head, and bathe.
Look at the child that is holding your hand,
and let your wife delight in your embrace.[3]

Problem

Let us now examine more closely this third stanza of Siduri's response.[4] In spite of its apparently straightforward meaning, the passage poses some difficulty. The quatrain is made up of two couplets, but their arrangement is odd. Precisely because of the common everyday

2. These lines (iii 14–16) might be read:

annâma ši-pi[r sinništim/awīlūtim]
[dGiš ēš tadâl]
ša ba-al-ṭú l[i-iḫ-du balāṭam]

This alone is the concern of woman/man.
Gilgamesh, whither do you rove?
Let him who is alive enjoy life.

Possibly, but less likely, line 16 might read:

ša ba-al-ṭú ⌜*la*⌝ *[i-ḫad-du-ú balāṭam]*
Should not he who is alive enjoy life?

I owe the restorations of lines 15–16 to Thorkild Jacobsen.

3. Translation: T. Jacobsen, "The Gilgamesh Epic: Romantic and Tragic Vision," in *Lingering over Words: Studies in Ancient Near Eastern Literature in Honor of William L. Moran* (ed. T. Abusch, J. Huehnergard, and P. Steinkeller; HSS 37; Atlanta: Scholars Press, 1990) 240–41. Because of its greater forcefulness, I cite Jacobsen's translation of these four lines, though I have suppressed "And" at the beginning of the first line.

4. In my estimation, my analysis of iii 10–13 is not materially affected by the broken lines 14–16.

meaning of the text, we are struck by the peculiar order of its elements: in the first couplet, wearing of clean clothes is enjoined prior to washing of head and body; in the second couplet, relationship with a child is mentioned prior to sexual relations with a woman. This ordering of elements contradicts a logical or, at least, a more usual causal or temporal sequence. Normally, one first washes before putting on clean clothes; so, for example, GE XI 262–267;[5] OB Gilg. P. iii 22–27 [= iii 106–111];[6] and elsewhere, cf., e.g., 2 Samuel 12:20.[7] And one normally imagines lovemaking as preceding the birth of a child; one expects that the mention of a relationship of an adult male with a woman will precede the mention of his relationship with a child. Why then did the composer order the elements in this unusual and somewhat jarring way?

Solution

a. Chiasm

The elements of each couplet seem to be inverted. Inversions or reversals are characteristic of chiastic form. The occurrence here of such characteristics should perhaps not surprise us, for I note that Siduri's speech contains other circular forms and chiasms[8] and, in line with chiastic structure, even takes the last part of Gilgamesh's speech as its point of departure.

Actually, the dialogue as a whole seems to be arranged chiastically. Not only do Gilgamesh's address and Siduri's answer run parallel to each other, but, as J. H. Tigay has also noted, these speeches also form a chiastic pattern:

> Gilgamesh had told the barmaid that: 1) Enkidu, whom he loves, is dead; 2) he mourned Enkidu for seven days and nights; and 3) he

5. "Ur-shanabi took him away and brought him to the washing-place. / He washed his matted hair with water like *ellu*. / He cast off his animal skin and the sea carried it off. / He moistened his body with fine oil, / and made a new wrap for his head. / He put on a royal robe worthy of him" (translation: Kovacs, *Gilgamesh*, 105).

6. "With water he washed / his hairy body, / rubbed himself with oil, / and became a man. / He put on a garment, / was like a young noble" (translation: Jacobsen, "Gilgamesh Epic," 237. Note that Jacobsen's translation follows the restoration [*mi*]-*i*; others restore [*ma-li*]-*i*, for which cf. GE XI 263, quoted above).

7. "Thereupon David rose from the ground; he bathed and anointed himself, and he changed his clothes" (translation: *Tanakh: A New Translation of The Holy Scriptures according to the Traditional Hebrew Text* [Philadelphia: Jewish Publication Society, 1985] 487).

8. Cf., e.g., iii 6–9, the middle stanza in Siduri's answer. See Abusch, "Gilgamesh's Request, Part II" [here, pp. 89–107], where I study the structure and meaning of both iii 6–9 and ii 5′–9′, the middle stanza in Gilgamesh's address.

> has not found the immortality he seeks. In reply, the barmaid tells Gilgamesh:
>
> > The life you pursue you shall not find.
> > When the gods created mankind,
> > Death for mankind they set aside,
> > Life in their own hands retaining.
> > As for you, Gilgamesh, let your belly be full,
> > Make merry day and night.
> > Of each day make a feast of rejoicing,
> > Day and night dance and play!
> > Let your garments be sparkling fresh,
> > Your head be washed; bathe in water.
> > Pay heed to a little one that holds on to your hand.
> > Let a spouse delight in your bosom,
> > For this is the task of [woman].
> >
> > (Gilg. Me. iii, 2–14)
>
> In this advice, the barmaid responds to Gilgamesh's plaint in inverse order: 3) You will never find immortality, because it is reserved for the gods; 2) eat, bathe, put on fresh garments and rejoice (the opposite of what mourners do); and 1) let your family fill the void left in your life by Enkidu's death. In sum: Embrace reality.[9]

Thus, the overall chiastic structure of this dialogue might possibly provide an explanation for the inverted order of elements in the last stanza of Siduri's response, for the second half of a chiasm will often be arranged in reverse. Influenced by his knowledge that the second half of a chiastic structure normally reverses the sequence of its first half, the composer here may thus simply have chosen to reverse also the order of individual elements within the last stanza.

Perhaps. But further reflection on the nature of chiastic construction suggests that the chiastic mode of composition neither requires nor adequately accounts for the composer's use of an apparently illogical sequence here and the disruption, thereby, of normal order. A chiasm should make sense. The structure of an entire chiasm follows a coherent train of thought. Certainly, gratuitous distortions of reality will be avoided. Thus, while the second half of a chiasm does indeed reverse the order of the first half, this reversal will normally achieve the rhetorical and psychological goals for which it is intended without grossly distorting reality. But, whereas a large unit can normally be repeated in

9. Tigay, *Evolution*, 50–51.

reverse order without disruption of logic, a small, tightly formed unit will usually retain its normal everyday order, since a reversal of the sequence of its internal elements will often create an impossible representation.[10] Thus, even when a literary work follows a chiastic order, elements of individual small units will ordinarily occur in their normal narrative order. Accordingly, the reversal of order in our last stanza and the subsequent presentation of events in an abnormal temporal sequence are, as such, not required by a chiasm and seem even to ignore the logical norms of chiastic composition. Therefore, we cannot simply explain the inversion as a normal feature of chiastic composition.

Still, it seems impossible to disregard chiastic patterning as a factor in the formation of the last stanza. Inversion of elements and chiastic mode of composition are closely associated, in our text and elsewhere. Thus, even though the chiastic structure of the dialogue as a whole does not seem to justify the inversion of elements in the last stanza, it is not possible to dismiss as coincidence the occurrence here of an inversion within a chiastic structure. We may neither treat the inversions as the natural consequence of chiasm nor dismiss the connection between the inversions and the chiastic mode of composition of the dialogue. Perhaps we should consider explaining the inversions as marks of clumsy craftsmanship. The poet may have carried out his task in a mechanical way. Knowing that in a chiasm, he was expected to reverse the elements in the second half, the poet may have inverted some scenes by reversing also the order of those elements which normally would have been left in their usual order.[11] Thus, it is possible that the structure of our stanza is

10. Accordingly, such inversions are quite infrequent. Thus, for example, W. G. E. Watson notes that "The only example of inversion in Hebrew poetry is Hosea 9,11 where the natural sequence of events is reversed—depicting utter negation" (*Classical Hebrew Poetry: A Guide to Its Techniques* [JSOTSup 26; Sheffield, UK: JSOT Press, 1984] 358). Hos 9:11b: "No childbirth, no gestation, no conception," is a good example of an "illogical" or unnatural sequence in which the elements of a small unit are inverted and listed in reverse order. For this verse, cf. also F. I. Andersen and D. N. Freedman, *Hosea: A New Translation with Introduction and Commentary* (AB 24; Garden City, NY: Doubleday, 1980) 538, 542–43. Certainly, Andersen and Freedman's claim that Hos 9:11b begins its unit (ibid., 538–39) supports the idea that such an inversion serves a distinct rhetorical purpose. For otherwise, the text would have followed a natural order, since the verse's position at the beginning of the unit would have militated against inversion and would certainly not have fostered it.

11. In further support of this characterization, note that this stanza remains an incomplete or partial chiasm within a larger chiasm, for while the elements of the quatrain under analysis are inverted, they are not a reversal of a corresponding set of elements in the first half of the dialogue. The elements in our stanza follow the order BADC;

simply the result of mechanical and uncorrected craftsmanship.[12]

Perhaps. But regardless of whether the inversions in our stanza are clumsily or skillfully formed, they are part of a chiastic structure, and we should not rule out too hastily the possibility that even here inversion conveys meaning. At best, what we have done thus far is establish that our text is written in a style that allows or encourages inversion. We have yet to ascertain whether or not the apparently illogical inversions have a special significance and serve a specific purpose.

b. Interpretation

i) Reexamining the passage now with an eye to spotting a possible special purpose to the inversions, we notice that the inversion is actually of significance and certainly deserving of an explanation. Enkidu having died, the composer in our passage now tries to convey to Gilgamesh the thought that to regain life he must seek a woman as the replacement for the dead friend for whom he grieved. The love that Gilgamesh felt for Enkidu was the love of a warrior for his comrade, a love that finds poignant expression in the story of Achilles and Patroclus as well as in the famous lament of David over Jonathan.

> How have the mighty fallen
> In the thick of battle—
> Jonathan, slain on your heights!
> I grieve for you,
> My brother Jonathan,
> You were most dear to me.
> Your love was wonderful to me
> More than the love of women.
> How have the mighty fallen,
> The weapons of war perished![13]

That love must now give way, be given up, and the void filled by a new, or expanded, relationship with a woman. Therefore, just as the chiasm began with Gilgamesh's mention of Enkidu (ii 1′ff.), so the "wife" who is to be Enkidu's replacement should find mention at its end.

---

thus neither do they relate directly to and reverse the elements in the first stanza of Gilgamesh's speech (which would require DCBA) nor do they form a miniature chiasm in themselves (ABBA).

12. Such a mistake would certainly be instructive, for it would show how some composers might have gone about shaping chiastic structures.

13. 2 Sam 1:25–27 (translation: *Tanakh*, 471).

Thus, the line citing the child (iii 12) is placed not after the mention of the woman, but rather before her mention so that the woman may appear at the end, in iii 13, as the counterpart of Enkidu. Here the need for emphasis overrides order. The change of order highlights the message. Final position is an emphatic and climactic position. It is thus a particularly appropriate and effective place to express and thereby emphasize the thought that a woman must replace Enkidu and take a central place in the protagonist's life. This idea appears to be one of the most important elements—perhaps the most important—of Siduri's message; in any case, it gives unity and significance to her overall advice. Thus, it is fitting that closure will occur here in Siduri's speech with that statement which for her would have represented the most powerful thought that she needed to impart.[14]

As for the couplet at the head of our stanza, we may now suggest that here also the composer intentionally inverted the order of elements. A possible explanation, if not a wholly satisfying one, is that he reversed these elements so that the order in the first couplet would be consistent with that of the second. By placing the wearing of clean clothes (iii 10) prior to washing and bathing the body (iii 11), the first couplet thus leads into and prepares us for the atemporal order of the second one.[15]

10. Let your clothes be clean,
11. Let your head be washed, in water may you bathe.
12. Look down at the child who holds your hand,
13. Let a wife ever delight in your lap.

The need to mention the woman at the end of Siduri's speech thus explains the strange order of the stanza. The stanza leads up to the affirmation of the importance in life of the "wife."[16] The speech ends with the mention of the human female partner in order thereby to recall the

14. Cf. B. Herrnstein Smith, *Poetic Closure: A Study of How Poems End* (Chicago: University of Chicago Press, 1968).

15. For an explanation of a different sort, we might suggest that the writer drew upon a source which presented the situation in a static form (e.g., a visual depiction of a festival scene). But when representing such scenes in a linguistic medium that stretches over time, the author need not present the scene in an atemporal order. And even when the underlying scene was actually made up of several simultaneous events or proceedings, the linear order chosen should have some significance.

16. The capping or climaxing of this thought would also find expression in line iii 14 if we restore *sinništim*: "For this alone is the conce[rn of woman]." Should this restoration be correct, it would further support my analysis.

very beginning of the speech and thus to link this woman with Enkidu and to emphasize her role as his replacement.

ii) But the woman's appearance at the end of the speech also serves another purpose. She replaces not only Enkidu of the beginning of Gilgamesh's speech but also recalls and replaces the divine woman (Siduri) mentioned at the end of Gilgamesh's speech. Thus, the text would seem to follow not only a chiastic structure, but also a parallel one. This observation will allow us to resolve a further difficulty of this text and to attain a deeper understanding of the message itself.

At the conclusion of Gilgamesh's first address to Siduri, he states in its very last lines (ii 12′–13′) that now that he has seen Siduri's face, he hopes no longer to see—that is, experience—death. What is the meaning of these lines? This statement has been taken to mean that Gilgamesh hopes that Siduri will enable him to reach Utnapishtim (by directing him to Urshanabi, the boatman, who, in turn, will convey Gilgamesh to Utnapishtim), and that he will thereby attain immortality. But this is neither the original meaning of these lines, nor indeed what the text actually says. We would suggest that these lines mean that Gilgamesh now realizes that he wishes to live with a woman rather than remain in spirit with his dead male friend. But instead of choosing a normal, mortal woman, he has focused on an immortal because he thinks her capable of endowing him with eternal life. Hence his statement:

ištu warkišu ul ūta balāṭam . . .
inanna sābītum ātamar pānīki
mūtam ša ātanaddaru ayāmur

Since his death, I have not found life, . . .
(but) now, alewife, that I have seen your face,
The death that I constantly fear may I not see.

He thinks that in her he has found life. He has not yet realized that for him now, his woman must be mortal.

Let us take up the text in detail. What does Gilgamesh's statement mean? Siduri is characterized as a *sābītu*, a tavernkeeper. She and her inn would function as a haven for the traveler and provide a place of rest, food and drink, companionship, merriment, and sex.[17] But she is also

17. Cf., e.g., R. Harris, "Images of Women in the Gilgamesh Epic," in *Lingering over Words: Studies in Ancient Near Eastern Literature in Honor of William L. Moran* (ed. T. Abusch, J. Huehnergard, and P. Steinkeller; HSS 37; Atlanta: Scholars Press, 1990)

a goddess, perhaps of the Ishtar type.[18] Apparently, Gilgamesh believes that having come to Siduri, he has, in effect, come to a goddess who is like Circe and Calypso and whose realm is similar to theirs.[19] In the *Odyssey*, these goddesses offered Odysseus "immortality" and a life of ease. It suffices to cite some passages from Odysseus's encounter with Calypso:

> So he (Hermes) spoke, and Kalypso, shining among divinities,
> shuddered, and answered him in winged words and addressed him:
> "You are hard-hearted, you gods, and jealous beyond all creatures
> beside, when you are resentful toward the goddesses for sleeping
> openly with such men as each has made her true husband.
>
> . . . .
>
> So now, you gods, you resent it in me that I keep beside me
> a man, the one I saved when he clung astride of the keel board
> all alone, . . .
>
> . . . .
>
> but the wind and the current carried him here and here they drove
> him,

222–25 and references there, and Dalley, *Myths*, 132 n. 106. More generally, see H. Hoffner, "The Arzana House," in *Anatolian Studies Presented to Hans Gustav Güterbock* (ed. K. Bittel, P. H. J. Houwink ten Cate, and E. Reiner; Istanbul: Nederlands Historisch-Archaeologisch Institut in Het Nabije Oosten, 1974) 113–22, especially p. 113 for Mesopotamian references and pp. 119–20 for the sexual activities in the Arzana house.

18. Cf. W. G. Lambert, "The Hymn to the Queen of Nippur," in *Zikir Šumim: Assyriological Studies Presented to F. R. Kraus on the Occasion of his Seventieth Birthday* (ed. G. van Driel et al.; Leiden: Brill, 1982) 208.

19. For a recent study of Odysseus's encounters with Calypso and Circe as well as of Circe's Near Eastern connections, see G. Crane, *Calypso: Backgrounds and Conventions of the Odyssey* (BKP 191; Frankfurt am Main: Athenäum, 1988), especially chapters 1–3. For the netherworld associations of these goddesses, see, e.g., pp. 15ff. For Circe as a netherworld goddess and her island as a netherworld, see pp. 33–34 with nn. 15 and 23 on pp. 46–47. For the view of Calypso as a netherworld goddess, see, e.g., p. 23 n. 7 and G. Levy, *The Sword from the Rock: An Investigation into the Origins of Epic Literature and the Development of the Hero* (London: Faber and Faber, 1953) 152 with n. 4. In comparisons of scenes from the *Epic of Gilgamesh* with Calypso and Circe materials, usually Circe and/or Calypso are compared to Ishtar in GE VI (e.g., Abusch, "Ishtar's Proposal," 161 [here, p. 29]; A. B. Lord, "Gilgamesh and Other Epics," in *Lingering over Words: Studies in Ancient Near Eastern Literature in Honor of William L. Moran* (ed. T. Abusch, J. Huehnergard, and P. Steinkeller; HSS 37; Atlanta: Scholars Press, 1990) 375; Crane, *Calypso*, 63–65) and not to Siduri. But see Dalley for a comparison of our story to that of Odysseus and Calypso: "The story of Odysseus and Calypso in *Odyssey*, V is recognized to have some close resemblances to the episode of Gilgamesh and Siduri: the lone female plies the inconsolable hero-wanderer with drink and sends him off to a place beyond the sea reserved for a special class of honoured people" (*Myths*, 48). In the course of this paper, it will be seen that our understanding of the comparison is quite different.

> and I gave him my love and cherished him, and I had hopes also
> that I could make him immortal and all his days to be endless."
> . . . .
> So she (Kalypso) spoke, a shining goddess, and led the way swiftly,
> and the man followed behind her walking in the god's footsteps.
> They made their way, the man and the god, to the hollow cavern
> and he seated himself upon the chair from which Hermes lately
> had risen, while the nymph set all manner of food before him
> to eat and drink, such things as mortal people feed upon.
> She herself sat across the table from godlike Odysseus,
> and her serving maids set nectar and ambrosia before her.
> They put their hands to the good things that lay ready before them.
> But after they had taken their pleasure in eating and drinking,
> the talking was begun by the shining goddess Kalypso:
> "Son of Laertes and seed of Zeus, resourceful Odysseus,
> are you still all so eager to go on back to your own house
> and the land of your fathers? I wish you well, however you do it,
> but if you only knew in your own heart how many hardships
> you were fated to undergo before getting back to your country,
> you would stay here with me and be the lord of this household
> and be an immortal, for all your longing once more to look on
> that wife for whom you are pining all your days here."
> . . . .
> Then resourceful Odysseus spoke in turn and answered her:
> "Goddess and queen, do not be angry with me . . .
> . . . .
> She is mortal after all, and you are immortal and ageless."[20]

Such boons are what Gilgamesh hopes to be offered now that he has found Siduri. For her house and her embrace partake of the immortal.[21]

Thus, if I am not mistaken, Gilgamesh is saying rather clearly that having finally reached Siduri, he hopes that she will now take him in and that he will thereby attain immortality. By saying that he has seen Siduri's face, Gilgamesh voices what might perhaps be a formula of

20. Homer, *Odyssey* 5.116–218, trans. R. Lattimore (New York: Harper & Row, 1975) 91–93.

21. Perhaps what Gilgamesh is seeking here is not eternal life, but rather a form of death different from the death which had overcome Enkidu and was the expected form of death for normal men. As it turns out, Gilgamesh cannot have even this different form of death at this point in the development of the epic. When finally he assumes the identity of a dead god, he attains, perhaps, something like that form of death. Cf. Abusch, "Ishtar's Proposal," 143–87 [here, pp. 11–57].

marriage or relationship. In marriage contexts, where a bride is veiled,[22] to see her face is to have attained a degree of intimacy with her.

> The unveiling of the bride, it may be added, was a cardinal element of ancient wedding ceremonies, and it has even been suggested that the familiar Biblical use of the word "know" to denote sexual relations referred originally to the bridegroom's coming to know the features of his bride by lifting her veil before the consummation of the marriage. The Arab bridegroom, we are told, often sees his bride's face for the first time on that occasion, and in Turkey, the present which he then gives her is known explicitly as "the gift of the seeing-of-the-face."[23]

Interpreters often read Gilgamesh's speech to Siduri as if it were his first encounter with her without regard to the fact that this speech occurs at the end of a large break. But I would surmise that in the break in the upper part of col. ii, prior to Gilgamesh's speech, Gilgamesh had already encountered the veiled Siduri and had persuaded her to unveil herself.[24] Originally, she was veiled, and it is surely no accident that in her first appearance in the Neo-Assyrian version, Siduri is associated with veiling or covering (GE X i 4: *kutummi kuttumatma* . . .), or that the name Calypso has been taken to mean "the covered/veiled one" and even treated as a translation of the Akkadian "cover."[25] Thus, when in our Old Babylonian passage Gilgamesh says that he has seen Siduri's face, he is stating that she has been unveiled and that some degree of intimacy has been established between them (though whether this intimacy extended also to sexual intercourse is unclear to me).[26] And

22. Cf. GE VIII ii 59.

23. T. H. Gaster, *The Holy and the Profane: Evolution of Jewish Folkways* (2nd ed.; New York: W. Morrow, 1980) 104. Cf. S. Greengus, "Old Babylonian Marriage Ceremonies and Rites," *JCS* 20 (1966) 72.

24. I thus disagree with Harris, who implies that unlike Shamhat, who undresses, Siduri remains veiled ("Images of Women," 225).

25. Cf., e.g., Dalley, *Myths*, 132 n. 108.

26. Here, "seeing the god's face" is not a cultic term referring to a divine manifestation. But for such a cultic manifestation, see, for example, the statement in the Nergal *šuilla, BMS* 27 (reedited recently by W. Mayer, *Untersuchungen zur Formensprache der babylonischen "Gebetsbeschwörungen"* [Studia Pohl, Series Maior 5; Rome: Biblical Institute, 1976] 478–81), lines 15–18 (esp. line 17: *aššum muppalsāta ātamar pānika*), which I would interpret as a seeking after a cultic manifestation of the deity, a seeking out of the actual face of the deity in the form of his statue. The theme reflects not the actual *Sitz-im-Leben* of the *šuilla*, but the temple experience of the liturgist responsible for the composition (cf. my remarks in "The Demonic Image of the Witch in Standard Babylonian Literature: The Reworking of Popular Conceptions by Learned Exorcists," in *Religion, Science, and Magic: In Concert and in Conflict* [ed. J. Neusner, E. S. Frerichs, and P. V. Mc. Flesher; Oxford: Oxford University Press, 1989] 36).

he now expresses the hope that she will take him in to live with her and to be her lover. For he believes that intimacy and cohabitation with a Calypso- or Circe-like goddess would bring immortality. Hence, "Now, alewife, that I have seen your face, may I not experience the death that I constantly fear."[27]

Gilgamesh takes Siduri to be a form of Ishtar, but unlike Tablet VI of the later version where Gilgamesh rejects Ishtar's proposal,[28] here he wishes to stay with the goddess in her realm in order to escape death. He imagines that she will consent. But Gilgamesh errs in his assessment, and Siduri must disabuse Gilgamesh of his belief and send him off. She tries to do so by means of her speech. In further support, then, of my interpretation of the last lines of Gilgamesh's speech, I would emphasize here that Siduri's speech to Gilgamesh is less than meaningful if his goal is other than to live with her. Their encounter gains in significance when we recognize that living with Siduri has now become Gilgamesh's goal; Enkidu is being pushed aside and Utnapishtim has not yet entered the scene. And her speech takes on a new force when we further realize that she is responding not only to his cry for Enkidu at the beginning of his speech, but also to his proposal to her at its end.

Siduri must dissuade Gilgamesh from his futile hope for immortality with her. Her purpose, then, is not only to encourage Gilgamesh to attach himself to a living female in place of Enkidu, but also to let him know that just as he cannot live forever with the dead Enkidu, so, too, he cannot live forever with an immortal female, a goddess, and must

27. Gilgamesh also uses the phrase "Now that I have seen your face" when addressing Urshanabi (Meissner iv 12). There is a repetition of several phrases in the speeches to Shamash, Siduri, and Urshanabi in the Old Babylonian Meissner + Millard fragments. For a listing of these repetitions, see Tigay, *Evolution*, 96–98. These repetitions represent an early stage of the process of assimilation of similar passages to each other, for which process, see Tigay, *Evolution*, 81–103. In my estimation, our phrase originates in Gilgamesh's address to Siduri (Meissner ii 12′) and is carried over from there to the address to Urshanabi as part of the aforementioned process of harmonization or assimilation of dialogues. This direction is indicated both by the fact that our phrase has a specific, not a general, meaning in the speech to Siduri and that the dialogue with Urshanabi empties it of specific meaning and links it with another general phrase, "Show me" (Meissner iv 13), that also occurs in Gilgamesh's address to Siduri (Millard iii 9′ [= iii 23]) but is there separated from "Now that I see your face" (Meissner ii 12′) by Siduri's first speech and by part of Gilgamesh's subsequent address. Thus, the speech to Urshanabi simply draws from speeches to Siduri, pulling together two separate phrases from two separate speeches. Also lines common to the speeches of Shamash and Siduri ("Gilgamesh, whither do you rove? . . .") were drawn from the Siduri dialogue; cf. below, n. 46.

28. For this interpretation of Tablet VI, see Abusch, "Ishtar's Proposal," 143–87 [here, pp. 11–57], and see below, Section II.

rather find fulfillment with a mortal female, a woman. It is not only to answer his points in the order of last to first, but also to disabuse him of his idea that he, a mortal, can enjoy immortality with her, a goddess, that she presents her reply as she does: the gods have designated immortality only for themselves (iii 1–5); instead, the mortal Gilgamesh should enjoy festivals to their fullest (iii 6–9) and find fulfillment, finally, with a mortal wife (iii 10–13).

Siduri must express even more than the thought that Gilgamesh cannot hope to find immortality with a goddess. The way for the erstwhile warrior to go on living and even to lead a meaningful life, when he must finally withdraw from the world of combat and adventure and surrender the love of his dead comrade, is for him to undertake normal activities and normal family relationships. At another time, Siduri might have been willing to be Gilgamesh's temporary sexual partner (see below). But here she must refuse him, for she must not only disabuse him of the notion that he can attain immortality through a relationship with her, but also convey to him the necessity of selecting a familial sexual partner rather than a non-familial one. Sex here is neither an act of immortality and eternity nor an act of the moment. For only through a familial context will Gilgamesh regain a normal life.[29] Hence, the poet is constrained to mention the child in iii 12 and to mention him prior to mentioning the woman. The mention of the child transforms the sexual relationship with the *marḫītum* into a family relationship. His partner is now also his "wife," and the birth of a child is a consequence of their relation. The woman, the child, both represent normality.

We are further prepared for this movement into "normal life" by the mention, even before the child, of clean clothes and body. Gilgamesh is to be washed and clothed in normal clothes (not regnal clothes [contra his role in Tablet VI] nor animal skins [contra his role as a wanderer]) so that he may reenter a normal state and be attractive to a human woman rather than a goddess.[30]

29. This understanding of Siduri's advice as serving to direct Gilgamesh back to normality agrees with the use of the tavern as a transition-point back to normal life for the patient who has undergone magical rites. See, e.g., R. I. Caplice, "The Akkadian Text Genre Namburbi" (Ph.D. diss., University of Chicago, 1963) 88–89; and idem, *The Akkadian Namburbi Texts: An Introduction* (SANE 1.1; Los Angeles: Undena, 1974) 12; and *CAD*, vol. S, p. 9: *bīt sābî* 2′. This function of the tavern has now been discussed by Stefan M. Maul in a paper ("Der Kneipenbesuch als Heilverfahren") read before the 38th Rencontre assyriologique internationale (Paris, 1991); Maul there cites our Gilgamesh text.

30. Cf. 2 Sam 12:20–25, where, after mourning, David bathes, anoints himself, and changes his clothes and subsequently has intercourse with Bathsheba, who then bears

The sexual act is now a procreative act which brings into being the posterity and future signalled by the child. Progeny implies death, and thus the woman and child also suggest mortality and are a most pronounced way for Siduri to impart to Gilgamesh the notion of his mortality and to express the hope that he accept his mortal nature. But progeny also implies immortality. A child is a form of immortality, and in our passage, this is the only form of immortality that Gilgamesh can hope for.

iii) To sum up our discussion thus far: the climax of Siduri's speech highlights the joy found in the relationship between mortal man and woman. Here the end of the second half of a chiasm resumes both the beginning and the end of its first half. Thus, Siduri's speech itself builds up to and concludes with the theme of a human wife so that this woman might replace both the male comrade Enkidu of the beginning of Gilgamesh's speech and the female goddess Siduri of its end. To enhance and give particular meaning to this climax, the poet inverted the order of the elements in the last stanza: clean clothes and bathing; a child and a wife.

Actually, the attempt to reintroduce Gilgamesh to normal life after his wandering in the wild recalls the humanization of Enkidu. The situation that is here meant to humanize and acculturate Gilgamesh is similar to that which served to humanize Enkidu and bring him out of the wild. The cleansing and clothing of Gilgamesh here remind us of the cleansing and clothing of Enkidu as an introduction to human life. Moreover, the prostitute Shamhat,[31] who humanizes Enkidu at the beginning of the tale, is like the alewife Siduri (as well as the "wife" of her advice), who humanizes Gilgamesh at the end of the tale. And just as the human prostitute attracts and introduces Enkidu to normal human life by means of sex, just so the divine alewife who may once have made love to the traveler now suggests that Gilgamesh make love with a woman and thereby return to a normal state.

But especially if this parallel is correct, a dissonant note is now heard, and perhaps it points up one more factor that is responsible for our inversions. The Enkidu tale may derive from a story of the humanization of a primitive by a prostitute that would have been told in the

him a son, Solomon. So, too, Gilgamesh's wandering in the steppe, away from civilization, unwashed and wearing skins—a trip, in effect, through the world of the dead—is a form or phase of mourning; washing and dressing and then taking a woman are stages in the termination of the state of mourning.

31. For the character of Shamhat, cf. recently Harris, "Images of Women," 222–24.

aštammu, 'tavern/inn'.[32] Similarly, Siduri's advice would also seem to derive from and have its setting in the *aštammu* or *bīt sabî/sābīti.*[33] But in "advice" or songs that emanate from institutions that provide drink and sex, places like the *bīt sābî/sābīti* or *aštammu*, one does not expect to find the injunction, "Look down at the little one who holds your hand." The point of such an institution is to encourage a man to undertake sexual pleasure with a woman and to provide him with the opportunity to do so, not to suggest that he undertake the responsibilities of caring for children and family.[34] Elsewhere, in a treatment devoted to the second stanzas of the Gilgamesh-Siduri dialogue, I will again examine the setting of portions of the text. Here, I would only mention that the Egyptian Harpers' Songs, sections of the biblical Ecclesiastes, and other texts that have been compared with portions of our written text, do not include a mention of children. Accordingly, just as the tale of the primitive human may have been taken up and made into the Enkidu tale by the bard responsible for the epic,[35] so too the *aštammu* prototype of Siduri's advice might also have been modified by the epic bard and the theme of the child introduced. Just as the acceptance of kingship was a necessary final step for Enkidu and added by the epic poet,[36] so too

32. See W. L. Moran, "Ovid's *Blanda Voluptas* and the Humanization of Enkidu," *JNES* 50 (1991) 121–27, especially pp. 126–27, for the suggestion that the pub may be the setting for the telling of a story of the humanization of primitive man by sex with a prostitute, by drinking, etc., a type of story that could have then served as the basis for the development of the Enkidu tale.

33. This setting, a place of drink and prostitution, is suggested by the fact that Siduri's establishment is such a place and by the fact that such an institution, or, at least, worldly drinking parties and banquets are assumed by the form and content of the advice itself (cf., e.g., J. Assmann, "Der schöne Tag—Sinnlichkeit und Vergänglichkeit im altägyptischen Fest," in *Das Fest* [ed. W. Haug and R. Warning; Poetik und Hermeneutik 14; Munich: Fink, 1989] 23–25). For feasting in the *aštammu*, see W. G. Lambert, *Babylonian Wisdom Literature* (Oxford: Clarendon Press, 1960) 256: 9–10: *ana qēret aštammi lā taḫâšma*, and pp. 339–40, especially p. 340, top. In "Gilgamesh's Request, Part II" [here, pp. 89–107] I suggest that portions of Siduri's advice reflect and play upon mortuary rites. This connection with mortuary rites does not contradict the association of Siduri's speech also with the *aštammu*, for the banquet of the dead draws upon the mundane banquet as its model and, in the context of the epic, is effectively refocused towards the living by the very character of the *aštammu* as an institution for the living.

34. Hence, for example, the ceremonial and therapeutic incantations and rituals of the *šaziga* corpus (see R. D. Biggs, *SÀ.ZI.GA. Ancient Mesopotamian Potency Incantations* [TCS 2; Locust Valley, NY: J. J. Augustin, 1967]) focus on restoring lost potency, but seem never to mention the desire for children and do not have reproductive goals. In my estimation, the *šaziga* materials originated or at least developed in the *aštammu*.

35. Moran, "Ovid's *Blanda Voluptas*," 126–27.

36. Ibid., 127.

the acceptance of children was a necessary ingredient in the advice to Gilgamesh and was also added by the epic poet.

Actually, it is useful to realize that iii 12 was probably an addition. This observation may allow us to recognize and come to terms with the fact that this line is odd. *Ṣubbi ṣeḫram ṣābītu qātika* (iii 12) is a strange formulation, a peculiar—or at least unusual—way to describe the father-son relationship that is being suggested to Gilgamesh. Perhaps the line is drawn from or influenced by another text. In any case, our line is reminiscent of *ṣabtat qāssu kīma . . . ireddešu*[37] of the Old Babylonian Gilg. Penn. tablet (ii 31–32 [= ii 73–74]). The formulation of the father-son relationship found in M iii 12 becomes understandable if we assume that the epic poet drew on the earlier Enkidu-Shamhat episode when he added the mention of the child to his *aštammu* prototype. He modeled M iii 12 on the earlier line in order, perhaps, to draw attention to the two passages and to link them together. This connection may perhaps also explain the use of the unusual *marḫītum*[38] in the following

37. The similarity of the two passages would be even greater were the conjectural reading *ṣeḫrim* (*ṣabtat qāssu kīma ṣehrim ireddešu*) for Gilg. Penn. ii 32 [= ii 74] again to find support. But for now, greater weight must be assigned to the reading preserved in later manuscripts from Boghazkoi (DINGIR-*lim*) and Uruk (DINGIR.MEŠ), for which see G. Wilhelm, "Neue akkadische Gilgameš-Fragmente aus Ḫattusa," *ZA* 78 (1988) 105: 7 (cf. pp. 108–9); and E. von Weiher, "Ein Fragment des Gilgameš-Epos aus Uruk," *ZA* 62 (1972) 224 = SpBTU 2, no. 30, obv. 11′. These readings support J. Renger's reading ("Gilg. P ii 32 [PBS 10/3]," *RA* 66 [1972] 190) of Gilg. Penn. ii 32 [= ii 74] as ⌜DINGIR!⌝. Note, however, that the text of the line preserved in Boghazkoi: [. . . *qá-as-sú ṣa-ab*]-*ta-at-ma ki-ma* DINGIR-*lim pa-ni-šu*, does not fully agree with that of P ii 31–32 [= ii 73–74] and that von Weiher in his commentary to the Uruk passage thought that "Die Wendung *kīma ilāni*[meš] steht hier wie ein Subjekt: 'wie die Götter (einen Menschen führen)',—so führt ihn (den Enkidu) die Dirne. In der altbabylonischen Version steht an dieser Stelle das Objekt: *kīma ṣeḫrim*! 'wie einen Kleinen' (führt sie ihn), s. noch W. von Soden, ZA 53 (1959), 210." The occurrence of *ṣeḫram* in M iii 12 and the connection between the two passages would certainly add considerable weight to the reading *ṣeḫrim* in P ii 32 [= ii 74] were all other evidence somehow equalized.

38. According to the dictionaries (see *AHw* and *CAD*, s.v.), the term *marḫītum*, with two exceptions, is limited to the *Epic of Gilgamesh*. It occurs here in OB M iii 13 and in SB Tablet XI. In Tablet XI, it serves as the designation for Utnapishtim's wife in the non-Flood section of that tablet (lines 212, 215, 219, 273). For the use of this and other terms for 'wife' in the epic, see Tigay, *Evolution*, 232–33. As Tigay has noted, the non-Flood sections of Tablet XI were introduced into the epic prior to the introduction of the Flood account. Note, however, that *marḫītum* in Tablet XI occurs always as part of the formulaic speech introduction. The occurrence of *marḫītum* in that tablet does not disprove my contention that Utnapishtim was not the original goal of Gilgamesh's journey and that even the non-Flood sections of Tablet XI dealing with Utnapishtim and his wife were additions to the epic (see below, Section II). These portions of Tablet XI could easily have been added subsequent to the existence already of an early form of

line (M iii 13), for *marḫītum* recalls *reḫû*, 'to pour, to have intercourse, to inseminate', of the contemporaneous Old Babylonian Enkidu-Shamhat encounter (P ii 8 [= ii 50] // SB I iv 194).[39] Through these and other connections the author links the Siduri-Gilgamesh encounter with the earlier Shamhat-Enkidu encounter and suggests that they parallel each other.

But the order of our last two lines is an inversion of the order of events in the earlier account, for there Enkidu first had intercourse with Shamhat and only then does she take him by the hand, while here Siduri's advice to Gilgamesh concludes with the suggestion that he look upon the child who is holding his hand and then have intercourse with a woman. Thus, in addition to its other purposes, it would seem that our inversion constitutes an attempt by the author to create a chiastic connection with the earlier Enkidu episode.[40] Perhaps the purpose of this chiasm is to round out the story and provide a (preliminary) closure to the epic by means of a larger chiasm.

* * *

The inversion conveys meaning on several levels. And yet, such writing remains strange to me. Its strangeness may reflect the reworking of an earlier literary form. But perhaps, this way of ordering elements serves also by its very strangeness and unexpectedness to emphasize and highlight Siduri's advice to Gilgamesh. (Thus, perhaps this is an example of what the Russian Formalists termed 'defamiliarization' or *ostraneniye* 'making strange'.)

---

the Meissner fragment, and they could thus have drawn upon and continued a term used by the older Old Babylonian text. The later writer's preference for *marḫītum* is simply a preservation of an earlier choice.

As for the meaning of *marḫītum* in our passage: especially if the Gilgamesh-Siduri dialogue is dependent on an earlier *aštammu* prototype in which *marḫītum* of iii 13 already occurred and if that dialogue is the primary instance of *marḫītum* in the epic, then we should probably translate *marḫītum* in M iii 13 not as 'wife', but as 'prostitute/harlot' or the like.

39. Note also that sex is joyful in both episodes: in the Siduri encounter, *marḫītum liḫtaddâm ina sūnika*; and in the earlier Shamhat account, the very name *šamḫat* is rendered most effectively by *Freudenmädchen*. In this regard, cf. also P i 20 and 32–34.

40. The chiastic form, then, is: sex—leading child (P) : : (leading) child—sex (M). While it might be possible, I hesitate to extend the chiasm to include the clothing and washing and the food and drink of the earlier lines of Siduri's advice and their corresponding mention in the P tablet.

Our efforts at interpretation have, I think, yielded further understanding. But I am not yet convinced that the odd forms do not also reflect a mechanical style of composition or redaction,[41] a mechanical way of articulating meaningful and significant thought. I cannot set aside the impression that the poet has chosen a stilted way of conveying an important idea and has thus failed to fully integrate form and meaning.

II. Historical Speculations

We ought now to rethink the significance of the encounter and examine its implications for the epic as a whole. For if Gilgamesh's goal is to live with Siduri and thereby attain immortality while her intention is to dissuade him from such a relationship and direct him to a normal life with woman and child, then the original meaning and context of this encounter are not those of a way station on the journey to Utnapishtim. While it is generally acknowledged that the Flood account itself is taken from elsewhere and was not part of the early version of the integrated Akkadian Gilgamesh epic, it is usually assumed that from its outset, Gilgamesh's journey after the death of Enkidu was a quest directed toward Utnapishtim. But it seems to me that this is not the case. For Gilgamesh's speech and Siduri's response in this section of the Old Babylonian dialogue make no sense if it is assumed that they were originally composed for a recension of the epic in which Gilgamesh was on his way to find Utnapishtim for the purpose of escaping death and attaining immortality. They make sense only if Siduri was, or had become, the goal of the journey. Originally, then, Utnapishtim was not part of the tale and Gilgamesh roamed without a goal until he met Siduri.

Here, then, we need to explain more fully several of the literary-historical implications for the *Epic of Gilgamesh* suggested by our study of the dialogue between Gilgamesh and Siduri.

41. Thus, one should perhaps modify statements about the spontaneity and freedom of Old Babylonian compositions and composers as well as the contrast drawn with later Standard Babylonian literature. The operation here of this mode of composition agrees with the notion that the poets of the Akkadian epics belong to the social layer of "the intelligentsia of the Old Babylonian age, the circle of the scribes, teachers, scholars of the schools and the royal court" (G. Komoróczy, "Akkadian Epic Poetry and its Sumerian Sources," *Acta Antiqua Academiae Scientiarum Hungaricae* 23 [1975] 62).

Old Babylonian

Originally, when Gilgamesh departs Uruk, he is reacting to the loss of Enkidu and embarking on a directionless journey. Even sections of the late text preserve this notion and are clear on this point. So, for example, in Tablet VII iii 146–147 of the Standard version, when Shamash comforts Enkidu by describing Gilgamesh's reactions to his death, he predicts:

> And he himself will neglect his appearance after you(r death) (= *arkika*[42]).
> Clothed only in a lionskin, he will roam the open country.[43]

And Gilgamesh himself speaks these very same words to Enkidu in Tablet VIII iii 90–91 of that version:

> And I myself will neglect my appearance after you(r death) (= *arkika*[44]).
> Clad only in a lionskin, I will roam the open country.[45]

With this assessment, our Old Babylonian fragment agrees, for Gilgamesh's speech to Siduri suggests that he was directionless until he encountered her and that it was his meeting with her that finally gave definition to his movement and transformed it into a quest.

Actually, Gilgamesh's meeting with Siduri changes everything. Till then, movement, wandering, travel were what Gilgamesh needed, though perhaps he also held out some hope for a solution for, or respite from, his existential/psychological pain. He acknowledges that he had been wandering aimlessly; hence his *attanaggiš*, 'roam' (*ištu warkišu ul ūta balāṭam / attanaggiš kīma ḫābilim qabaltu ṣēri*) rather than Siduri's later *tasaḫḫuru*, 'pursue' (*balāṭam ša tasaḫḫuru lā tutta*).[46] For him, *balāṭam* in ii 10′ meant a meaningful life or perhaps the state of being/feeling alive, not eternal life. He was wandering aimlessly because he had lost and could not recover his own sense of being alive. When he first comes

---

42. Cf. *ištu warkišu* M ii 10′.
43. Translation: Dalley, *Myths*, 88.
44. Cf. *ištu warkišu* M ii 10′.
45. Translation: Dalley, *Myths*, 93.
46. *^{d}Gilgameš ēš tadâl / balāṭam ša tasaḫḫuru lā tutta* (M iii 1–2) also occurs in Shamash's speech (M i 7′–8′). For the problem, see n. 27 above. As with the lines common to the speeches of Siduri and Urshanabi, so, too, these lines are original to Siduri's speech, for it is only here in the dialogue between Gilgamesh and Siduri that there is a play between *balāṭam ša tasaḫḫuru lā tutta* and Gilgamesh's earlier *ul ūta balāṭam* and that the lines in question have a specific referent. In this context, I should again note that Siduri's use of the phrase *ša tasaḫḫuru* serves to redefine Gilgamesh's earlier wandering (*attanaggiš . . . qabaltu ṣēri*) as a purposeful act. The use of *tadâl* alone without *tasaḫḫuru* simply affirms Gilgamesh's own sense of purposeless wandering.

upon Siduri, he begins to regain focus and structure. He recognizes that he now wishes to stop roaming and stay with her.

Gilgamesh is seeking an experience, not information or advice about the road to Utnapishtim, and so says to Siduri, "Now that I have seen your face, may I not see death," rather than "Now that I have seen your face, tell me where to go," as Gilgamesh had in fact said to Ur-shanabi: *inanna Sursunabu ātamar pānīka kullimanni ūtanaʾištim rēqam* (M iv 12–13). His unrealistic wish not to experience death does not mean that he believes that in finding Siduri he has found the way to Utnapishtim. Rather, it means that he wants to stay with the goddess because he thinks her capable of endowing him with eternal life.

At the beginning of their encounter, Gilgamesh has begun to emerge from an almost total identification with the dead and to seek a focus. He can no longer tolerate the chaotic existence symbolized by roaming the steppe, but he is not yet able to let go of death and fantasy and return to normal life. He looks for a way that will allow him to find rest from wandering, but still to escape from natural death. He thinks that he can find these by living with the goddess Siduri. In actuality, Gilgamesh has not yet completely put the dead aside; he remains obsessed with death. His continued grief for the dead is tantamount to a wish to remain with them. And in his mind, living with Siduri allows him to continue to live with the dead, for he thinks that through her he can move away from an overt state of grief without having to surrender his attachment to the dead and reenter the normal world. In his attempt, then, to free himself from the anguish of his grief for his friend Enkidu, Gilgamesh tries to enter into a marriage with the goddess Siduri. Hers is a world in which he can live without living and die without dying. He can thus live life through fantasy and need not let go of the dead.

By becoming a goal for him, Siduri does Gilgamesh a service, for her appearance provides structure and direction to what had been a chaotic, aimless existence. But she recognizes that such a union is untenable for the mortal man Gilgamesh who remains under the shadow of death. On an ontological level, their union cannot be, for it is a mingling of human and god, life and death. It is even more destructive on a psychological level, for it is a fantasy that denies death and leaves unresolved the losses of life and one's own mortal destiny. To live forever with a beautiful woman, a goddess, is a pleasant fantasy for a man, but it is also a death wish. Gilgamesh could never again regain human life.

Accordingly, Siduri herself proposes a new course. She advises him to return to a normal life. (In an earlier form, she would then have advised his immediate return home to Uruk and the resumption there of a normal life.) Thus, she first gives form and definition to what was aimless wandering by using the term *tasaḫḫuru*, and then suggests the futility of a quest which seeks to set fantasy in place of reality. She redefines his wanderings as having been in the service of a goal, but then tells him that this goal is attainable only if it is realistic. She tells Gilgamesh that even now that he no longer wanders, but is beginning to define and seek ways of "living," he cannot find eternal life or even succeed in escaping death.

But it may well be that it is also Siduri who is responsible, in part, for the eventual inclusion of Utnapishtim in the tale. Staying with Siduri had become Gilgamesh's goal, but by rejecting Gilgamesh and thus denying the possibility of some kind of relationship, she not only redefines his journey, but unwittingly also directs it in a way which neither she nor he had originally considered. Initially, Gilgamesh said that he was searching for life; he had not said that he was pursuing eternal life. But Siduri turns what was originally an aimless activity into a quest for eternal life by redefining his aimlessness as *saḫāru*, 'pursue', and by juxtaposing iii 1–2: "Gilgamesh, whither do you rove? The life (*balāṭam*) that you pursue (*tasaḫḫuru*) you shall not find," with iii 3–5: "When the gods created mankind, death they appointed for mankind, life (*balāṭam*) in their own hands they held."[47] Inadvertently, perhaps, she suggests by her speech the new goal of Utnapishtim: by introducing the notion that mankind had not been granted immortality by the gods, she introduces the notion of immortality and puts Utnapishtim into his mind. She thus redirects Gilgamesh's gaze towards the new goal of Utnapishtim-like immortality and redefines or gives new meaning to his search for life.

Put somewhat differently: Gilgamesh had been roaming aimlessly. His desolation, his despair, his loneliness, his fear of death had impelled him to keep on moving. But when once he stopped, thinking that he might escape death, Siduri tried to tell him that he would not be able to find a life or a love that does not include—or that allows one to avoid—death. There is no human life without death, but the fear of death must not be allowed to spoil life. Gilgamesh must fear and suffer death, Siduri says, but can still enjoy a good life even though it will terminate in death. But Gilgamesh could neither accept her advice nor think of another realistic solution. Instead, he focused on the idea of

47. For a related but still different formulation of this thought, cf. Utnapishtim's remark in the SB version, Tablet X vi 319–322 (and *Atrahasis* OB III vi 47ff.).

immortality, and the thought of Utnapishtim took form in his mind. Thus, instead of heeding Siduri's advice, he heard in her speech the possibility of attaining immortality, for he had heard of Utnapishtim (or rather, Ūtanaʾishtim as he is called in the Old Babylonian text) and knew that, contrary to Siduri's contention, a human being had once attained immortality. To be sure, Siduri's speech does not mention Utnapishtim by name, but the aptness of seeking him out was promoted in the present context by the obvious connection and play between (*ul*) *ūta balāṭam* and *Ūtanaʾištim*/Utnapishtim.[48]

Utnapishtim has now become a part of the story. Thus, while our Old Babylonian text still emphasizes the original idea of Gilgamesh as an aimless wanderer, that Old Babylonian piece already represents a step in the transition from the earlier perspective to the later form of the epic that sets Utnapishtim as a goal. Our Old Babylonian text represents a stage in the development of the epic.[49] In its evolution, the epic will

48. Note that Komoróczy has also noticed the verbal play between the name Utnapishtim and the statements that Gilgamesh has not/will not find life ("Akkadian Epic Poetry," 61):

> The name [scil. Uta-napishtim] means "He has found life." In the epic we find the statement several times that Gilgameš will not find "life," thus for example in Fragm. Meissner I. 8 = line III. 2: "Life that you search for, you will not find" (*ba-la-ṭam ša ta-sa-aḫ-ḫu-ru la tu-ut-ta*), ibidem II. 10: "I do not find life" (*u-ul ú-ta ba-la-ṭam*). In the contexts of the epic it refers to the name Ūta-naʾištim, and it is a play of words contrasting Gilgameš with the immortal hero of the deluge. The name of the human hero of the Sumerian deluge epic is Ziʾusudra (zi-u_4-sud-rá). It is obvious that the Old Babylonian Akkadian poet deliberately chose another name, serving also his idea.

Cf. also Speiser, *ANET*, 90 n. 164; for a different slant on the connection, see Tigay, *Evolution*, 229–30.

Here I should mention that Gilgamesh's response to Siduri: "Why, my good alewife, do you talk thus? / My heart is sick for my friend! / Why, my good alewife, do you talk thus? / My heart is sick for Enkidu!" (iii 18–21; translation: Jacobsen, "Gilgamesh Epic," 241) does not contradict my understanding of Gilgamesh's statement in ii 12′–13′ as a wish to live with Siduri. It is true that, on the face of it, Gilgamesh's words do not seem to be an appropriate response to the rejection of such a request. But, neither do they agree with any other interpretation of his request, e.g., the wish to find Utnapishtim or attain immortality. Gilgamesh's response seems to reflect the fact that he has been thrown back to his earlier fixation on his friend by the rejection. Unable to accept her advice that he give her up and take up instead with a mortal woman, Gilgamesh reverts to his earlier attachment to Enkidu, although he had already moved beyond it. Hence, his response and wish to find Utnapishtim.

49. Note also that the text is fluid and seems to represent a literary stage of change and experimentation. One can almost identify different hands at work. I note, for example, that the writing in the Old Babylonian text seems uneven, with different sections appearing to be composed in different styles. Thus, I would suggest, for example, that the

eventually take as its focus the journey to Utnapishtim and the quest for immortality. But while Utnapishtim seems already to have been introduced into and become part of the Old Babylonian sequence,[50] he has not yet become the focus of the journey from its inception, and Gilgamesh's and Siduri's first set of speeches still represents the earlier context.

Standard Babylonian

The transformation of Utnapishtim into Gilgamesh's goal from the outset of his journey must await a further evolution of the epic evident in the final version. For although the late version still preserves sections that express the original sense of initial emotional distress and chaos, the nature of Gilgamesh's travel has been changed into a more directed journey. Thus, for example, Tablet IX of the Standard version takes up Gilgamesh's travels at their beginning and opens with a presentation of the travels different from that quoted above:

> Gilgamesh mourned bitterly for Enkidu his friend,
> And roamed open country.
> "Shall I die too? Am I not like Enkidu?
> Grief has entered my innermost being,
> I am afraid of Death, and so I roam open country.
> I shall take the road and go quickly
> To see Ut-napishtim, son of Ubara-Tutu."[51]

It would appear that Tablet IX is a later addition; in any case, it is an integral part of the late recension in which Gilgamesh now directs his movement from early on to a goal, the attainment of Utnapishtim.

With the emergence of Utnapishtim as the new focus of the journey from almost its beginning, the text changed in various ways. One consequence of this new development was a change in the presentation of Siduri, for the new configuration and quality of the work explains the differences between the figure and role of Siduri of the Old Baby-

middle stanza has been introduced into each of the two speeches, and that the original speeches contained only the first and third stanzas.

50. This, on the assumption that Utnapishtim is actually one of the foci of the action in the Meissner-Millard fragments, which seems to be the case, and that Urshanabi, in Siduri's instructions to Gilgamesh, no longer plays the role of one who will directly lead Gilgamesh back to Uruk. But, the evidence in the Old Babylonian text for the new role of Utnapishtim is limited; see Meissner iv 13 (cf. iv 6) and Millard iv 1′ [= iv 16] (restored).

51. Tablet IX i 1–7. Translation: Dalley, *Myths*, 95.

lonian version and of the later Standard version. For now that Gilgamesh's travels have Utnapishtim as their original goal, Siduri loses her earlier function. She is no longer a newly discovered goal, but rather one more person along the way to hear Gilgamesh's tale, bear witness to his state, and direct him toward Utnapishtim. Gilgamesh does not want to stay with Siduri; rather, he wants to move on to Utnapishtim. Her famous *carpe diem* speech is now superfluous and is suppressed; the task of directing Gilgamesh back to normality and reality now falls to Utnapishtim and his wife. The altered dialogue between Gilgamesh and Siduri in this version is consonant with the new construction of the epic. Their encounter has changed from one in which Siduri refuses to provide a home for Gilgamesh and advises him instead to return to his own home to one in which she highlights his plight and helps him reach Utnapishtim.

Earlier Stages

If our Old Babylonian piece does not preserve the latest form of the encounter between Gilgamesh and Siduri, it also does not preserve the original form. However, it may still be possible to reconstruct earlier forms of the story. A prior form of the story—earlier even than that preserved on the Old Babylonian fragment—may well have ended with Siduri sending Gilgamesh back to Uruk in the care of a boatman, perhaps Urshanabi, who here serves as a form of Hermes.[52] Thus, this earlier account would have proceeded from the Gilgamesh-Siduri dialogue (and perhaps some version of the encounter with Urshanabi) to Tablet XI 253–261, where originally it would have been Siduri, and not Utnapishtim, who advised the boatman to wash Gilgamesh and return him to Uruk. From there, it would have moved on to the return voyage

52. I would go so far as to suggest that originally Urshanabi did not serve as the boatman who took Gilgamesh to Utnapishtim, but rather as the guide who would have brought Gilgamesh directly from Siduri back to Uruk, the land of the living. He is like Hermes, a mediator between this world and the next. This understanding of Urshanabi is not inconsistent with W. G. Lambert's suggestion ("The Theology of Death," in *Death in Mesopotamia: Papers Read at the XXVIe Rencontre assyriologique internationale* [ed. B. Alster; Mesopotamia 8; Copenhagen: Akademisk Forlag, 1980] 59) that Urshanabi may be an altered form of the tradition of the boatman who ferries people across to the netherworld; but note that Hermes (*psychopompos*) is the guide rather than the ferryman and is only secondarily linked up with the river of the underworld and Charon's ferry. For Hermes in the role of mediator between this world and the next, in general but particularly in the *Odyssey*, see, e.g., W. Burkert, *Greek Religion* (Cambridge, MA: Harvard University Press, 1985) 157–58; and Crane, *Calypso*, 16–19, 34–40.

presently preserved in Tablet XI 271–272, 319–321, and perhaps 322–328.[53] Utnapishtim was not originally part of the tale.[54]

Actually, even the form of the story in which Siduri sends Gilgamesh back to Uruk may not have been the earliest form of the episode. Gilgamesh's original mistake regarding what he could expect from Siduri suggests an interesting possibility and allows for some further historical speculation. Surely, Gilgamesh did not construct out of whole cloth the possibility that he might be able to stay with Siduri. Rather, he made this mistake because he saw in her a type of goddess like Calypso and Circe. And if Gilgamesh's expectations were not wholly far-fetched, and if Siduri did, in fact, share at least some of the characteristics of

53. Actually, our speculation about early stages helps us to better understand how the late version emerged. Our reconstruction of an earlier form of the text (Gilgamesh-Siduri + XI 253–261 + return journey [= XI 271–272, 319–321, and perhaps also 322–328]) agrees with, finds support in, and explains the disjunctions that we sense in the present Tablet XI between the episodes associated with Utnapishtim (encounter, Flood account, test of sleep, plant-of-life episode) and the instructions to Urshanabi to wash and clothe Gilgamesh and return him to Uruk. The redactor created the present composite text largely by framing the instructions to Urshanabi with the initial encounter with Utnapishtim, on the one hand, and the plant-of-life episode, on the other, as well as by repeating the instructions in the form of a narration (XI 262–270).

Disruption and clumsiness in the movement of the story make evident the composite nature of the text: especially good examples are provided by the interruption of the return to Uruk by the joining on of the plant-of-life episode in XI 273ff. and the clumsy, after-the-fact way in which Gilgamesh and Urshanabi turn back toward Utnapishtim's shore, after having already begun their journey, and carry on a long-distance conversation with Utnapishtim from their boat offshore. Further support for this reconstruction is provided by the secondary nature of the narrative passage XI 262–270, which tells of Urshanabi's carrying out of his instructions. Its derivative nature is evidenced by the inclusion of lines 268–270 (= 259–261) within that narrative. These lines refer to the future and are clearly a dittography. This conclusion is suggested by the inappropriateness of a future reference in the narrative, but its appropriateness in the original instructions; it is confirmed by the absence of lines 268–270 in manuscripts: see simply Thompson, *Epic of Gilgamesh*, 65 n. 37. (The original text could have included the narration minus lines 268–270 instead of, or in addition to, the instructions. But the dittography and the frequent use of instructions in the Old Babylonian versions suggest that we give preference to the instructions.)

54. After completing this essay, I was pleased to discover that also I. M. Diakonoff and N. B. Jankowska have noticed that the Utnapishtim episode was not part of the original epic and that "the Siduri episode, of little importance in the Nineveh version, must have originally been the final *dénouement* of the epic" ("An Elamite Gilgameš Text from Argištihenele, Urartu (Armavir-blur, 8th century, B.C.)," *ZA* 80 [1990] 104, cf. p. 111). They think that originally the plant of life was part of the Siduri episode and that the purpose of Gilgamesh's visit was to ask Siduri for the plant of life (ibid., 110–11, 116). For the time being, at least, I do not accept this as the purpose of Gilgamesh's visit, though it is an ingenious interpretation and would also provide a reasonable context and meaning for M ii 12′–13′: "now that I have seen your face, may I not see death."

Calypso and Circe and of their stories, then it seems quite possible that in some earlier tradition, Siduri acceded to Gilgamesh's proposal and allowed him to stay with her and that in an even earlier tradition, she was the initiator and even suggested that he stay with her. Her invitation would have been like the invitations proffered to Odysseus by Circe and Calypso. Presumably, the original story and perhaps even its several early forms involved not Gilgamesh but rather another traveler or wanderer; Gilgamesh was made into the hero of the story when later this theme of the wandering hero and the goddess was taken over and developed by the Gilgamesh tradition.

In any case, in the earliest version Siduri's invitation would also have been like Ereshkigal's invitation to Nergal in *Nergal and Ereshkigal*, and it is not irrelevant that in Tablet X i 15–22 of the Standard version we are told:

> The alewife looked at him and locked [her door],
> She locked her door, locked it [with a bolt].
> Then he, Gilgamesh, noticed [ ]
> Raised his chin and [ ]
> Gilgamesh spoke to her, to the alewife;
> "Alewife, why did you look at me [and lock] your door,
> Lock your door, [lock it] with a bolt?
> I will smash the door, I will shatter [the bolt]!"[55]

This theme is known to us from such other netherworld contexts as *The Descent of Ishtar, Nergal and Ereshkigal*, and GE, Tablet VI,[56] and its association with Siduri further links her to the netherworld and suggests that like the other Mesopotamian and Greek goddesses mentioned, she too had a netherworld dimension.

Furthermore, it may well be that the original Gilgamesh or pre-Gilgamesh/Siduri encounter paralleled Ishtar's proposal to Gilgamesh in Tablet VI of the Standard Babylonian version of the epic, sharing with it the topos of the goddess proposing to the hero that he become her mate and join her in her infernal home.[57] It is of interest that the epic would introduce the same basic topos more than once. But the two episodes are surely not the same in the traditions before us. For even if Siduri was originally an Ishtar figure, in our Old Babylonian

55. Translation: Dalley, *Myths*, 100.
56. Cf. Tigay, *Evolution*, 173–74 for a discussion of this theme in these three myths.
57. For this interpretation of Tablet VI, see Abusch, "Ishtar's Proposal," 143–87 [here, pp. 11–57].

composition the Siduri-Gilgamesh encounter is in effect a reversal of the Ishtar-Gilgamesh encounter of Tablet VI, for there Ishtar proposes and Gilgamesh refuses and here Gilgamesh proposes and Siduri refuses. Siduri has assumed a role like that of the prostitute Shamhat, who humanized Enkidu and led him to the city. It is, therefore, of even greater significance and perhaps ironic value that the two occurrences of the topos would be polar variations of each other. The Ishtar-Gilgamesh episode offers Gilgamesh what he desires but cannot attain in the Old Babylonian version and also points up the implication of living with a goddess, i.e., death. But these two polar variants of the topos were probably not present in the same recension of the epic. The Ishtar-Gilgamesh episode of Tablet VI was not part of the Old Babylonian version;[58] rather, it was part of the late Standard version, a version that also transformed the Siduri-Gilgamesh encounter into simply one more meeting on the way to Utnapishtim in order to learn how the latter had attained immortal life. It is perhaps significant for the development of the epic that in its earlier Old Babylonian stage, the epic emphasized a form of the topos in which Gilgamesh seeks the goddess because he thinks she represents life absolute and is refused by her because she recognizes that her acquiescence would mean his death, while at a later stage, the epic emphasized a different form of the topos, one in which the goddess proposes, but the hero refuses the proposal because he realizes that its acceptance means death rather than an enhanced life. In either case, the hero is not yet ready to accept the inevitability of death.

III. Reformulation

Elsewhere, I shall examine in detail the poetic structure and meaning of the second stanza of both Gilgamesh's and Siduri's speeches. Here, therefore, I may end by reformulating the dialogue between Gilgamesh and Siduri in somewhat abstract terms.

The dialogue is structured around the major events of the life cycle: birth, but especially marriage and death. The sequence, however, is

58. See Abusch, "Ishtar's Proposal," 180–87 [here, pp. 49–56]. Only with the insertion of Tablet VI at a later stage, do we get the introduction of a form of the story in which a goddess invites the hero to live with her. It is perhaps not a coincidence that the later version has suppressed wholly the theme of living with a goddess in the Siduri encounter and eliminated this goddess's need to convince Gilgamesh to leave her and return to life. In this context, note also the contrast in that later version between the handsomeness of Gilgamesh's person and clothes and his attractiveness to Ishtar in VI 1–6 and his worn-out appearance and negative impact on Siduri in X 5–16 and 40–52.

from death with its attendant funeral to marriage. But like funerals, marriage can also be an entrance into death and, thus, a marriage that is a form of death must be replaced by a normal marriage that carries with it a reaffirmation of life. Operating with the polarities of funeral and marriage, on the one hand, and death and life, on the other, the text links these elements in several ways and moves from funeral/death (ii 4′–9′) through marriage/death (ii 12′–13′) to marriage/life (iii 6–13): in his attempt to free himself from his attachment to his dead friend Enkidu, a relationship that had not been resolved by the funeral and mourning rites, Gilgamesh tries to enter into a marriage with the goddess Siduri. But such a marriage is untenable for the man Gilgamesh, for it is a union of life and death, human and god. Siduri is a divinity, and death and divinity are alike in their absoluteness and eternity. Recognizing both the initial impasse as well as the final sterility and death that are inherent in the union of human and divine, the goddess tries to save Gilgamesh from the destruction to which their union would lead by disengaging him from herself and directing him instead to a normal marriage with its attendant births and family life, for only so may he free himself from death and enter into a new stage of life. She tries to disengage Gilgamesh both from death and from fantasy, from his attachment to a dead human male as well as from his hope to be attached to an immortal female.

Thus, the end of Siduri's speech responds not only to the beginning of Gilgamesh's speech but also to its end. For while forming a chiasm, the two speeches also run parallel to each other with the first, second, and third stanzas of each corresponding sequentially to those of the other: The first stanza of Gilgamesh's speech centers upon a narration of his personal past and upon human destiny, while the first stanza of the goddess's speech centers upon a narration of mythic past and responds to the cry in his first stanza by pointing to the contrast between human and divine destiny and to the inevitability of human death. Their second stanzas are organized poetically around unconventional centers and deal with the failure of conventional funeral forms; the middle stanza of Gilgamesh's speech exposes the problem while the middle stanza of Siduri's suggests a way of resolving it.[59] Gilgamesh's third stanza expresses his solution to the problem formulated in his first stanza, a solution which tries to deal with the loss of Enkidu by acknowledging his death and

59. See Abusch, "Gilgamesh's Request and Siduri's Denial, Part II" [here, pp. 89–107].

replacing him with a goddess whose partnership bestows immortality upon Gilgamesh. After responding in her first stanza both to the specific loss of Enkidu and to the general problem evoked by that loss, Siduri, in her third stanza, then rejects the solution proposed by Gilgamesh in his third stanza and provides the poem's solution. Thus, the third stanzas suggest, on the one hand, Gilgamesh's hope for his future and, on the other, Siduri's correction of this thought and its redirection to an alternate goal. She suggests that he take up the normal life of a mortal man who experiences the pleasures and bears the responsibilities of human family and society.[60]

60. G. A. Anderson studies some of the same issues treated in the present essay and its companion pieces in *A Time to Mourn, A Time to Dance: The Expression of Grief and Joy in Israelite Religion* (University Park: Pennsylvania State University Press, 1991), especially pp. 74–82. This work is an interesting and useful treatment. Unfortunately, it appeared after my studies of the Gilgamesh-Siduri dialogue were completed and could no longer be incorporated into the essays.

Gilgamesh's Request and Siduri's Denial, Part II

An Analysis and Interpretation of an Old Babylonian Fragment about Mourning and Celebration

I. Introduction

The purpose of this essay is to provide an analysis of two of the most powerfully evocative stanzas in Akkadian poetic literature. Such a study is surely fitting in a volume honoring Professor Yochanan Muffs. Yochanan's understanding of ancient texts is almost preternatural; one can only marvel at his ability to grasp and bring to life the emotions and metaphors that govern these texts. It seems appropriate, then, to celebrate a great scholar and dear friend with a study of the form and emotional force of passages from the *Epic of Gilgamesh*, passages that center upon themes which have also interested Yochanan.

The two stanzas are part of the justly famous exchange between Gilgamesh and the divine tavernkeeper Siduri in an Old Babylonian (OB) version of the *Epic of Gilgamesh*. The preserved part of their encounter begins with a request that Gilgamesh addresses to Siduri followed by her response (= OB Gilg., Meissner, ii–iii).[1] Each speech contains three stanzas. In translation, the two speeches read:

This essay and its companion study ("Gilgamesh's Request and Siduri's Denial, Part I: The Meaning of the Dialogue and Its Implications for the History of the Epic" [here, pp. 58–88]) have benefited greatly from the comments of several scholars. Stephen A. Geller discussed the text with me in great detail, and both he and Kathryn Kravitz read the several drafts and made a number of helpful comments and suggestions. William L. Moran also discussed the text with me, Mordechai Cogan critiqued an early draft, and Diane Feinman suggested improvements in the final draft. I am grateful to all these friends for their interest and help.

1. The Meissner fragment was published by B. Meissner, *Ein altbabylonisches Fragment des Gilgamosepos* (MVAG 7.1; Berlin: Peiser, 1902). More recently, it has been joined to a fragment in the British Museum; see A. R. Millard, "Gilgamesh X: A New Fragment," *Iraq* 26 (1964) 99–105. For translations of both the Old Babylonian text and the later Standard Babylonian version of the epic, see, e.g., E. A. Speiser and A. K. Grayson in *ANET*, 72–99, 503–7, and S. Dalley, *Myths from Mesopotamia: Creation, The*

col. ii * My friend, whom I love dearly,
1′ Who with me underwent all hardships,
2′ Enkidu, whom I love dearly,
3′ Who with me underwent all hardships,
4′ Has gone to the fate of mankind.

5′ Day and night I wept over him,
6′ I would not give him up for burial—
7′ (saying) "My friend perhaps will rise up to me at my
cry!"—
8′ Seven days and seven nights
9′ Until a worm dropped out at me from his nose.

10′ Since his death, I have not found life.
11′ I keep roaming like a hunter in the open country.
12′ Now, alewife, that I have seen your face,
13′ The death that I constantly fear may I not see.

14′ The alewife spoke to him, to Gilgamesh:

col. iii 1 Gilgamesh, whither do you rove?
2 The life that you pursue you shall not find.
3 When the gods created mankind,
4 Death they appointed for mankind,
5 Life in their own hands they held.

6 You, Gilgamesh, let your stomach be full.
7 Day and night keep on being festive.
8 Daily make a festival.
9 Day and night dance and play.

10 Let your clothes be clean,
11 Let your head be washed, in water may you bathe.
12 Look down at the child who holds your hand,
13 Let a wife ever delight in your lap.[2]

Flood, Gilgamesh and Others (Oxford: Oxford University Press, 1989) 39–153. For studies of the epic, cf., e.g., T. Jacobsen, *Treasures of Darkness: A History of Mesopotamian Religion* (New Haven, CT: Yale University Press, 1976) 195–219; J. H. Tigay, *The Evolution of the Gilgamesh Epic* (Philadelphia: University of Pennsylvania Press, 1982); T. Abusch, "Ishtar's Proposal and Gilgamesh's Refusal: An Interpretation of *The Gilgamesh Epic*, Tablet 6, Lines 1–79," *History of Religions* 26 (1986) 143–87 [here, pp. 11–57].

2. Following the end of the third stanza of Siduri's speech, there are an additional three lines that are largely broken. These lines might read:

"This alone is the conce[rn of woman/man.]

Gilgamesh's speech encapsulates his emotional state: past, present, and future. Beginning with a description of the death of his friend, it moves on to an expression of his present anguish, and finally to his proposal for a solution. Siduri's speech provides her response and her advice. Elsewhere, I have examined the overall structure of this first set of speeches in the encounter between Gilgamesh and Siduri and there paid particular attention to the last, that is, the third stanza of each of the two speeches.[3] Here, I shall take up questions of poetic form and meaning of the second, that is, the middle stanza of these two speeches.

In the aforementioned study, we noted that the two speeches run parallel to each other, but also form a chiasm. In either structural form, the second or middle stanzas (ii 5′–9′ and iii 6–9) correspond to each other and form the center of each speech. The middle stanza of Gilgamesh's speech contains the impassioned statement of his distress, and the middle stanza of Siduri's speech contains the goddess's direct response to that statement. The stanza iii 6–9 forms Siduri's solution to the personal and cultural crisis that Gilgamesh articulates in ii 5′–9′. Her injunction has been treated as a Babylonian form of *carpe diem*. This interpretation of her advice perhaps distorts its meaning but, certainly, does not exhaust it. For her advice is not simply the urging of a hedonistic philosophy, a call for sensual pleasure: "Let us eat and drink, for tomorrow we die" (Isa 22:13b). Rather, as we shall see, it is a prescription for healing, for therein the goddess draws a mourner away from the desert of grief and leads him back to the city of life.

The middle stanzas rightly form the centerpiece of each speech and of the dialogue as a whole. In fact, each of these central stanzas itself revolves around a central element. Thus, the poem directs our gaze to the center(s) of the center(s) and requires us to pay particular attention to them. Yet, the meaning of the central element, especially in Siduri's speech, is far from clear, for we do not know the form or force of the feasts or festivities that she urges Gilgamesh to undertake. Moreover, the two stanzas exhibit difficulties—perhaps irregularities—of poetic form, especially at their centers, and the very placement of these centers would seem to be responsible for unusual forms elsewhere in the stanzas.

[Gilgamesh, whither do you rove?]
Let him who is alive [enjoy life]."

The first of these lines and perhaps the two that follow seem to be a concluding summary construction of Siduri's message.

3. Abusch, "Gilgamesh's Request, Part I" [here, pp. 58–88].

II. Analysis and Interpretation

To understand the meaning of the two stanzas as well as the cultural and existential issues at stake, we do well to allow their peculiarities to guide us to an understanding of the message.

A. Gilgamesh's description of his distress, ii 5′–9′:

5′ *urrī u mūšī elišu abki*
6′ *ul addiššu ana qebērim*
7′ *ibrīman itabbe'am ana rigmiya*
8′ *sebet ūmi u sebe mušiātim*
9′ *adi tūltum imqutam ina appišu*

The center of the stanza is an utterance: "My friend perhaps will rise up to me at my cry!" Each of the four other lines of the stanza is sundered from its logical connection, and all four are set loosely around the center, for properly speaking, ii 5′ and 8′ belong together as do ii 6′ and 9′.

B. Siduri's central advice, iii 6–9:

6 *attā* ᵈ*Gilgameš lū mali karaška*
7 *urrī u mūšī ḫitaddu attā*
8 *ūmišam šukun ḫidûtam*
9 *urrī u mūšī sūr u mēlil*

Lines iii 7–8 parallel each other and form the center of the stanza; for their part, iii 6 and 9 open and close the stanza and also parallel each other. As parallel lines, the two inner lines are unduly repetitive and strike one as vague and generic. On the other hand, the outer lines, while sharing elements with the core lines (*attā* in iii 6 and 7, *urrī u mūšī* in iii 7 and 9), are quite specific. This marked difference creates an imbalance.

Note, moreover, that in both Gilgamesh's and Siduri's speeches, it is only the middle two stanzas that are built around a central element, while the first and third stanzas are not. This contrast highlights the significance of the construction.

The poetic structures in these stanzas are part of the composer's way of conveying a message. To understand these stanzas, we must examine them more closely and answer several questions: What thought is expressed by the central themes and perhaps highlighted by the deviations and imbalances? Why did the poet build these stanzas around central points? What is the effect of this construction in each of the two different stanzas?

A. Gilgamesh's Distress: col. ii 5′–9′

We begin with the second stanza of Gilgamesh's speech (ii 5′–9′). The stanza describes Gilgamesh's mourning for Enkidu, but Gilgamesh's act of mourning is neither traditional nor effective:

5′. Day and night I wept over him,
6′. I did not give him up for burial—
7′. (Saying) "My friend perhaps will rise up to me at my cry!"—
8′. Seven days and seven nights
9′. Until a worm dropped out at me from his nose.

1. Form

The stanza shows a breakdown of poetic form. Rather than being constructed in the form of groups of parallel lines, the poetry is loose and informal. The clause begun in line 6′ continues beyond the end of its line and is only concluded in line 9′. Line 8′, an adverbial phrase which modifies line 5′ and/or line 6′, has been separated from them and appears disconnected. At the mid-point of the stanza (line 7′), is a parenthetical remark; its occurrence is disruptive and creates an anacoluthon. Altogether, the stanza is characterized by disjunction. Instead of poetic calm, there is a rush of words. All this conveys Gilgamesh's confused, disruptive, and disjointed feelings. To appreciate the force of the stanza we need only notice how sharply it contrasts with the immediately preceding stanza. That stanza is formal and orderly:

My friend, whom I love dearly,
Who with me underwent all hardships,
Enkidu, whom I love dearly,
Who with me underwent all hardships,
Has now gone to the fate of mankind.

By contrast, our stanza is both broken and tense.

Especially given the formal quality of the first stanza, we need to explain why the second stanza differs and follows a freer form. That we are right in highlighting this contrast between the two stanzas is further indicated by the form of the second stanza in Tablet X ii 58–60 of the Standard Babylonian (SB) version; in that version, the stanza possesses the formal quality characteristic of the first stanza of the OB version. Thus, we might have expected that the OB version, too, would have a text form in line with the poetic structure of its first stanza. Accordingly, the freer manner of articulation of the OB stanza must be of particular significance.

2. Comparison of Versions

By contrasting the differing SB and OB forms of the same stanza, we may understand the OB (and the SB) forms better.

Standard Babylonian (X ii 58–60)	Old Babylonian (ii 5′–9′)
6 urrī u 7 mušâti elišu abki	*urrī u mūšī elišu abki*
ul addinšu ana qebēri	*ul addiššu ana qebērim*
	ibrīman itabbeʾam ana rigmiya
	sebet ūmī u sebe mušiātim
adi tūltu imquta ina appišu[4]	*adi tūltum imqutam ina appišu*
For 6 days and 7 nights I wept over him;	Day and night I wept over him,
I did not give him up for burial	I did not give him up for burial—
	(saying) "My friend perhaps will rise up to me at my cry"—
	seven days and seven nights
Until a worm dropped out at me from his nose.	until a worm dropped out at me from his nose.

In the SB version, ii 5′b and ii 8′ of the OB version are joined together in X ii 58, and OB ii 6′ and ii 9′ are joined together in X ii 59–60. Thus, in the SB version, the amount of time that has elapsed (the number of days and nights) is joined to the statement of Gilgamesh's mourning over Enkidu, and Gilgamesh's refusal to give up Enkidu for burial is followed by the event—the appearance of the worm—which forces him to give up the body of Enkidu. While this version contains some elements of drama and surprise, it is fundamentally cast in narrative form. In the main, its organization is in line with prosaic logic and prosaic story-telling.

In the OB version, SB X ii 58 is split apart, and X ii 59 and 60 are separate. Gilgamesh's weeping (ii 5′) is followed by his refusal to give Enkidu up for burial (ii 6′) but is not preceded by—or in any way directly connected with—a number of days and nights (ii 8′); and his refusal to give up Enkidu is followed not by the appearance of the worm (ii 9′), but rather by his cry of futile hope that Enkidu might still rise (ii 7′), a cry that is itself followed by "seven days and seven nights" (ii 8′). Thus, whereas logically, OB ii 5′ and ii 8′, and ii 6′ and ii 9′

4. See X ii 58–60 (speech to Siduri), restored from X iii 135–137 (speech to Urshanabi) and X v 235–237 (speech to Utnapishtim).

might belong together, in fact line 8′ is separated from line 5′, and line 9′ from line 6′.

In both versions, the appearance of the worm brings home the point that Gilgamesh should have buried Enkidu much earlier and lets us know how grossly inappropriate Gilgamesh's behavior was. Here, however, I would emphasize the importance in our text of the different treatments of time durations and placements of the elapsed number of days and nights.

Joined together, *6 urrī u 7 mušâti* / *sebet ūmī u sebe mušiātim* and *elišu abki* (SB X ii 58 // OB ii 5′b + 8′) are a formulation of a standard mourning motif and reflect the ceremonial reality of a period of mourning subsequent to the burial of the dead. Usually, burial would follow immediately upon death and only then would a seven-day period of mourning ensue.[5] In both texts there is a delay in the recognition of the significance of Gilgamesh's mourning, but the recognition occurs at different points and becomes known by different means in each text with the result that the audience is affected differently in each case.

In the OB version, line 8′ is separated from line 5′ and linked with line 6′. Consequently, in contrast to the SB version, the continuous day-and-night mourning of line 5′ is not of limited duration; instead, it is of unknown or indefinite length. Line 8′ tells us only how many days Gilgamesh did not give up Enkidu before the reality of line 9′ intervened.

But whereas the OB text presents mourning as indefinite and undefined, the writer of the SB text begins in line 58 by presenting the mourning as six/seven days in duration. This would appear to be proper behavior. But in line 59 we learn that Gilgamesh had not yet buried Enkidu and therefore that this six/seven-day period of mourning was prior to burial. When, in the SB version, the reader learns that Gilgamesh has not yet buried Enkidu, it comes as a surprise. Retroactively, the reader realizes that the seven days of weeping were not days of mourning subsequent to a funeral, but rather, days of suspension of funeral rites. Precisely because the number of days of weeping in line 58 is the same as the number of days of mourning after a funeral, the mention of a

5. The assumption of a seven-day period of mourning in Mesopotamia seems reasonable, though I cannot recall a study that has established or examined the custom. Seven days seems to be the standard period of mourning in Israel; see, e.g., P. K. McCarter, Jr., *II Samuel: A New Translation with Introduction, Notes, and Commentary* (AB 9; Garden City, NY: Doubleday, 1984) 288 on v. 27 and 301 on v. 18; and cf. W. W. Hallo, "The Death of Kings: Traditional Historiography in Contextual Perspective," in *Ah, Assyria . . . : Studies in Assyrian History and Ancient Near Eastern Historiography Presented to Hayim Tadmor* (ed. M. Cogan and I. Ephʿal; ScrHie 33; Jerusalem: Magnes, 1991) 159.

precise number of days rather than a generalized period introduces an ironic twist by showing how the rites of burial and mourning have been reversed.[6] For with the recognition that these seven days came before the burial, we realize that the mourning has served a purpose opposite to that which it was meant to serve. The period that should have been devoted to honoring the dead resulted instead in their dishonor, and this point is then brought home by the appearance of maggots.

The SB text seems precise and does not hold back information. The OB version is less precise but more dramatic and powerful. It conveys the impression of uncontrollable grief and manages to convey the inner life of the hero and to involve us in that life. In the OB version, mourning is generalized. Mourning day and night is followed by Gilgamesh's refusal to bury Enkidu. At this point in the text we cannot yet know either the full significance of the mourning or of the refusal to bury, for a precise number of days has been mentioned alongside neither the weeping nor the refusal. Instead, the refusal is followed by an expression of hope.

In itself, Gilgamesh's statement, "my friend perhaps will rise up to me at my cry," is not wholly unreasonable.[7] But the true significance of also this statement is not clear until the mention of seven days and seven nights in the following line. For only then do we realize how long Gilgamesh had failed to give up Enkidu for burial and how delusional his hope had been. Surely, his statement of hope was only believable when we thought that Enkidu had only just died and had been kept out of the grave for a short time. Until the mention of seven days and seven nights

6. A comparable irony or reversal is perhaps presented to the onlookers by David's behavior in 2 Sam 12:15–23, where David apparently mourns for seven days before the death of his sick child, but not after the death.

7. It is sometimes necessary to ascertain that the deceased is actually dead and has not simply fallen into a suspended state from which he might revive. Hence, prior to burial, one function of mourning is to attempt to revive one who seems to have died, but may yet be brought back to life (cf. *muballiṭ mīti*). For the latter reason, David, in the incident in 2 Sam 12:15–23, did not continue to mourn the child after his death. For not only did he probably lack emotional engagement with the infant and had in any case already performed virtual rites of mourning for the child when he was alive for the sake of doing penance for him in order to revive him, he also knew that the child was irrevocably dead: "He replied, 'While the child was still alive, I fasted and wept because I thought: "Who knows? The Lord may take pity on me, and the child may live." But now that he is dead, why should I fast? Can I bring him back again? I shall go to him, but he will never come back to me'" (2 Sam 12:22–23; translation: *Tanakh: A New Translation of The Holy Scriptures according to the Traditional Hebrew Text* [Philadelphia: Jewish Publication Society, 1985]).

in line 8′, recognition has been delayed. Were we told the number of days originally, in line 5′, we would have immediately known the impropriety of Gilgamesh's refusal to give up the body and the profoundly delusional character of his hope. His statement would then have had little impact, for it would have been unbelievable.

The delay is longer and the surprise and shock all the greater in the OB text, for the delay has allowed us to be privy to, and has brought us to accept, both Gilgamesh's unlimited grief and his belief that Enkidu might actually not be dead and might shake off his deep sleep and rise up. The mention here of seven days and seven nights introduces reality in such an explosive way that we condemn what we before accepted. And this recognition is now capped off by a sense of revulsion at the appearance of the maggots.[8]

3. Emotional Logic of the Text

But let us now review the OB version of the second stanza in greater detail, but this time more from the point of view of Gilgamesh's experience. While the text is not ordered in conventional poetic terms, it seems to represent Gilgamesh's reality more faithfully than the SB version. It follows an emotional logic and is forceful and expressive. Every line is different from and contrasts with every other line, and as we read the OB version, we become increasingly conscious of its dynamic, almost chaotic, and pressured quality:

Line 5′: Gilgamesh tells us that he weeps over his friend day and night. Rather than being finite, the weeping and mourning are indefinite.

---

8. Rather than basing the analysis of the OB text on the number of days, one might instead focus on the delusional statement: "My friend perhaps will rise up to me at my cry!" (ii 7′). For it is possible that this statement immediately informs the audience, even prior to the mention of six/seven days (ii 8′), that the mourning over Enkidu and the delay in his burial were not acceptable forms of behavior. If this is correct, the audience of the OB text hears the mention of six/seven days knowing already that it was wrong to act so instead of burying Enkidu immediately. It is possible that Gilgamesh's statement was understood as a delusion immediately upon its mention in the text. But even if it is acknowledged that the delusional quality of line 7′ is immediately sensed, the full delusional force would probably only have been fully recognized and understood with the mention of the days in line 8′. For initially, the reader would not be sure how to interpret line 7′: on the one hand, he might agree that it was possible that Enkidu was only asleep; but on the other, even one who fully sympathizes with Gilgamesh's grief recognizes that the reality of death is obvious. Only with the mention of the seven days/nights would the full force of the delusion become evident, and the reader would realize how horrendous and unacceptable Gilgamesh's behavior had been and that he had acted solely on the basis of his delusion.

Line 6′: Gilgamesh is not able to bury and separate from the dead Enkidu. Instead of burying his friend immediately and then weeping over him for seven days, he holds back his body from burial.

Line 7′: For he grasps at the delusion that his friend might rise up from the bier upon hearing his lament. The statement expressing this thought, this delusion, is here inserted into the text and disrupts the passage—as it disrupts Gilgamesh's life. It is set in the middle of the stanza and governs it from beginning to end.

Line 8′: "Seven days and seven nights." His chaotic thoughts and behavior have persisted for these many days. The days that should have defined the period of mourning instead designate the number of days of delusion. The absence of a verb highlights the emotional and behavioral disjunctions. The line that indicates duration here applies not to Gilgamesh's mourning or weeping, but to his resistance or inability to bury Enkidu, and it specifies the number of days that he was in the grip of delusion before reality forced him to bury his friend.

Line 9′: The rotting of dead human flesh shocks Gilgamesh and forces him to recognize the failure of his attempt to keep Enkidu alive. The climactic events of this line call a halt to his deluded and futile behavior. His failure throws him back into a despairing reality.[9]

4. Psychological and Cultural Significance

The appearance of the worm demonstrates how perverse and topsy-turvy Gilgamesh's world had become. The outcome of preventing Enkidu's burial is ironic. Leaving the dead unburied is actually the worst treatment that can be accorded them. By not giving Enkidu's body over for burial, Gilgamesh wished to keep Enkidu present in the hope that his friend might come back to life. But Enkidu's body could not remain in a state of preservation, and, therefore, rather than expressing his love for Enkidu, Gilgamesh's behavior actually resulted in the mistreatment and dishonor of Enkidu. Gilgamesh has committed an offense against Enkidu and has deprived him of that which he had been promised: a proper burial. For it is not his friend that he has preserved, but his own delusion. He has become so self-centered that he has forgotten his friend. Gilgamesh needed to be reminded of this as, in another epic, did Achilles. In Patroclus' words to Achilles:

9. Notice also that the text never states explicitly that Gilgamesh finally gave Enkidu up for burial.

> Sleeping so? Thou has forgotten me, Akhilleus.
> Never was I uncared for in life but am in death.
> Accord me burial in all haste: let me pass the gates of death.[10]

As Whitman noted regarding this passage, "What can be the meaning of this accusation, when Achilles can think of nothing but Patroclus? While his friend was alive, Achilles had listened to him, considered his nature, yielding to his claim upon him. Now he is dead. Achilles' actions are appropriate to himself, but not to Patroclus. What the dead wants is burial, burial in human decency."[11] So, too, Gilgamesh has thought only of himself and has allowed Enkidu's beautiful body to suffer disfigurement. And the worm brings this horror home to Gilgamesh in a profoundly shocking way.

Especially in our OB stanza, there is a mixture of order and confusion, continuity and disjunction. Order and continuity are visible to an outsider looking upon a burial scene which stretches over time and shows the duration of mourning activity. The confusion and disjunction, on the other hand, are most palpable when we step into the scene and experience the emotional pressure that compels and impels Gilgamesh.

Gilgamesh's state of mind is one of confusion and disorder, and his grasp of reality is weakened. He is driven by his feelings and is unable to follow the burial customs of his society. Funerary rites have failed him, and he is thus unable to separate from his dead friend and come to terms with reality. His special status allows him to flout the customary practices of his community; as with other aspects of his life, he rebels here against accepted norms. But, in effect, his idiosyncratic performance of the rites merely mimics them and thus conveys both their expected form as well as their distortion.

The stanza conveys to the audience the collapse of Gilgamesh's world and his identity within it. The various literary means give verbal expression to Gilgamesh's anguish and disintegrated state. Especially the breakdown of literary form, the deviations from poetic order, convey a breakdown of internal order and of cultural forms of mourning and burial.

Both versions describe the failure of funerary rituals. But unlike the SB version, the OB version does not simply present this failure and

10. Homer, *Iliad* 23.69–71, trans. R. Fitzgerald (Garden City, NY: Anchor, 1974) 537.

11. C. H. Whitman, *Homer and the Heroic Tradition* (Cambridge, MA: Harvard University Press, 1958) 214.

Gilgamesh's recourse to unconventional mourning and burial rites in a formal or schematic fashion, that is, in a ritualized form of poetic expression, but rather uses free form and emphasizes the centrality—the power—of the delusion and the long period in which Gilgamesh was deluded and could not surrender his friend to the grave. Whereas the SB version presents the events from the perspective of one looking back on a completed event, the OB version actually carries the speaker and the audience back to the experience itself. It presents the event as if it were ongoing and causes the audience to share in it. The OB text expresses, imitates, and draws us into Gilgamesh's state.

Delusion is shown to be central to the thought of the stanza by the placement of the delusional statement—"My friend perhaps will rise up to me at my cry"—at its center, and the stanza is built around this line. The disorder and poetic tension in ii 5′–9′ make clear the failure of the mourning rites, for Gilgamesh could not bury his friend immediately after death, as he should have done in accordance with standard rites.

Even delusional behavior did not succeed, and finally Gilgamesh was forced to recognize that Enkidu was dead. But even then, he was unable to bury and truly separate from Enkidu. By the same token, Gilgamesh was unable to accept his own mortality and finiteness. Mourning in all its different forms has failed. Hence, his flight and eventual movement towards the alewife. Hence, also, the necessity for her to pry him loose from his attachment to the burial place and bring him back to everyday life. This, then, brings us to the middle stanza of Siduri's speech, to which we now turn.

B. Siduri's Advice: col. iii 6–9

6. You, Gilgamesh, let your stomach be full.
7. Day and night keep on being festive, (you).
8. Daily make a festival.
9. Day and night dance and play.

1. Joy

The whole of Siduri's speech has more than once been compared with the Egyptian Harpers' Songs. And for our purposes, it is worth attending to the Harpers' Songs and related orchestra songs,[12] for the core of the

12. For this literature, see M. Lichtheim, "The Songs of the Harpers," *JNES* 4 (1945) 178–212; E. F. Wente, "Egyptian 'Make Merry' Songs Reconsidered," *JNES* 21 (1962) 118–28; M. Lichtheim, *Ancient Egyptian Literature*, vol. 1: *The Old and Mid-*

second stanza of Siduri's speech seems to represent or be based upon a set phrase, a phrase which would seem to have been taken over from elsewhere. In any case, the phrase repeats a refrain found in the Harpers' Songs: *ir hrw nfr*, "enjoy a festive day."[13]

These texts have a holiday or feast-day setting and are normally associated with festive banquets where they may have been sung. J. Assmann has recently provided an apt characterization of the Harpers' Songs:

> Es gibt eine Gattung, die wir—ungenau—"Harfnerlieder" nennen, und die ihre typische Aufführungssituation, ihren "Sitz im Leben" in der geselligen oder intimen Festfeier des "Schönen Tages" hat. Diese Gattung ist Ausdrucksform einer ganz spezifischen Lebensweisheit. Der bedeutendste Text steht . . . im Londoner Papyrus Harris 500. . . .
>
> Der Text ist zweigeteilt . . . Die erste beklagt die Vergänglichkeit alles Irdischen, die zweite fordert zum Festgenuss auf. . . .
>
> Der zweite Teil fordert zum Festgenuss auf. Zwei Elemente sind uns vertraut: der hier als "Refrain" eingeführte Trinkspruch *jrj hrw nfr* "feiere den schönen Tag," und die Aufforderung, sich durch weisse Kleidung, duftende Salben und Öle und die Gemeinschaft der "Schönen" dem Fest hinzugeben. Diese Elemente stammen unmittelbar aus der Festsituation. Es scheint mir evident, dass das "Anteflied" eine literarisch-poetische Elaboration solcher Lieder und Trinksprüche darstellt, wie sie in der mündlichen Überlieferung des Festes seit alters ihren Ort haben.[14]

While Siduri's first stanza, like the first part of the Harpers' Song, tries to convey the theoretical underpinnings of the transitoriness of life, it is actually Gilgamesh's speech itself which conveys that sense with power and poignancy. Siduri's speech is focused more on the second part, the theme of enjoyment, and here, therefore, we deal only with aspects of the second of the two parts of the Harpers' Song.

---

dle Kingdoms (Berkeley: University of California Press, 1973) 193–97; vol. 2: *The New Kingdom* (Berkeley: University of California Press, 1976) 115–16; M. V. Fox, "A Study of Antef," *Or* 46 (1977) 393–423; idem, "The Entertainment Song Genre in Egyptian Literature," in *Egyptological Studies* (ed. S. Israelit-Groll; ScrHie 28; Jerusalem: Magnes, 1982) 268–316; J. Assmann, "Der schöne Tag—Sinnlichkeit und Vergänglichkeit im altägyptischen Fest," in *Das Fest* (ed. W. Haug and R. Warning; Poetik und Hermeneutik 14; Munich: Fink, 1989) 3–28. For several further references, see Assmann, "Der schöne Tag," 18 n. 70.

13. For this phrase, see, e.g., Fox, "Entertainment Song Genre," 293–96; Lichtheim, "Songs of the Harpers," 207–8; idem, *Ancient Egyptian Literature*, 1:195.

14. Assmann, "Der schöne Tag," 18–20.

The Harpers' Songs and related orchestra songs emphasize the theme of *ir hrw nfr*, "enjoy a festive day." This theme recalls our iii 7–8: *urrī u mūšī ḫitaddu attā // ūmišam šukun ḫidûtam*, "day and night keep on being festive, daily make a festival." This Egyptian motif and our lines iii 7–8 are parallel formulations of the same thought and possibly reflect or derive from similar settings. For this reason, these lines have, as we have noted, a general quality. The general theme forms the centerpiece of our stanza, around which are arranged the more specific lines 6 and 9. Like Gilgamesh's second stanza, the stanza is created from the middle outward. Lines 7 and 8 parallel each other. Line 8 is the less poetic and its concrete formulation of a command to act suggests that it represents the original festival prescription (*ḫidûtam šakānu* may well be a technical term) and that line 7, which has richer poetic texture, was then formulated to serve as its poetic parallel and as the first line of the pair. Lines 6 and 9 detail and make explicit the main pleasures of the day: food in iii 6; music and dance in iii 9. They thus specify aspects of the more general festival occasion and render the occasion concrete.

The structured repetition in our stanza conveys a sense of order. In fact, the stanza forms an interpenetrated or interlocking circular structure. Line 7 ends with *attā* (you), which word also begins line 6. The repetition of the word links lines 6 and 7, and personalizes the event and directs the advice to Gilgamesh. And line 9, the last line of the stanza, repeats *urrī u mūšī* of line 7 (rather than *ūmišam* of line 8). The repetition of *urrī u mūšī* from line 7 may serve to achieve variety by avoiding the repetition of *ūmišam*[15] from the immediately preceding line. It may also be used here because it recalls the parallel stanza in Gilgamesh's speech where this same phrase opens the stanza (ii 5′). But most of all, the use of this phrase in line 9 serves precisely to highlight its use in line 7. In line 7, the words *urrī u mūšī* and *attā* bracket *ḫitaddu*; thus, the repetitions in lines 6 and 9 in concert highlight the remaining and central word of line 7 and of the text: *ḫitaddu*. Graphically, this emphasis may be represented as follows:

6.			*attā* . . .
7.	*urrī u mūšī*	*ḪITADDU*	*attā* . . .
9.	*urrī u mūšī* . . .		

The composer plays with and highlights line 7 rather than line 8 because this line may have been his own poetic formulation of the central

15. Note also the alliteration of *ūmišam* and *mūšī*.

theme. Lines 6 and 9 are not simply added to create a stanza. They personalize its central message; they lead up to and highlight the fundamental purpose of the festival: joy. Hence, the use of forms of *ḫadû* in the two center lines.

The stanza's several devices create a central assertion of the joy of this life and a reaffirmation of its goodness and value. This emphasis on joy as a way of affirming life then achieves a further climax in line 13 of the next stanza, for in that final line the climactic act of integration, the relationship with the woman, is expressed by the same verb *liḫtaddâm*.

2. Funeral and Festival

Emphasis on joy does more than just affirm the goodness or pleasure of life. Here we may remember that the parallel of the second stanza of Siduri's speech in the Egyptian materials is part of a song that gives concrete expression to the banquet of the festive day.[16] Examples of Harpers' Songs and related orchestra songs have been collected and interpreted by M. Lichtheim and others. A short example from the tomb of Haremhab at Thebes reads:

> For thy *ka*! Make holiday in thy beautiful house of eternity, thy dwelling of everlastingness. . . . Receive garlands, anoint thyself with fine oil. Take part in a holiday in the favor of that good god of the west of Thebes.[17]

Egyptologists have tried to determine whether the banquet and the accompanying Harpers' Songs are primarily of a mundane or of a mortuary character.[18] Without entering into that debate, it is worth noting that the Egyptian materials are usually attested in mortuary contexts and are associated with the dead.[19] In view of this association, it is tempting to wonder whether the banquet song here in Gilgamesh might not also have had primary or secondary associations with rituals for the dead. It

16. Although iii 10–11, the first two lines of Siduri's third stanza, are not treated here in my analysis, these lines parallel elements in the Harpers' Songs and may originally also have been part of the "mortuary/festive banquet" background of our passage. I have not included them here because I have focused my analysis on the formally defined central stanzas. For a study of these two lines, see Abusch, "Gilgamesh's Request, Part I" [here, pp. 58–88].

17. Lichtheim, "Songs of the Harpers," 183.

18. Contrast, e.g., ibid., 178–212, with Wente, "Egyptian 'Make Merry' Songs," 118–28, and cf. Fox, "Entertainment Song Genre," 268–316.

19. Cf., e.g., Lichtheim, "Songs of the Harpers," esp. pp. 182–83 and 208–9; Fox, "Entertainment Song Genre," esp. pp. 270–71 and 275–78; idem, "Study of Antef," 396–97.

is not unusual to find festive activity associated with funerals in the Near East (cf., e.g., the *bêt marzēaḥ*).[20] And funerals in Mesopotamia include feasts; sometimes dying people seem to have been called to the banquet of the gods at their death.[21] These scenes also recall traditions of dead or translated heroes feasting continuously in Elysium,[22] traditions which in turn recall Gilgamesh's original hope to live forever with Siduri (// Calypso/Circe).[23]

The banquet Siduri urges on Gilgamesh surely takes place in this world. But, here, in the context of a response to Gilgamesh's uncontrolled grief and futile desire to remain with the dead and live forever with Enkidu, the evocation of a banquet scene might well even be an ironic reuse of a scene resonant with netherworld associations. Siduri, too, perhaps mimics and distorts the rites for the dead. The irony turns on her suggestion that instead of performing the act of feasting as part of a mortuary ritual or in the netherworld itself, he ought to do it in this life; instead of taking destructive pleasure in netherworld celebrations he ought to feast in this world. But it remains ambiguous/unclear to the

20. Cf., e.g., Jer 16:5–9 and see M. H. Pope, "The Cult of the Dead at Ugarit," in *Ugarit in Retrospect: Fifty Years of Ugarit and Ugaritic* (ed. G. D. Young; Winona Lake, IN: Eisenbrauns, 1981) 174–79; K. Spronk, *Beatific Afterlife in Ancient Israel and in the Ancient Near East* (AOAT 219; Kevelaer: Butzon & Bercker; Neukirchen-Vluyn: Neukirchener Verlag, 1986) 196–202 and 248; T. J. Lewis, *Cults of the Dead in Ancient Israel and Ugarit* (HSM 39; Atlanta: Scholars Press, 1989) 80–94.

21. See R. Harris, "The *Naditu* Woman," in *Studies Presented to A. Leo Oppenheim* (ed. R. D. Biggs and J. A. Brinkman; Chicago: Oriental Institute of the University of Chicago, 1964) 120, and cf. eadem, "Independent Women in Ancient Mesopotamia?," in *Women's Earliest Records: From Ancient Egypt and Western Asia* (ed. B. S. Lesko; BJS 166; Atlanta: Scholars Press, 1989) 154.

22. See, e.g., Homer, *Odyssey* 4.561–70, trans. R. Lattimore (New York, Harper & Row, 1965) 79–80; and Hesiod, *The Works and Days*, lines 167–75, in *Hesiod: The Works and Days, Theogony, The Shield of Herakles* (trans. R. Lattimore; Ann Arbor: University of Michigan Press, 1959) 37–39. Cf. W. Burkert, *Greek Religion* (Cambridge, MA: Harvard University Press, 1985) 198; G. Crane, *Calypso: Backgrounds and Conventions of the Odyssey* (BKP 191; Frankfurt am Main: Athenäum, 1988) 15 with pp. 22–23 nn. 1–6, and pp. 40–41 (the reference there to *Theogony* should be changed to *Works and Days*); and especially E. Rohde, *Psyche: The Cult of Souls and Belief in Immortality among the Greeks* (trans. W. B. Hillis; London: K. Paul, Trench, Trubner; New York: Harcourt, Brace, 1925) 55–87 for the translation of heroes to the Elysian plain or the islands of the blessed, especially in Homer and Hesiod, and chap. 14, part 2, esp. pp. 535–39 and 564–65 n. 99, for the later periods.

23. For this interpretation, see my "Gilgamesh's Request, Part I" [here, pp. 58–88] where I suggest that Gilgamesh hoped that the goddess Siduri would allow him to live with her in her realm, thus attaining the boon of eternal life. I also note there that Siduri was viewed as a Calypso-like character and would therefore have had netherworld associations.

hearer whether it is Siduri or Gilgamesh who is distorting the convention, for the possibility of a double meaning inherent in the use of the banquet scene remains present, and it can be construed or misconstrued as a meal for the living or for the dead.

Especially if this portion of the text originally had a mortuary context, here the author's use of the topos allows Siduri to acknowledge Gilgamesh's struggle—his clinging to death and mortuary rites, his confused identification of death and life—and to help him disentangle life from death. Thus her advice to enjoy life now effectively serves to redirect his energies away from the dead and back to this world. At the very least, her advice means that Gilgamesh ought to perform the reintegrating funeral meal in a proper and effective way.

Of course, the banquet Siduri urges on Gilgamesh is surely also a worldly one. As well as being a goddess who may originally have had netherworld associations, Siduri, it should be remembered, is the goddess of the tavern. Speeches like that of Siduri are associated with worldly parties and celebrations.[24] Thus, for our purposes, it is unimportant whether the speech is primarily of a mundane or a funerary nature, for it belongs not only to the funereal setting, but also to the tavern, the drinking party, and even the more formal banquet. This mundane association allows and even fosters the re-focusing toward this world of the topos of festivity and thereby the re-direction of Gilgamesh's psychic energy and human attachments. Thus, Siduri is able to impart different resonances of meaning to the topos of the banquet. And now she is able to refocus the scene away from its mortuary dimension and transfer it back to the mundane enjoyment of the pleasures of this world.

Elsewhere, I have argued that iii 12, "Look down at the child who holds your hand," is secondary and was inserted into a tavern song by the epic poet responsible for the Gilgamesh epic. By introducing this new theme of progeny he introduces both mortal and immortal dimensions into the vision of Gilgamesh's future.[25] Here, we would notice that yet another reason for the insertion is the redefinition of the banquet scene. The mention of the child in line 12 of the next stanza would seem to move the banquet scene back into this world in an unambiguous way. Even the enjoyment (*liḫtaddâm*) of the woman (line 13), as the enjoyment of the feast (lines 7–8: *ḫitaddu, ḫidûtam*), may be part of the

24. Cf. Assmann, "Der schöne Tag," 23–25.
25. See Abusch, "Gilgamesh's Request, Part I" [here, pp. 58–88].

eternal banquet of dead or translated heroes, but the mention of the child surely transfers the scene from the world of the dead and defines it as having a mundane setting. Certainly, the evocation of this scene of human celebration in a context in which hope for eternal life is explicitly denied (iii 2–5) serves to emphasize the this-worldly joy of the festivity and thus re-directs Gilgamesh's attention away from his futile quest for immortality and towards the world of the living.

But whatever the case—whether the festivities only reflect a this-worldly celebration or also have funerary associations—the final effect is the same: the use of the banquet scene serves to celebrate the pleasures of life and to reaffirm life itself.

C. Complaint and Response

Thus far, we have explained the elements which occur in Siduri's speech, but we must also explain the repetitive structured quality that characterizes her speech. We do this best in the context of an answer to our original query regarding the significance of the poet's construction of the second stanza of both Gilgamesh's and Siduri's speeches around central elements and the disposition of strange patterns around them. It is surely valid to consider the two stanzas together. For whether the two speeches run parallel to each other and/or are chiastic in relationship, these two stanzas correspond to each other. Moreover, the connection is drawn tighter by the occurrence of similar formulations in each: *urrī u mūšī . . . sebet ūmī u sebe mušiātim* ("day and night . . . seven days and seven nights") in Gilgamesh's second stanza and *urrī u mūšī. . . . ūmišam . . . urrī u mūšī* ("day and night . . . daily . . . day and night") in Siduri's second stanza.

Gilgamesh states that he constantly grieved and daily participated in mourning rituals. Siduri responds that he should not feast only when a beloved dies, that he should not restrict his feasting to mourning rites; rather than consuming his own life over the beloved's death, he should instead lay out a feast every day. The meal she urges here is a daily meal (*urrī u mūšī // ūmišam*)[26] and not a holiday feast or funerary meal. The two stanzas are intended to speak to each other with the cen-

26. Cf. the use of "every day" in the Egyptian entertainment songs associated with the netherworld; see, e.g., Fox, "Entertainment Song Genre," 278: "The majority of entertainment scenes have no special ties to a particular occasion, funerary or festival. One help in identifying representations of the daily mortuary meal is the use of a phrase signifying daily recurrence of the entertainment, as, for example, when Djeserkerasonb (TT 38) is advised to 'do it (sc. make merry) every day.'"

tral thought of Siduri responding to the central thought of Gilgamesh. The second stanza of Gilgamesh's speech represents a description of the failure of mortuary rites; the responding second stanza in Siduri's speech represents an attempt to free a human being from overly strong identification with the dead and to redirect him to enjoyment with the living. It is this shared enterprise that explains the use of similar literary structures.

Siduri's stanza conveys a new center and a new orderliness to existence by means of content and form. Here we would recall the crucial contrast between the two stanzas: chaos and order. Gilgamesh's speech is chaotic; one word tumbles out before the preceding one is finished; it is a flood of words and emotions. Siduri's stanza, on the other hand, introduces calm by means of a repetitive, almost unchanging structure of discourse—a calm Gilgamesh himself started to introduce in ii 12′–13′ when he spoke of seeing Siduri's face. Whereas Gilgamesh's second stanza centers on a delusional thought around which is set a range of chaotic actions, Siduri's speech places at its center a realistic thought and surrounds it with ordered statements. Counseling a new way of thinking, it conveys the notion that we can impose joy on existence by means of orderly disposition and behavior.

Siduri's advice here in the epic is more than just a trite Mesopotamian version of *carpe diem*. The composer's purpose in formulating and structuring these stanzas as he did was to suggest that there are occasions when grief is so very great that the standard rites of mourning do not suffice to allow the bereaved to separate from the dead and to resume a normal life. Having once recognized the potential for failure of standard forms of separation, he emphasizes, perhaps in an exaggerated way, the wisdom of celebration as a way of vigorously reaffirming life.[27]

27. G. A. Anderson studies some of the same issues treated in the present essay and its companion pieces in *A Time to Mourn, A Time to Dance: The Expression of Grief and Joy in Israelite Religion* (University Park: Pennsylvania State University Press, 1991), especially pp. 74–82. This work is an interesting and useful treatment. Unfortunately, it appeared after my studies of the Gilgamesh-Siduri dialogue had been completed and could no longer be incorporated into the essays.

Mourning the Death of a Friend: Some Assyriological Notes

My friend, whom I love dearly,
Who with me underwent all hardships,
Enkidu, whom I love dearly,
Who with me underwent all hardships,
Has gone to the fate of mankind.

With these words Gilgamesh began his lament over the death of his friend Enkidu. In a volume dedicated to the memory of Professor Frank Ephraim Talmage, I might similarly express the love and loss that I feel when I recall the many years and the many joys and sorrows that Frank and I shared, experiences shared also by my wife and sons. We all mourned for him. On the Yom Kippur following Frank's death, I delivered a talk, in his memory, on the rituals of the Day of Atonement and their similarities to rites of mourning. Here, in this memorial volume, I would offer a brief essay on the Akkadian text from which the lament cited above derives, a text that deals with grief and mourning.

This text is the justly famous encounter between Gilgamesh and the divine tavernkeeper Siduri found in an Old Babylonian version of the *Epic of Gilgamesh* and preserved on the Meissner Fragment.[1] Column ii of this Old Babylonian fragment begins with Gilgamesh's address to Siduri

---

My work on this Gilgamesh text has benefited greatly from discussions with several friends. I am particularly grateful to Stephen A. Geller and Kathryn Kravitz, as well as Mordechai Cogan and William L. Moran, for their valuable suggestions.

1. The Meissner fragment was published by Bruno Meissner, *Ein altbabylonisches Fragment des Gilgamosepos* (MVAG 7.1; Berlin: Peiser, 1902). More recently, it has been joined to a fragment in the British Museum; see A. R. Millard, "Gilgamesh X: A New Fragment," *Iraq* 26 (1964) 99–105. For translations of both the Old Babylonian text and the later Standard Babylonian version of the epic, see, e.g., E. A. Speiser and A. K. Grayson in *ANET*, 72–99, 503–7; and S. Dalley, *Myths from Mesopotamia: Creation, The Flood, Gilgamesh, and Others* (Oxford: Oxford University Press, 1989) 39–153. For studies of the epic, cf., e.g., T. Jacobsen, *Treasures of Darkness: A History of Mesopotamian Religion* (New Haven, CT: Yale University Press, 1976) 195–219; J. H. Tigay, *The Evolution of the Gilgamesh Epic* (Philadelphia: University of Pennsylvania Press, 1982); T. Abusch, "Ishtar's Proposal and Gilgamesh's Refusal: An Interpretation of *The Gilgamesh Epic*, Tablet 6, Lines 1–79," *History of Religions* 26 (1986) 143–87 [here, pp. 11–57].

and continues with her response (= OB Gilg., Meissner, cols. ii–iii). It is to this opening exchange that I shall direct my remarks. The text has interested me for some time, and I have prepared for publication two detailed, technical studies of this text and of some of the issues that it raises. Here, I want to present in general terms some of my conclusions about the meaning of the text. The detailed argumentation in support of my interpretations and conclusions is presented in the aforementioned studies.[2] Frank saw the need to write about his field in general humanistic terms, and I hope that he would have appreciated this attempt.

Turning to the text, we may begin by characterizing the opening exchange. Gilgamesh's speech encapsulates his emotional state: past, present, and future. Beginning with a description of the death of his friend, it moves on to an expression of his present anguish, and finally to his proposal for a solution. Siduri's speech provides her response and her advice. Each speech contains three stanzas. In translation, these two speeches read:

col. ii * My friend, whom I love dearly,
1′ Who with me underwent all hardships,
2′ Enkidu, whom I love dearly,
3′ Who with me underwent all hardships,
4′ Has gone to the fate of mankind.

5′ Day and night I wept over him,
6′ I would not give him up for burial—
7′ (saying) "My friend perhaps will rise up to me at my cry"—
8′ Seven days and seven nights
9′ Until a worm dropped out at me from his nose.

10′ Since his death, I have not found life.
11′ I keep roaming like a hunter in the open country.
12′ Now, alewife, that I have seen your face,
13′ The death that I constantly fear may I not see.

14′ The alewife spoke to him, to Gilgamesh:

2. The two more technical studies are "Gilgamesh's Request and Siduri's Denial, Part I: The Meaning of the Dialogue and Its Implications for the History of the Epic," in *The Tablet and the Scroll: Near Eastern Studies in Honor of William H. Hallo* (ed. M. E. Cohen, D. C. Snell, and D. B. Weisberg; Bethesda, MD: CDL Press, 1993) 1–14 [here, pp. 58–88], and "Part II: An Analysis and Interpretation of an Old Babylonian Fragment about Mourning and Celebration," in *Comparative Studies in Honor of Yohanan Muffs* = *JANESCU* 22 (1993) 3–17 [here, pp. 89–107].

col. iii
Gilgamesh, whither do you rove?
The life that you pursue you shall not find.
When the gods created mankind,
Death they appointed for mankind,
Life in their own hands they held.

You, Gilgamesh, let your stomach be full.
Day and night keep on being festive.
Daily make a festival.
Day and night dance and play.

Let your clothes be clean,
Let your head be washed, in water may you bathe,
Look down at the little one who holds your hand,
Let a wife ever be festive in your lap.[3]

I

In the epic, Enkidu has died; in his grief, Gilgamesh withdraws from his life as king of the city-state Uruk and starts to wander in the wild. In his wanderings, in both the Old Babylonian version and the later Standard Babylonian version of the epic, Gilgamesh encounters Siduri, a divine alewife who dwells near the shores of the faraway ocean. In the Standard Babylonian version, Gilgamesh is seeking Utnapishtim, the Babylonian Noah who survived the Flood and was granted immortality, in order to gain the secret of immortality for himself. The encounter with Siduri is simply a step along the way; she serves as one more person to hear Gilgamesh's tale, bear witness to his state, and direct him to Utnapishtim.

Gilgamesh's first speech in the Old Babylonian text has usually been understood as a description of his plight, an enunciation of his desire to attain immortality, and a request of Siduri that she direct him to Utnapishtim. Siduri's speech has been understood as a rejection of this request. The quest is futile: immortality is reserved for the gods; mankind cannot attain immortality. Hence, enjoy life. Her advice has been treated as a Babylonian *carpe diem* comparable to Ecclesiastes 9:7–9. Thus, the

3. Following the end of the third stanza of Siduri's speech, there are an additional three lines that are largely broken. These lines might be read:

This alone is the conce[rn of man/woman.]
[Gilgamesh, whither do you rove?]
Let him who is aliv[e enjoy life.]

The first of these lines and perhaps the two that follow seem to be a final summation of Siduri's message.

Old Babylonian version of the encounter has been read as if it shared the same literary context as the later Standard Babylonian version. This, in spite of the fact that the contours of the two versions of the epic are quite different, and much of what defines the character of the passage in the Old Babylonian text and renders it justly famous and powerful (e.g., Siduri's specific advice to Gilgamesh) is not present in the later Standard Babylonian version.

In an attempt to explain some discrepancies in the order of statements in the Old Babylonian version of the dialogue between Gilgamesh and Siduri, but especially in Siduri's speech, as well as some oddities of formulation, I have tried to work out the structure of the passage, the force of some of the formulations, and the overall movement and meaning of the dialogue. These studies have led me to the conclusion that the aforementioned understanding of the Old Babylonian dialogue is not wholly correct; they have suggested a different reading of the passage, a reading which I would sketch out here in partial form.

In my estimation, the Old Babylonian version belongs to a literary and cultural context different from that of the Standard Babylonian version, has a different force, and thus requires a different reading. Initially, Gilgamesh was not searching for Utnapishtim. He was wandering aimlessly, seeking but not finding his own lost sense of being alive. Agitated movement was what he needed, though perhaps he held out some hope for a respite or release from his existential/pschological pain. He was directionless until he encountered Siduri. When he meets her, he describes to her the loss of his beloved Enkidu and his inability to give up the dead Enkidu for burial and thus separate from the dead. Seeing her, he becomes aware of his wish to stop roaming and to remain with her, and he states that having seen Siduri's face, he hopes never to see—that is, experience—death.

His unrealistic wish not to experience death does not mean that he believes that in finding Siduri he has found the way to Utnapishtim. Rather, it means that he wants to stay with the goddess and, thereby, attain immortality. He is proposing to the goddess. Meeting Siduri, he recognizes that he now wishes to live with a woman rather than remain in spirit with his dead male friend. But instead of choosing a normal, mortal woman, he has focused on a goddess. He wishes to live with an immortal woman because she is capable of endowing him with eternal life. In Gilgamesh's eyes, at least, Siduri is a Calypso-like character. Her house and her embrace partake of the immortal. To have sexual relations with her and to live with her is to attain the boon of eternal life and to escape death.

But in actuality, Gilgamesh has not yet completely put the dead aside; he remains obsessed with death. His continued grief for the dead is tantamount to a wish to remain with them. And in his mind, living with Siduri allows him to continue to live with the dead, for he thinks that through her he can move away from an overt state of grief without having to surrender his attachment to the dead and to reenter the normal world. Uniting with the goddess is a fantasy that denies death and leaves unresolved the losses of life and one's own mortal destiny, but it is also a death wish. Siduri's is a world in which Gilgamesh can live without living and die without dying. He can thus live life through fantasy and need not let go of the dead.

In his attempt, then, to free himself from the anguish of his grief for his friend Enkidu, Gilgamesh tries to enter into a marriage with the goddess Siduri. But such a marriage cannot be, for ultimately it would bear the consequence that Gilgamesh could never again regain human life.

Not only psychologically, but also ontologically, such a union is untenable for the mortal man Gilgamesh. Siduri is a divinity, and on an ontological level, their union would be a mingling of human and god, life and death. Both death and divinity are alike in their absoluteness and eternity; both exist on a nonhuman—an absolute—plane. To the human being, both the dead and the immortal represent death.

Gilgamesh believes that Siduri might take him in and that he could thereby escape death. But he errs in his belief, and Siduri must disabuse him of it and send him off. Siduri wishes his welfare. The goddess recognizes both the initial impasse and the final sterility and death of the union of human and divine. A similar fate is exemplified in the *Odyssey* by the breakdown of the relationship of Calypso and Odysseus, by Odysseus's inability to live with Calypso and his recognition of the need to leave the goddess and reengage with his wife and family:

> [Calypso speaks]
>
> "So, now, you gods, you resent it in me that I keep beside me
> a man, the one I saved when he clung astride of the keel board all alone.
> . . . .
> and I gave him my love and cherished him, and I had hopes also
> that I could make him immortal and all his days to be endless."
> . . . she, the queenly nymph, when she had been given the message
> from Zeus, set out searching after great-hearted Odysseus,
> and found him sitting on the seashore, and his eyes were never
> wiped dry of tears, and the sweet lifetime was draining out of him,

as he wept for a way home, since the nymph was no longer pleasing
to him. By nights he would lie beside her, of necessity,
in the hollow caverns, against his will, by one who was willing,
but all the days he would sit upon the rocks, at the seaside,
breaking his heart in tears and lamentation and sorrow
as weeping tears he looked out over the barren water.
She, bright among divinities, stood near and spoke to him:
"Poor man, no longer mourn here beside me nor let your lifetime
fade away, since now I will send you on, with a good will."[4]

Recognizing the sterility that threatens a coupling of human and divine, Siduri tries to save Gilgamesh from the destruction to which their union would lead by disengaging him from her and directing him instead to a normal marriage, for only so may he free himself from death and enter into a new stage of life. She tries to disengage Gilgamesh both from death and from fantasy, from his attachment to a dead human male as well as from his hope to be attached to an immortal female.

Siduri tries to redirect Gilgamesh by means of her speech. She responds not only to his cry for Enkidu at the beginning of his speech, but also to his proposal to her at the end of his speech. Especially to disabuse him of the idea that he, a mortal, can enjoy immortality with her, a goddess, does she present her reply as she does: the gods have designated immortality only for themselves (iii 1–5); instead, the mortal Gilgamesh should enjoy festivals to their fullest (iii 6–9) and find fulfillment, finally, with a mortal wife (iii 10–13). He cannot find a life or love that does not include death. She concludes her speech on the theme of a mortal woman not only to encourage Gilgamesh to attach himself to a living female in place of a dead male, but also to let him know that just as he cannot live forever with the dead Enkidu, so, too, he cannot live forever with an immortal female, a goddess, and must rather find fulfillment with a mortal female, a woman.

But her speech is not only an appeal for renewed human pleasure; even more it is a call for the adoption of a normal human life, for normal activities and relationships. To that purpose, she adapts what might once have been a pleasure-song of the tavern and brothel. Now, she not only highlights the woman at the end of her speech, as in the original song, but also introduces the important theme of the child immediately before mentioning the woman. Siduri is now advising sexual pleasures not

4. Homer, *Odyssey* 5.129–131, 136–136, 149–161, trans. R. Lattimore (New York: Harper & Row, 1975) 91–92.

with a casual partner, but rather with a familial partner, so that a child may be born who will normalize life and define its mortal and immortal dimensions. The sexual act is now also a procreative act which brings into being the postery and future signalled by the child. Progeny implies death, and thus the woman and child also suggest mortality and are a most pronounced way for Siduri to impart to Gilgamesh the notion of his mortality and to express the hope that he accept his mortal nature. But a child is also a form of immortality, and in our passage, this is the only kind of immortality that Gilgamesh can hope for.

Our story is one in which Siduri refuses to provide a home for Gilgamesh and advises him instead to return to his own home. But Gilgamesh can neither accept her advice nor think of another realistic solution. Instead, he focuses on the idea of immortality and the thought of Utnapishtim. Thus, instead of heeding her advice, he perceives in Siduri's speech the possibility of attaining immortality, for he has heard of Utnapishtim (or rather Utanaʾishtim as he is called in the Old Babylonian text) and knows that, contrary to Siduri's contention, a human being actually once attained immortality. And the appropriateness of seeking out Utnapishtim in the present context is promoted by the obvious connection and play between *ul ūla balāṭam*, "I did not find life," in ii 10′, and *Ūta-naʾištim*/Utnapishtim.

In its evolution, the epic will eventually take as its focus the journey to Utnapishtim and the quest for immortality, and the Gilgamesh-Siduri encounter will change into a meeting which serves primarily to highlight Gilgamesh's plight and further his progress toward Utnapishtim. These developments have surely taken place in the later Standard Babylonian version. But even our Old Babylonian text represents a stage in the development of the epic. For already in the Old Babylonian recension before us, Utnapishtim seems to have become part of the story. Thus, while our Old Babylonian text still emphasizes the original idea of Gilgamesh as an aimless wanderer, that Old Babylonian piece already represents a step in the transition from the earlier perspective to the later idea that set Utnapishtim as the goal.

The Old Babylonian fragment preserves neither the original nor the latest form of the encounter. A form of the story earlier than that preserved on the Old Babylonian fragment may well have ended with Siduri sending Gilgamesh back to Uruk in the care of a boatman, perhaps Urshanabi, who here serves as a form of Hermes. Thus, this earlier account would have proceeded from the Gilgamesh-Siduri dialogue (and perhaps some version of the encounter with Urshanabi) to SB Tablet XI

253, where originally it would have been Siduri, and not Utnapishtim, who advised the boatman to wash Gilgamesh and return him to Uruk (XI 253–261). Utnapishtim was not originally part of the tale.

Actually, even the form of the story in which Siduri sends Gilgamesh back to Uruk may not have been the earliest form of the episode. Gilgamesh's original mistake regarding what he could expect from Siduri suggests an interesting possibility and allows for some further historical speculation. Surely, Gilgamesh did not construct out of whole cloth the possibility that he might be able to stay with Siduri. Rather, he made this mistake because he saw in her a form of goddess like the later Calypso and Circe. And if Gilgamesh's expectations were not wholly farfetched, and Siduri did, in fact, share at least some of the characteristics of Calypso and Circe and of their stories, then it seems quite possible that in an earlier tradition, Siduri acceded to Gilgamesh's proposal and allowed him to stay with her.

Actually, Calypso and Circe are examples of a goddess who invites the traveling or returning hero to dwell with her. This tradition is known in the ancient Near East and even appears in the Standard Babylonian version of the *Gilgamesh Epic* in the form of Ishtar's proposal to Gilgamesh in SB Tablet VI. And if, as we think, Siduri is indeed like Calypso and Circe, she too may have once proffered an invitation to Gilgamesh. Thus, we may speculate further and suggest that in another—probably earlier—form of the story, Siduri was the initiator and herself proposed that Gilgamesh stay with her. Indeed, we need not rely on Greek or even Canaanite analogues (e.g., *Anat and Aqhat*), for on the Mesopotamian side, Siduri's invitation would have been like Ishtar's proposal to Gilgamesh and Ereshkigal's to Nergal in *Nergal and Ereshkigal.*

In any case, the theme of the wandering hero and the goddess did not originate with Gilgamesh. Presumably, the story and perhaps even its several earliest forms involved a different traveler or wanderer. Only later would the theme be taken over and developed by the Gilgamesh tradition, and Gilgamesh made into the hero of the story.

II

There are several other interesting observations to be made regarding the text. Here, I would address the meaning of the advice contained in Siduri's second stanza.

> You, Gilgamesh, let your stomach be full.
> Day and night keep on being festive.

Daily make a festival.
Day and night dance and play.

Earlier we observed that Siduri's advice to Gilgamesh, "Let a wife ever be festive in your lap," is not simply a call to sensual pleasure, but also a call to family life, responsibility, and progeny, and that the progeny represents the mortality and immortality of the progenitors. Similarly, the second stanza of Siduri's speech is not merely a call to merriment and is thus different in attitude from the forms of *carpe diem* found, for example, in Horace, *Odes* 1.11, Ecclesiastes 9:7–9a, or Isaiah 22:13b, "Let us eat and drink, for tomorrow we die." Her advice is not a simple call for pleasure, but rather a response to Gilgamesh's earlier statement:

Day and night I wept over him,
I would not give him up for burial—
(saying) "My friend perhaps will rise up to me at my cry!"—
Seven days and seven nights
Until a worm dropped out at me from his nose.

Gilgamesh has failed to come to terms with reality and free himself for life. He has been unable to observe correctly the several funeral and mortuary rites of his society. Consequently, he has neither given the dead their due nor separated from his dead friend. Actually, he has distorted the rites, for he is governed by the delusion that his friend might rise up from the bier upon hearing his lament. Thus, he does not bury his friend immediately after death, but holds back his body from burial; he mourns before—rather than after—burial, and continues to mourn indefinitely. The purposes of the mourning rites have not been achieved.

In response, the alewife tries to pry him loose from the burial place and bring him back to everyday life. She advises that he enjoy and celebrate life through the vehicle of the feast (note the centrality of forms from *ḫadû*, 'to rejoice', in the two central lines). The feast represents the affirmation of the goodness or pleasure of life. But it is more. The banquet and this type of advice are often attested in mortuary contexts. Banquets are festive occasions for the living, but they may also be associated with the dead; the eternal daily (and festival) banquet of the dead, a banquet concretized and punctualized in such occasions as the funeral and the periodic offerings in which the living participate. In the context of a response to Gilgamesh's uncontrollable grief and futile desire to live forever with Enkidu and remain with the dead, the evocation of the banquet seems to be also an ironic reuse of a scene resonant with netherworld associations. Siduri recalls—mimics—the rites for the dead. She advises Gilgamesh to utilize a rite which is associated with both death and life—but to use it for life—and thereby to come to terms with death as well as with life. By using a *topos* with both netherworld and mundane associations, Siduri is able to acknowledge Gilgamesh's struggle, his struggle with grief, his clinging to death and mourning, his confused identification of death and life, and to help him disentangle life from death. Thus her advice to enjoy life now effectively serves to redirect his energies away from the dead and back to this world. And the reuse and redirection are made easier by the fact that banquets of the dead and their songs not only sometimes involve the living, but were originally also modeled on banquets of the living. She refocuses the scene away from its mortuary dimensions and transfers it back to the mundane enjoyment of the pleasures of the world.

The second stanza of Gilgamesh's speech represents a description of the failure of mortuary rites. The corresponding second stanza in Siduri's speech represents an attempt to free a human being from attachment, even identification with the dead and to redirect him to enjoyment with the living.

Just as Siduri directed Gilgamesh back to normalcy by transforming a physical, perhaps even a sexual involvement with a dead man or a living goddess into a familial/sexual relationship with a woman, so she changes the banquet of the dead into a feast of this world, a feast in which the living participate and by which they reaffirm their lives. Perhaps she is telling him to have a festive meal every day—not just on the occasion of a death.

Siduri has attempted to transform a grief which had taken the form of clinging to the dead, refusal and paralysis, failure to disengage and attach anew—even an active wish to live with the dead. In its place, Siduri urges Gilgamesh to celebrate life through its everyday, yet joyful activities.

The Gilgamesh who comes to Siduri might originally have seconded David's lament over Jonathan in 2 Samuel 1:25–27:

> How have the mighty fallen
> In the thick of battle—
> Jonathan, slain on your heights!
> I grieve for you,
> My brother Jonathan,
> You were most dear to me,
> Your love was wonderful to me

More than the love of women.
How have the mighty fallen,
the weapons of war perished![5]

Siduri's response is intended to draw the mourner away from the desert of grief back to the city of life. Some of the confusion in interpretation of her advice results from the fact that her words would sound equally natural an age and a world away, where a more hedonistic version of the *carpe diem* theme occurs in the Hebrew poetry of the Spanish Golden Age, a period and tradition that Frank loved:

Immerse your heart in pleasure and in joy,
And by the bank a bottle drink of wine,
Enjoy the swallow's chirp and viol's whine.
Laugh, dance, and stamp your feet upon the floor!
Get drunk, and knock at dawn on some girl's door.

This is the joy of life, so take your due.
You too deserve a portion of the Ram
Of consecration, like your people's chiefs.
To suck the juice of lips do not be shy,
But take what's rightly yours—the breast and thigh![6]

We visited Frank's resting place on Har ha-Menuḥot in the mountains of Judah. We wept over his death and our loss. But the location of his grave compelled us to see more. Around us rose the mountains of Judah and the city of Jerusalem that he treasured. By his grave, we could see and again feel the joys of the life and of the world that Frank so loved. May his memory be a blessing.

5. *Tanakh: A New Translation of the Holy Scriptures according to the Traditional Hebrew Text* (Philadelphia: Jewish Publication Society, 1985) 471.

6. Moses Ibn Ezra. Translation: R. P. Scheindlin, *Wine, Women, and Death: Medieval Hebrew Poems on the Good Life* (Philadelphia: Jewish Publication Society, 1986) 91.

The Epic of Gilgamesh *and the Homeric Epics*

My purpose in this study is to relate a few of the results that I have previously reached regarding the *Epic of Gilgamesh* (GE) to the Homeric corpus. This is not an unreasonable undertaking, for it has been suggested more than once that the *Iliad* and the *Odyssey* were influenced by the *Epic of Gilgamesh*. Parallels and connections between the *Epic of Gilgamesh*, on the one hand, and the *Iliad* and the *Odyssey*, on the other, have been noticed and established by a number of scholars. Limiting myself to classicists, I note particularly the work of Burkert,[1] the recent book by West,[2] and the earlier observations and sustained arguments by others such as Beye,[3] Crane,[4] Gresseth,[5] Page,[6] Webster,[7] and Wilson.[8] Accordingly, in this study, I shall take the connection for granted and try to link together larger developments and structures in the hope of producing a provocative argument rather than definitive results.

I shall carry out the comparison of the Akkadian and Greek materials in two parts. (1) First, I shall look at the Homeric materials to see if these works reflect some of the same issues and stages that I have postulated elsewhere for the *Epic of Gilgamesh* and if they thus provide some support for the ideological constructions that I have posited. (2) Then, I shall suggest that some of the literary developments that I have noted in the *Epic of Gilgamesh* may have been operative also in the construction of the *Odyssey*. Finally, I shall leave the reader with an unresolved

1. See especially W. Burkert, *The Orientalizing Revolution: Near Eastern Influence on Greek Culture in the Early Archaic Age* (Cambridge, MA: Harvard University Press, 1992).

2. M. L. West, *The East Face of Helicon: West Asiatic Elements in Greek Poetry and Myth* (Oxford: Clarendon Press, 1997).

3. C. R. Beye, "The Epic of Gilgamesh, the Bible, and Homer: Some Narrative Parallels," in *Mnemai: Classical Studies in Memory of Karl K. Hulley* (ed. H. D. Evjen; Chico, CA: Scholars Press, 1984) 7–19.

4. G. Crane, *Calypso: Backgrounds and Conventions of the Odyssey* (BKP 191; Frankfurt am Main: Athenäum, 1988).

5. G. K. Gresseth, "The Gilgamesh Epic and Homer," *The Classical Journal* 70, no. 4 (1975) 1–18.

6. D. Page, *Folktales in Homer's Odyssey* (Cambridge, MA: Harvard University Press, 1973) 51–69, esp. pp. 59–60.

7. T. B. L. Webster, *From Mycenae to Homer* (London: Methuen, 1964).

8. J. R. Wilson, "The Gilgamesh Epic and the Iliad," *Echos du Monde Classique/Classical Views* 30, n.s. 5, no. 1 (1986) 25–41.

question, in line with the rabbinic dictum that "You are not obliged to finish the task, but neither are you free to neglect it" (*Pirkei Avot* 2:21).

I

First, then, to the ideological stages.[9] But before examining these, I would be remiss if I did not acknowledge that there are also significant differences in mood and tone between the Akkadian and Greek epics, and these affect the manner in which we experience the different ideological constructions. Thus, Homer is more pessimistic and his heroes do not resolve their conflicts with the decisiveness and finality of Gilgamesh: rather than going home, Achilles dies; Odysseus, for his part, must look forward to further journeys after his homecoming.

As a literary form, the epic draws upon and grows out of songs of lament and songs of praise. But the grand epics like Gilgamesh or the *Iliad*, whether oral or written, introduce a note of tragedy; they view heroism not from the perspective of the battle, as if it were now taking place, but from a time after the war, and they explore the inevitable conflict that the new circumstances call forth. Thus, the epic is often a meditation upon and an exploration of the inevitable conflict between, on the one hand, the forces represented by the absolute commitment by the powerful and heroic male to energy and battle and, on the other, the forces that represent newly emerging social structures and value systems.

Gilgamesh is an epic hero and in his epic we find a constant conflict between the heroic values that the warrior Gilgamesh represented and those other values that define Mesopotamian culture, values that appear in the form of Gilgamesh's various identities. For, in addition to being a hero, Gilgamesh is also a man, a king, and a god, and he must come to terms with these several identities. The basic conflict is that between the extraordinary and the normal. In the Old Babylonian version of the epic, the conflict is that of hero vs. man; in the eleven-tablet version, it is that of hero vs. king; and in the twelve-tablet version, it is that of hero vs. god. In each version, the heroic identity breaks down as an approach to life because of the occurrence of an event, and a new solution must be found in order to resolve the conflict that (re)emerges thereupon. In the Old Babylonian version, Gilgamesh finds a meaningful context

9. I have written about these stages in "The Development and Meaning of the *Epic of Gilgamesh*: An Interpretive Essay," *JAOS* 121 (2001) 614–22 [here, pp. 127–43]; a popular version has appeared as "Gilgamesh: Hero, King, God and Striving Man," *Archaeology Odyssey* 3, no. 4 (July/August 2000) 32–42, 58–59.

within the bosom of the family, begetting children who represent him in the future. In the eleven-tablet version, he becomes a responsible ruler who rules his community with wisdom and creates human cultural achievements that outlast his own reign and are passed down to future generations. In the twelve-tablet version, he readies himself to become a normal god who judges dead human beings for eternity.

The struggles between the desires of the warrior and those of the normal man (Old Babylonian version) seem to find their parallel in the *Iliad*. That work is less about the Trojan War and more about Achilles. Achilles stands apart from his social and literary environment, and the work describes his emotional journey. It is thought that his story forms a discrete and late strand in the evolution of the *Iliad*. It has been noticed that Near Eastern themes and influences are particularly evident in the Achilles story and that a significant number of parallels exist between Achilles and Gilgamesh. Accordingly, it has been suggested that the *Epic of Gilgamesh* had a part in the formation of the Achilles story.

For us, it is significant that Achilles experiences some of the deepest human emotions. In his story, we see a struggle in the person of the hero between his commitment to the absolute values of the hero and the need to compromise; that is, a struggle between the vengeful warrior and the empathic human being. Although Achilles' commitment to absolutes defines the course of public events, his human side—his acceptance of his self as one who experiences normal sympathies—defines the private evolution of his character. He stands apart, but, in the end, his love of Patroclus, his reconcilation with Priam, and his thoughts about his father represent the ascendancy of his human side, of his identification with the human family.

In any case, I would suggest that the first stage of development of the *Epic of Gilgamesh*, that stage which centers upon the conflict between standing apart and being a member of a human family and leading a normal life, parallels the story and journey of Achilles, and thus finds its reflection (and our construction perhaps finds some support) in the *Iliad*.

For the second stage of the development of the *Epic of Gilgamesh*, I suggest that we turn to the story of Odysseus. Again, parallels have been found between the two accounts, and the influence of the *Epic of Gilgamesh* has often been noticed. For our purposes, it is therefore significant that the wanderings of Odysseus tell the story of the warrior-king who after a war wanders for ten years and experiences many adventures prior to returning to a peaceful milieu wherein he resumes the social responsibilities of a king. True, the *Odyssey* seems sometimes to be primarily about Odysseus's homecoming and the resumption of his role as master of his household and husband of his wife. But clearly, the theme of kingship and the regaining of the kingship by Odysseus have been incorporated into this tale. For he is the ideal leader; he must therefore learn self-control and struggle against temptations and his own impulses in order to hold the course and return to his kingdom and kingship. Thus, our second stage of development, the version which focuses upon the struggle between the values of the warrior and those of the king (a version in which also Gilgamesh must learn self-control), finds its parallel in the wanderings of Odysseus.

Thus, the first two stages of development of the *Epic of Gilgamesh* seem to find their parallel (and our construction some support) in the Homeric materials. But when we examine the Homeric materials in light of the third stage of development of the *Epic of Gilgamesh*, we are led to wonder whether in this instance the Greek materials might not reflect a different process of development. In the third stage, Gilgamesh attains immortality by first resisting but then assuming the cultic role as judge of the netherworld by means of Enkidu's descent and ascent in Tablet XII. But whereas in the *Epic of Gilgamesh*, the cultic vision seems to define the third and last stage of development of the epic itself, it has been asserted that the Greek hero attains actual immortality through cult[10] and not through epic. I refer to Nagy's argument that Greek cult and epic treat the hero in two separate ways. The hero is both human and divine. Epic asserts the hero's humanity; through fame and praise, he achieves a human form of immortality. But it is in cult and not in epic that he becomes a divinity and thereby attains actual immortality.[11]

II

Perhaps the Greek materials do not provide a parallel to the cultically oriented third stage that I have posited for the *Epic of Gilgamesh*. But in thinking about the problem and especially about the relationship of GE Tablet XII to the Greek material, I note that Book 11 of the *Odyssey*, Odysseus' visit to the netherworld, appears to parallel Tablet XII of the *Epic of Gilgamesh*, at least on a thematic and structural level. This observation suggests a specific connection between the Akkadian and Greek

10. Needless to say, Gilgamesh attains immortality also through the actual cult.

11. See G. Nagy, *The Best of the Achaeans: Concepts of the Hero in Archaic Greek Poetry* (Baltimore: Johns Hopkins University Press, 1979) x–xi (foreword by J. M. Redfield) and 114–17.

epics and points to the possibility that some literary developments that took place in the *Epic of Gilgamesh* may also have taken place in the *Odyssey*. And at this juncture, it is especially gratifying to observe a concrete literary connection, for however interesting the comparison of ideological stages may be, they sometimes suffer (as here perhaps) from too much abstraction and generalization.

This, then, brings me to my second topic, the suggestion that some literary developments may be common to both the *Epic of Gilgamesh* and the *Odyssey*. For this purpose, I shall make use of some well-known observations made by classicists about the *Odyssey* together with my own conclusions about the history of the *Epic of Gilgamesh*, conclusions originally reached without recourse to the *Odyssey*.

First, the historical conclusions about the *Epic of Gilgamesh*.

1. In the original epic, Gilgamesh's wanderings ended with Siduri. She informed Gilgamesh that he could not attain immortality by remaining with her and advised him to live a human life of celebration and family relationship. She then sent him with the boatman directly back to Uruk. The epic did not originally include a section dealing with Utnapishtim.[12]
2. Subsequently, the Utnapishtim episode was developed in Tablet XI, and Siduri's role was diminished. Her famous speech was suppressed, and she became only one more stop on the way to Utnapishtim.[13]
3. Into this new version, the Ishtar episode of Tablet VI was inserted.[14]
4. Finally, during the last stage of the development of the epic, Tablet XII was added after the visit to Utnapishtim and in response to Tablet VI.[15]

Turning to the *Odyssey*, we may recall the oft-made observations that:

1. The netherworld scene in Book 11 disrupts the Circe episode, causing Odysseus to leave and then to return to Circe.
2. The Circe episode itself is a doublet of sorts to that of Calypso.

---

12. See "Gilgamesh's Request and Siduri's Denial, Part 1: The Meaning of the Dialogue and Its Implications for the History of the Epic," in *The Tablet and the Scroll: Near Eastern Studies in Honor of William W. Hallo* (ed. M. E. Cohen, D. C. Snell, and D. B. Weisberg; Bethesda, MD: CDL Press, 1993) 1–14 [here, pp. 58–88], esp. pp. 9–13 [here, pp. 77–86].

13. Ibid., 12 [here, pp. 82–84].

14. "Ishtar's Proposal and Gilgamesh's Refusal: An Interpretation of *The Gilgamesh Epic*, Tablet 6, Lines 1–79," *History of Religions* 26 (1986) 143–87 [here, pp. 11–57], esp. pp. 179ff. [here, pp. 48–52].

15. Ibid., 183–87 [here, pp. 52–56].

It has been argued repeatedly that Book 11 of the *Odyssey* is an insertion into the text. Note, for example, the elegant argument offered by Page.[16] This conclusion seems reasonable; moreover, it parallels and finds support in the generally accepted opinion that also Tablet XII, which centers on a visit to and report about the netherworld, constitutes a late addition to the *Epic of Gilgamesh.* On a structural level, therefore, we should compare Book 11 and Tiresias to GE Tablet XII and Enkidu, rather than to (or in addition to) GE Tablet XI and Utnapishtim. Accordingly, there can be little doubt that Odysseus's encounter with Circe and his trip to the netherworld in Book 11 parallel Tablets VI and XII of the *Epic of Gilgamesh.* And should further support be necessary for the link that I posit between Tablets VI and XII, then the juxtaposition of the Circe episode and Book 11 provides it. In any case, if my relative chronology regarding Tablets VI and XII is correct, we may suggest that an analogous development took place in the *Odyssey*, namely, the late addition of the Circe scene to Odysseus' narration and the subsequent insertion of Book 11 into that scene. This is supported by the fact that while Circe has been compared to Siduri, she has also been compared to and seems actually to be more like Ishtar. Hence, the functional parallel Calypso//Siduri belongs to an earlier version and is supplemented by a later Circe//Ishtar parallelism.[17]

More generally, we may ask our classicists to test the *Odyssey* in light of the following historical scheme suggested by the *Epic of Gilgamesh.*

1. Originally, the early version of the *Epic of Gilgamesh* reaches its climax in Gilgamesh's visit to Siduri, followed immediately by his journey home. Parallel to this stage, an early version of the *Odyssey* presented the wanderings of Odysseus as having ended with his visit to Calypso, followed by his journey home to Ithaca.
2. Subsequently, the Utnapishtim episode is added in the *Epic of Gilgamesh* between Gilgamesh's departure from Siduri and his arrival in Uruk; following this, the actual retelling of the Flood story is inserted

16. D. Page, *The Homeric Odyssey* (Oxford: Clarendon Press, 1955) 21–51. For a unitarian position, see A. Heubeck and A. Hoekstra, *A Commentary on Homer's Odyssey* (3 vols.; Oxford: Clarendon Press, 1988–92) 2:75–77; cf., e.g., C. Sourvinou-Inwood, *"Reading" Greek Death: To the End of the Classical Period* (Oxford: Clarendon Press, 1995) 70–76, for a recent discussion which takes a middle position.

17. Note that the role of Siduri is downplayed in later Akkadian versions and therefore her impact on an early stage of development of the Greek tradition is more plausible than her impact on later materials. Moreover, the later Circe would more likely have been modeled on Ishtar, who similarly became important only at a later stage of the development of the *Epic of Gilgamesh.* This supports the argument that Calypso belongs to an earlier layer of the *Odyssey* than does Circe.

into that episode. Parallel to this, the Phaeacian episode is added between Odysseus's departure from Calypso and his arrival in Ithaca, and an account of some of the earlier wanderings is subsequently inserted.[18]

3. Finally, the encounter with Ishtar is inserted in GE Tablet VI, to which is then added the account of Enkidu's descent to and ascent from the netherworld in GE Tablet XII. Parallel to this, the Circe account is added to the series of tales recited by Odysseus and, subsequently, the descent to the netherworld of Book 11 is inserted into that account.

This historical reconstruction seems to me to be useful in several regards. It may provide an additional set of tools for the analyst of the *Odyssey*. In any case, it should resolve a set of apparent contradictions that I have noticed in the secondary literature regarding the relationship between the *Epic of Gilgamesh* and the *Odyssey*. It is obvious that Ishtar and Siduri have very different natures and functions. All the same, Circe is compared by some to Ishtar, by others to Siduri, and sometimes to both. Utnapishtim and Enkidu and their environs are surely different from each other, as are Alcinous and Tiresias. And yet, Utnapishtim has been compared by some to Alcinous and the Phaeacians and by others to Tiresias and the netherworld setting, as has Enkidu. It may therefore be suggested that the drawing of contradictory parallels between the two works may sometimes be simply a result of the fact that as the *Odyssey* developed, later patterns were imposed on or introduced alongside earlier ones, and new characters took their place alongside older ones. In this sense, also the *Odyssey* is a palimpsest or, rather, a mosaic.

I am not certain whether the developments that seem to be common to both the *Epic of Gilgamesh* and the *Odyssey* reflect actual contact or are in the nature of parallel developments. We may therefore end by asking whether the parallels between the *Epic of Gilgamesh* and (the *Iliad* and) the *Odyssey* are an indication of similar developments, thereby providing material for arguments by analogy, or whether they indicate actual contact and influence of one work on the other. Parallel independent development seems unlikely because the similarities are much too specific, and thus we should probably assume actual contact. If so, then presumably the *Epic of Gilgamesh* influenced the *Odyssey* rather than the reverse. But if that is the case, then we may have to consider the possibility that contact took place at the several stages of literary development that we have suggested.

18. Note the occurrence, in both the Phaeacian and Utnapishtim episodes, of the literary device of retelling past events (Odysseus's earlier wanderings : Flood account).

But multiple contacts seem very unlikely. The difficulty of assuming multiple contacts may not be unrelated to the fact that different levels of the *Epic of Gilgamesh* seem to show up alongside each other in the individual Homeric works. Thus, as noted earlier, the story of Achilles seems to parallel the first stage of development of the *Epic of Gilgamesh*, the conflict between the warrior and the man, and the story of Odysseus seems to parallel the second stage. Yet, the Achilles story is said to contain parallels to the latest version of the epic as well, and the *Odyssey* surely contains parallels to its earliest version. So given that a series of several contacts seems problematic, as does the apparent mixing of early and late in the Greek materials, perhaps the Homeric works and the *Epic of Gilgamesh* initially developed independently, though they may have drawn upon a common narrative tradition. But, at a later stage, the Homeric tradition came into contact with the developed Gilgamesh account, a contact that allowed for the assimilation of the developed pattern or structure of the twelve-tablet version.

I usually hesitate to make suggestions in fields in which I am not a specialist, but comparison often requires just that, and I have welcomed the opportunity to compare Akkadian and Greek materials, both because the comparison of materials from the classical and the Mesopotamian worlds is methodologically valid and because the results of such comparison may be significant for our understanding of the history of Western culture. So I am happy to end by apologizing to my classical colleagues and leaving the resolution of this problem to them.

The Development and Meaning of the Epic of Gilgamesh

An Interpretive Essay

Introduction

The *Epic of Gilgamesh*[1] combines the power and tragedy of the *Iliad* with the wanderings and marvels of the *Odyssey*. It is a work of adventure, but it is no less a meditation on some fundamental issues of human existence. The epic explores many issues; it surely provides a Mesopotamian formulation of human predicaments and options. Most of all, the work grapples with issues of an existential nature. It talks about the powerful human drive to achieve, the value of friendship, the experience of loss, the inevitability of death.

The story draws together the many strands that make up the identity of Gilgamesh: man, hero, king, god. Gilgamesh must learn to live. He must find ways to express his tremendous personal energy but still

---

Versions of this essay were read to the California Museum of Ancient Art, November 1998, and to the annual meeting of the American Oriental Society, March 2000. A popular version has appeared as "Gilgamesh: Hero, King, God and Striving Man," in *Archaeology Odyssey* 3, no. 4 (July/August 2000) 32–42, 58–59. A discussion of the relationship of the Gilgamesh epic and the Homeric epics, especially the *Odyssey*, appears in "The *Epic of Gilgamesh* and the Homeric Epics," in *Mythology and Mythologies: Methodological Approaches to Intercultural Influences* (Melammu Symposia 2; Helsinki: Neo-Assyrian Text Corpus Project, 2001) 1–6 [here, pp. 119–26]. I should like to thank Kathryn Kravitz for reading and commenting on versions of this paper.

1. An excellent and up-to-date translation of the epic in its various Akkadian versions as well as of the Sumerian tales of Gilgamesh is presented by A. R. George, *The Epic of Gilgamesh: A New Translation* (New York: Penguin, 1999). I have drawn all translations from this work. Needless to say, I have learned much from such general studies of the epic as T. Jacobsen, *The Treasures of Darkness* (New Haven, CT: Yale University Press, 1976) 193–219; idem, "The Gilgamesh Epic: Romantic and Tragic Vision," in *Lingering over Words: Studies in Ancient Near Eastern Literature in Honor of William L. Moran* (ed. T. Abusch, J. Huehnergard, and P. Steinkeller; HSS 37; Atlanta: Scholars Press, 1990) 231–49; G. S. Kirk, *Myth: Its Meaning and Functions in Ancient and Other Cultures* (Berkeley: University of California Press, 1973) 132–52; W. L. Moran, "The Gilgamesh Epic: A Masterpiece from Ancient Mesopotamia," in *Civilizations of the Ancient Near East* (ed. J. M. Sasson; 4 vols.; New York: Scribner, 1995) 4: 2327–36; J. H. Tigay, *The Evolution of the Gilgamesh Epic* (Philadelphia: University of Pennsylvania Press, 1982); and George's introductions in the volume of translations cited above.

act in a manner that accords with the limits and responsibilities imposed upon him by his society and universe. But the work emphasizes the theme of death and explores the realization that in spite of even the greatest achievements and powers, a human is nonetheless powerless against death. Thus, in the final analysis, Gilgamesh must also come to terms with his own nature and learn to die, for he is both a man and a god, and as both he will experience loss and will die.

In the present essay, I shall discuss the changing emphases of three major versions of the Akkadian *Epic of Gilgamesh.* About 1700 B.C.E., a Babylonian author created a unified epic about the hero Gilgamesh. The new epic "bear[s] witness to a wholesale revision of Gilgamesh material to form a connected story composed around the principal themes of kingship, fame, and the fear of death."[2] This Old Babylonian (OB) account of Gilgamesh is the earliest, perhaps also the most immediately felt and compelling, version of the Akkadian epic. Subsequent to the Old Babylonian period, the epic circulated throughout the ancient Near East. Not surprisingly, the work underwent many changes and developments, and a number of new versions took form in Akkadian as well as in other languages. The Babylonian version(s) changed and developed during the course of the second and early first millennium. While a number of new recensions and versions took form, the Standard Babylonian (SB) eleven- and twelve-tablet versions represent without doubt the two most important post–Old Babylonian Akkadian versions that we possess. Accordingly, in this essay we will examine the Old Babylonian, the eleven-tablet, and the twelve-tablet versions.[3]

2. George, *Epic of Gilgamesh,* xxi.

3. My understanding of the development of the epic and, especially, the interpretation of the epic in terms of its underlying conflicts are basically my own. In the course of this essay, I have worked from the following assumptions: (1) The earliest form of the epic did not contain the Utnapishtim episode, but the meeting with Siduri was the climax of Gilgamesh's wanderings. (2) The encounter with Ishtar in Tablet VI was a post–Old Babylonian insertion. (3) The addition of Tablet XII was meaningful. These conclusions derive from study of the dialogues between Gilgamesh and Ishtar, and Gilgamesh and Siduri. For conclusion one, see my "Gilgamesh's Request and Siduri's Denial, Part 1: The Meaning of the Dialogue and Its Implications for the History of the Epic," in *The Tablet and the Scroll: Near Eastern Studies in Honor of William W. Hallo* (ed. M. E. Cohen, D. C. Snell, and D. B. Weisberg; Bethesda, MD; CDL Press, 1993) 1–14 [here, pp. 58–88]; and "Mourning the Death of a Friend: Some Assyriological Notes," in *The Frank Talmage Memorial Volume, Part I* (ed. B. Walfish; Haifa: University of Haifa Press, 1993) 53–62 [here, pp. 108–18] (repr. in *Gilgamesh: A Reader,* ed. J. Maier [Wauconda, IL: Bolchazy-Carducci, 1997] 109–21). For conclusions two and three, see my "Ishtar's Proposal and Gilgamesh's

The Epic: Development and Meaning

To understand the epic, we should now turn to its inner development and meaning. But first we must say a few words about the nature of epic itself, and then we shall assess the evolving meaning of the work by identifying and explicating the particular conflict that is central to it at each major stage of its development.

Epic. Epic deals with a hero,[4] that is, a powerful warrior who shows his mettle in battle. He is aggressive and courageous, even impetuous, and battles strong enemies. He shows little concern for his own safety and focuses all of his energy upon battle, obligation, honor, and victory. As a literary form, the epic draws upon and grows out of songs of lament and songs of praise.[5] In the Sumerian tales of Gilgamesh, we encounter such praises of the warrior as the following passage from *Gilgamesh and the Bull of Heaven*:

> Hero in battle, hero in battle, let me sing his song!
> Lord Bilgames, hero in battle, let me sing his song!
> Lord with beard of black, hero in battle, let me sing his song!
> Fair of limb, hero in battle, let me sing his song![6]
> Merry one, hero in battle, let me sing his song!
> Rampaging against wrongdoers, hero in battle, let me sing his
>   song! (1–8)

The glorious warrior exists at a time before the emergence of the developed state and of civilization. He usually represents the force needed to fight the enemy prior to the institutionalization of power in the form of the state. But the grand epics like *Gilgamesh* or the

---

Refusal: An Interpretation of *The Gilgamesh Epic*, Tablet 6, Lines 1–79," *History of Religions* 26 (1986) 143–87 [here, pp. 11–57].

4. While there may be some objections to the use of the term "hero" for Gilgamesh, I must use it all the same because I know no better term for what I want to express.

5. It grows out of the earlier praise of the living hero, praises that were recited in his presence and were meant to glorify him and to enhance his power, as well as out of laments for heroes who died in battle. See C. M. Bowra, *Heroic Poetry* (London: Macmillan, 1952; repr., London: Macmillan, 1964) 8–10. My understanding of "epic" draws from and builds upon some ideas set out by Bowra, chapter 1 ("The Heroic Poem") and chapter 3 ("The Hero").

6. A longer version here adds:

> Young lord, mightiest of the mighty, hero in battle, let me sing his song!
> [Expert] in wrestling and trials of strength, [hero in battle, let me sing his
>   song!]

Iliad, whether oral or written, introduce a note of tragedy; they view heroism not from the perspective of the battle itself, as if the battle were now taking place, but from outside or after the battle, from a time after the war. For not only do they recall the inevitable death in battle of the courageous warrior but, even more, they reflect upon the poor fit between the values of power and war and those of the present moment, and they explore the inevitable conflict that the new circumstances call forth. These circumstances may be the requirement that one return to a peaceful occupation and pursue a normal life or that one submit to the discipline of the state and become a warrior or king and leader in its service. Thus, for the individual who chooses to remain a traditional hero, the epic is often a meditation upon and an exploration of the inevitable conflict between, on the one hand, the forces represented by the absolute commitment of the powerful and heroic male to energy and battle and, on the other, the forces that represent some newly emerging situations and value systems.

Growing out of traditions of praise for the heroic warrior, the Akkadian *Epic of Gilgamesh* tells of courageous deeds, but it does this only to highlight the pain caused by these deeds and the new problems that must be faced. Gilgamesh, as we shall see, struggles against the world and is as deeply committed to his own personal absolutes as is Achilles, but there is moral growth: he learns, he changes. As with Odysseus, the growth is symbolized by wanderings, wanderings which both reflect and elicit changes in the hero. His wanderings are the mechanism and backdrop for change, but the death of Enkidu is the catalyst for change. By making Enkidu Gilgamesh's friend, the composer has turned the epic into a tale of growth—of discovery of human suffering, limitation, death, and, finally, human meaning. Without Enkidu's death, there is no development. But without the wandering, there would be no possibility for development, and Enkidu's death would have left Gilgamesh, literally, at a dead end.

In our epic, then, there is moral growth, and Gilgamesh is able to resolve the conflict, even if this is accomplished in pain, and find a life that does not depend solely on violence, impulsiveness, and battle. Conflicts and their resolutions turn the work into an epic about growth.

Conflict. Basic to the *Gilgamesh Epic* is the issue of death. In the course of the epic, we witness the transformation of Gilgamesh's heroic indifference to death into an all-consuming knowledge of his mortality and dread of death. But death is not treated in a vacuum, for there are several layers of meaning and stages of development in the work; each resolves the problem of death in its own terms. To understand these levels of meaning and stages of development, we must try to understand the nature of the underlying conflict or conflicts that define and impart power to the work. Gilgamesh is an epic hero, and in his epic we find a constant conflict between the heroic values that the hero Gilgamesh represented and those other existential values that define Mesopotamian culture. These values are of a social, political, and religious nature and appear in the epic in the form of Gilgamesh's various identities. For in addition to being a hero, Gilgamesh is also a man, a king, and a god, and he must come to terms with these several identities.

The basic conflict is that between the extraordinary and the normal. In the Old Babylonian version, the conflict is that of hero versus man; in the eleven-tablet version, it is that of hero versus king; and in the twelve-tablet version, it is that of hero versus god. If I am not mistaken, each version is organized around and presents in sequence its view of (a) the original situation of Gilgamesh, that is, the status quo of that version, (b) an event or experience that causes the original status to break down or to fail as a basic identity or approach to life, and (c) the new solution or resolution. In this way, each version resolves a form of the basic conflict. And it is the various conflicts themselves and their resolutions that turn the work into an epic about growth.

There is, to be sure, a core of common narrative elements shared by all the versions: Gilgamesh, the warrior-king of Uruk, his friendship with Enkidu and their adventure in search of fame, the death of Enkidu, Gilgamesh's flight and encounters, his eventual return to Uruk. From version to version, the core story is modified in various ways, but mainly through major additions at the beginning (Tablet I, 1–28), middle (Tablet VI), and end (the development of the Flood account and the addition of Tablet XII). Narrative logic is present in each version, but the emphasis in each is on a different thematic strand. This is especially true of the twelve-tablet version, which follows a logic of theme more than of linear plot. I should also emphasize that from version to version earlier elements are often retained and given a new meaning as part of a new structure. Although Gilgamesh's form of heroism is that of a warrior-king throughout, the understanding of kingship seems to change—king as warrior, king as builder, king as ruler who deposits inscriptions telling of his experiences and achievements, king as god—along with the development of Gilgamesh's character from one version to another, for the work explores the different aspects of his identity in the different versions.

We turn now to the interpretations of each of the three versions.

The Old Babylonian Version: Man

In the Old Babylonian version, the following tale is told: Gilgamesh is the warrior-king of Uruk whose extraordinary energy oppresses his people. Enkidu is created by the gods so that Gilgamesh may have a companion who is his equal and can channel his energy. Enkidu is seduced and humanized by a prostitute who then leads him to Uruk where he encounters Gilgamesh. They forge a deep friendship. In search of fame, they undertake an expedition to the Cedar Forest where they defeat and kill Huwawa. Enkidu is sentenced to death by the gods as a punishment for that killing. Gilgamesh is devastated by his loss and flees the city for the wild. In the course of his wanderings, he finally encounters Siduri, a divine tavernkeeper at the edge of the world. She tells him that he cannot attain immortality and advises him to resume normal life. In an early form, this Gilgamesh tale did not include the Utnapishtim episode. Rather, Siduri was his final stop prior to returning to Uruk. But already, the Old Babylonian tale hints at the presence of an embryonic form of the Utnapishtim episode.

Interpretation. In the Old Babylonian version, the original situation is that of heroic battle and the search for fame. This comes to expression first in the original introduction to the work (now preserved in SB I, 29ff.):

> Surpassing all other kings, heroic in nature,
> brave scion of Uruk, wild bull on the rampage!
> Going at the fore he was the vanguard,
> going at the rear, the trust of his brothers!
>
> A mighty bank, protecting his warriors,
> a violent flood-wave, smashing a stone wall!
> Wild bull of Lugalbanda, Gilgamesh, the perfect in strength,
> suckling of the august Wild-Cow, the goddess Ninsun!

In this version, Gilgamesh and Enkidu mount an armed expedition against the monster Huwawa because of Gilgamesh's belief that he would thereby maintain his role as a warrior, experience the excitement of adventure, and win fame. For it is the accomplishment of great acts of valor that is the highest achievement of life and one that serves as the basis of lasting fame, fame in the form of stories of one's great deeds that are told and retold by future generations:

> Gilgamesh opened his mouth,
> saying to Enkidu:
>
> "Who is there, my friend, can climb to the sky?
> Only the gods [dwell] forever in sunlight.
> As for man, his days are numbered,
> whatever he may do, it is but wind.
>
> "Here are you, afraid of death!
> What has become of your mighty valour?
> Let me walk in front of you,
> and you can call to me, 'Go on without fear!'
>
> "If I should fall, let me make my name:
> 'Gilgamesh joined battle with ferocious Huwawa!'"
> (OB Yale Tablet, 138–150)

But this situation—the quest for adventure and fame—proves untenable; it breaks down when Enkidu is struck down by the gods because of the hubris, the arrogance, of the two friends. With this, Gilgamesh is thrown into despair, for he has lost his dearest companion and experiences a real fear of death for the first time. After failing to bring his friend back to life, he rejects all human identities and obligations, flees to the wild, where he assumes the identity of his dead friend, and finally goes in search of actual, physical immortality. Here, the barmaid Siduri tries to teach him that he cannot have immortality, but can only find meaning in normal human activities.

> Said the tavern-keeper to him, to Gilgamesh:
> "O Gilgamesh, where are you wandering?
>
> "The life that you seek you never will find:
> when the gods created mankind,
> death they dispensed to mankind,
> life they kept for themselves.
>
> "But you, Gilgamesh, let your belly be full,
> Enjoy yourself always by day and by night!
> Make merry each day,
> dance and play day and night!

"Let your clothes be clean,
Let your head be washed, may you bathe in water!
Gaze on the child who holds your hand,
Let your wife enjoy your repeated embrace!"
(OB Sippar Tablet, ii 14′–iii 13)

This passage has been virtually eliminated from the later versions, but may represent the very message of our Old Babylonian version. Here, emphasis is placed on normal life as the form of existence that provides meaning. Thus, Gilgamesh the hero must learn to be satisfied with the normal pleasures of everyday human life if he is not to destroy himself. It is significant that just as a prostitute, a woman, humanized and acculturated Enkidu at the beginning of this version, so a tavernkeeper, another woman, humanizes and acculturates Gilgamesh at the end. Women here represent the values of life and its affirmation in the face of the heroic and the absolute, which can only lead to death.

As noted above, in an early form of the Old Babylonian version, Gilgamesh's quest was directed to Siduri and not to Utnapishtim. Thus, subsequent to his meeting with Siduri, Gilgamesh returns to Uruk and there assumes his identity as a man. He concludes the work by directing the attention of the boatman (and therefore ours) to the grandeur and significance of the human city in which he lives and rules and to its walls which he built:[7]

"O Ur-shanabi, climb Uruk's wall and walk back and forth!
Survey its foundations, examine the brickwork!
Were its bricks not fired in an oven?
Did the Seven Sages not lay its foundations?

"A square mile is city, a square mile date-grove, a square mile is clay-pit, half a square mile the temple of Ishtar:
three square miles and a half is Uruk's expanse."
(SB XI, 323–328)

7. The end of Tablet XI (323–328) does not mention that Gilgamesh built the walls; but this act is ascribed to him in the prologue (I, 11; note that line 12 ascribes to him also the building of Eanna). It is often assumed that XI, 323–328 originate at the end of Tablet XI and were only later added to the beginning of the epic where they were then expanded. Thus, it remains possible that XI, 323–328 did not assume or, at least, did not wish to convey the message that Gilgamesh was the builder of the walls. But this seems unlikely, especially since an Old Babylonian royal inscription from Uruk already mentions Gilgamesh as the builder of the walls of Uruk; see D. Frayne, *Old Babylonian Period (2003–1595 BC)* (RIME 4; Toronto: University of Toronto Press, 1990) 474–75, Anam no. 4: 5–8.

He has given up the role of hero and accepted his identity as a normal man of the royal class, who can hope for no more than achievements and descendants.

The Eleven-Tablet Version: King

The eleven-tablet version may be said to have assumed its present form during the latter part of the second millennium. In gross terms, this form of the text is identical with the text of the first eleven tablets of the Standard Babylonian version. This new text is longer than the Old Babylonian epic; it appears to have taken a narrative sequence similar to that of the older version as its basis and to have developed it by means of various modifications, expansions, and inclusions of new sections. We find the developed form of Gilgamesh's encounter with Utnapishtim and the latter's recital of the story of the Flood. (The Flood account was taken over from the Akkadian myth *Atrahasis.*) Moreover, the work is now framed, at the beginning of Tablet I and the end of Tablet XI, by passages describing the walls of Uruk (SB I, 11–23; XI, 323–328). The description originally appeared only once and served as the conclusion of the Old Babylonian version; it highlighted the kind of achievement of which one could be proud and a form of immortality available to a mortal man. In the eleven-tablet version, the description was repeated at the beginning of the work, and thus the theme of the walls of Uruk served as a frame for the whole. In contrast to the Old Babylonian version, which seems to have had the form or at least the self-representation and image of a work of oral literature, this new version sees and represents itself as a work of written literature. For, in the new expanded prologue, it contains two stanzas that direct our attention to a written text that Gilgamesh had written and that then served as the basis of the epic (SB I, 5–10, 24–28).

One other important development is the insertion of the famous Gilgamesh-Ishtar episode in Tablet VI. This episode was not part of the Old Babylonian version. It tells of Ishtar's proposal that Gilgamesh marry her and his rejection of that proposal on the grounds that marriage to Ishtar would result in his death.

Interpretation. Gilgamesh was the king of Uruk and had probably attained that position because of his extraordinary energy, courage, and power. He had been the perfect hero, but the work must now explore the question of whether he is able to be a successful king. The eleven-tablet version explores this question and resolves the issue. Gilgamesh's initial situation is represented by the prologue that originally opened the work and described his strength and heroism as a king who led his troops in battle (see SB I, 29–34, quoted above). When the narrative opens, we find Gilgamesh ruling over his people. Because of his extraordinary energy, his rule is oppressive and he stands in isolation from other human beings. His subjects cry out to the gods for relief from his rule.

> In Uruk-the-Sheepfold he walks [back and forth],
> like a wild bull lording it, head held aloft.
> He has no equal when his weapons are brandished,
> his companions are kept on their feet by his contests.
>
> The young men of Uruk he harries without warrant,
> Gilgamesh lets no son go free to his father.
> By day and by night his tyranny grows harsher,
> Gilgamesh, [the guide of the teeming people]!
>
> It is he who is shepherd of Uruk-the-Sheepfold,
> [but Gilgamesh] lets no [daughter go free to her] mother.
> [The women voiced] their [troubles to the goddesses],
> [they brought their] complaints before [them].
>
> (SB I, 63–74)

The author thereby tells us that Gilgamesh is unable to rule successfully because of the very energy that made him a successful hero. His heroism defined his being and perhaps even allowed him to assume the role of king. But it is this very heroic energy that brings about his failure as a ruler of a normal people in normal times. The qualities that were virtues for a warrior, and even allowed him to become a king, have now become faults. To be a just and effective ruler requires more than just energy and heroism; and Gilgamesh must learn that a just kingship, a caring shepherdship of his people, is a greater good in peacetime than the heroism of the warlord.

The work presents Gilgamesh as an extraordinary being, one greater than his fellows. The narrative opens with a description of Gilgamesh's failure as a king. Gilgamesh withdraws from his people and from his role as ruler and now loses himself again in mock-heroics against monsters and in his new and exclusive friendship with Enkidu. But with Enkidu's death, this form of supranormal existence and human connection also fails. Gilgamesh now goes in search of Utnapishtim, thinking that Utnapishtim is an extraordinary being from whom he can wrest the boon of immortality. The resolution of the conflict between the virtues of individualistic heroism and public responsibility and leadership will come when Gilgamesh recognizes that he must give up the illusion of living on an extraordinary plane, learn to value normality, and assume the role of a normal and, therefore, effective ruler. This is achieved upon Gilgamesh's recognition that Utnapishtim is no more than a normal man, who received immortality not because of his heroic acts, but because he was obedient to the command of his god.

> Said Gilgamesh to him, to Uta-napishti the Distant:
> "I look at you, Uta-napishti:
> your form is no different, you are just like me,
> you are not any different, you are just like me.
>
> "I was fully intent on making you fight,
> but now in your presence my hand is stayed.
> How was it you stood with the gods in assembly?
> How did you find the life eternal?"
>
> (SB XI, 1–7)

Here Gilgamesh rejects fighting and begins to realize that he must learn from one who is not a *qarrādu*, a warrior. Utnapishtim exemplifies normal kingship.[8] But in addition to his example, he imparts wisdom both by reciting his history and the history of the Flood, and by explaining that never again would the gods assemble to grant immortality to a human being. Just as Siduri had told Gilgamesh that when the gods created mankind, they assigned death to humanity and reserved life for themselves, so now Utnapishtim informs Gilgamesh that the gods had granted immortality only once, on that one and never repeatable occasion when they assembled after the Flood. Siduri's message was meant to teach Gilgamesh the man to accept his humanity; Utnapishtim's message was meant to teach Gilgamesh the king that even the unique warrior cannot remain extraordinary and must throw in his lot with the rest of humanity and accept his role. And the story of the Flood sets Gilgamesh's age, and all ages, into the context of universal history and under the rule of divine law.

8. For a recent discussion of the royal status of the Flood hero in Mesopotamian tradition, see J. R. Davila, "The Flood Hero as King and Priest," *JNES* 54 (1995) 199–214. As regards the *Epic of Gilgamesh*, Davila notes that "the Standard Babylonian Gilgamesh epic followed the tradition of the royal Flood hero" (p. 206).

Gilgamesh now returns to Uruk, where he himself emphasizes the greatness of the city and resumes his role as king, brings back the wisdom and the lessons that he learned in the course of his exhausting wanderings, and sets down in writing his tale and his new-found knowledge. All this we are told in the new prologue to the work. We recall that the transformation of the Old Babylonian version into the later eleven-tablet version involved, among other changes, not only the development of the story of the Flood hero Utnapishtim and the recounting of the story of the Flood, but also the addition of a new prologue. This new prologue reads:

He who saw the Deep, the country's foundation.
[who] knew . . . , was wise in all matters!
[Gilgamesh, who] saw the Deep, the country's foundation,
[who] knew . . . , was wise in all matters!

[He] . . . everywhere . . .
and [learnt] of everything the sum of wisdom.
He saw what was secret, discovered what was hidden,
he brought back a tale of before the Deluge.

He came a far road, was weary, found peace,
and set all his labours on a tablet of stone.
He built the rampart of Uruk-the-Sheepfold,
of holy Eanna, the sacred storehouse.

See its wall like a strand of wool,
view its parapet that none could copy!
Take the stairway of a bygone era.
draw near to Eanna, the seat of Ishtar the goddess,
that no later king could ever copy!

Climb Uruk's wall and walk back and forth!
Survey its foundations, examine the brickwork!
Were its bricks not fired in an oven?
Did the Seven Sages not lay its foundations?
[A square mile is] city, [a square mile] date-grove, a square mile is clay-pit, half a square mile the temple of Ishtar:
[three square miles] and a half is Uruk's expanse.

[See] the tablet-box of cedar.
[release] its clasps of bronze!
[Lift] the lid of its secret,
[pick] up the tablet of lapis lazuli and read out
the travails of Gilgamesh, all that he went through.

(SB I, 1–28)

In the eleven-tablet version, there is an emphasis on wisdom, on Gilgamesh's travels, suffering, and toils in search of wisdom, and on his acquisition of this wisdom as a result of his travels and meeting with Utnapishtim. This is the message that he brought back to Uruk and that forms the basis of the text that he wrote and that the epic poet has written for us. Hence, Gilgamesh, the king, now deposits an inscription based on his experience: like a *narû* (a royal inscription intended for the instruction of posterity), this inscription is intended to instruct future generations, generally, and later kings, specifically.

In the new prologue, we learn that the epic has now become a work of written literature, for the author tells us that Gilgamesh's inscriptions serve as the basis for the literary epic (SB I, 24–28). The difference between the Old Babylonian version as an oral tale and the eleven-tablet version as a written work of literature parallels and perhaps gives expression to the difference between the respective lessons of the two versions. Their messages are directed towards—and find fulfillment in—different contexts. The oral epic focuses on family and the present, the written epic on community and the future. The former speaks to one's contemporaries and immediate descendants; the latter to the community in both its present and future existence. The past and future of community are longer and have greater depth than those of family. Its memory and ability to remember the past is proportionally longer, especially when the past is preserved in writing, for writing lasts for many generations, whereas memorialization through one's child(ren) lasts no more than several generations. The eleven-tablet version thus tells the story not only of Gilgamesh but also the story of the distant and constitutive past, the Flood; and as a written work, it can be read in the distant future.

In the eleven-tablet version, there is thus greater emphasis on the community, on universal history, and on continuity than on the individual, his private story, and immediate future. This is to be expected of a recension that focuses on Gilgamesh's acceptance of communal responsibility rather than on his growth as an individual.

The Twelve-Tablet Version: God

Following the development of the eleven-tablet version, a further version was created by the addition of what is now the last, or twelfth, tablet of the work. This last tablet is a translation of the second half of the Sumerian tale *Gilgamesh, Enkidu, and the Netherworld.* It tells how Enkidu descends to the netherworld in search of Gilgamesh's *pukku* and *mekkû* but is seized by the netherworld and loses his life. He then returns to Gilgamesh in the form of a shade and describes the fate of the various classes of inhabitants of the netherworld. It is true that this tablet was added in a mechanical fashion and contradicts earlier parts of the work. This form of redaction, namely simple addition rather than some form of actual revision, is understandable if—and this is a reasonable assumption—at this point in its development, the text of the epic had already assumed a stabilized frozen form.[9] Be that as it may, the addition is meaningful and intentionally changes the nature of the work.

Interpretation. In Gilgamesh, the cultic vision seems to define the third and last stage of development of the epic itself.

Gilgamesh is part god and part man.

> Who is there can rival his kingly standing,
> and say like Gilgamesh, "It is I am the king"?
> Gilgamesh was his name from the day he was born,
> two-thirds of him god and one-third human.
> It was the Lady of the Gods drew the form of his figure,
> while his build was perfected by divine Nudimmud.
> (SB I, 45–50)

There is a conflict between these two identities. Gilgamesh must choose one or the other, or seek a way out of the dilemma.

As the king of Uruk, he participated in some form of the sacred marriage and had intercourse with the goddess Išḫara in the guise of a human female, whether a priestess or a new bride.

> For the goddess of weddings the bed was laid out,
> Gilgamesh met with the maiden by night.
> (OB Pennsylvania tablet, 196–199)

In this way, the text seeks a way out of the dilemma. But this solution, which represents the original status or customary mode of behavior, is destroyed by Enkidu.

> Forward came (Enkidu), he stood in the street,
> blocking the path of Gilgamesh.
> (OB Pennsylvania tablet, 200–203)

Gilgamesh and Enkidu fight and then become inseparable friends. With this new development, Gilgamesh abandons the practice of intercourse with the goddess and gives up the attempt to bridge his divine and hu-

9. My thanks to Bruce Zuckerman for reminding me to include this point.

man sides. But Gilgamesh must choose one or the other side, and ultimately he must choose his divine side.

In Tablet VI, he is given one more chance. Ishtar invites him to become her husband.

> On the beauty of Gilgamesh Lady Ishtar looked with longing
> "Come, Gilgamesh, be you my bridegroom!
> Grant me your fruits, O grant me!
> Be you my husband and I your wife!"
>
> (SB VI, 6–9)

True, the wedding would take the form of a *hieros gamos*. But Gilgamesh sees through Ishtar's proposition. He recognizes that were he to accept her proposal and marry her, he would not be entering into a normal or even sacred marriage. Rather, he would be accepting an offer to assume the role of a deity in the netherworld. He would be taking on the identity of Ishtar's prototypical consort Tammuz (Dumuzi) (cf. SB VI, 46–47). The offer thus constitutes immortality, but also a loss of actual human life. Gilgamesh is not yet prepared to give up the heroic quest of the live hero, and so he rejects Ishtar's offer.

But with the subsequent death of Enkidu, a life of heroism loses its meaning, and for Gilgamesh now, only immortality as a human seems to remain as an acceptable option; but such is unattainable, for only gods are immortal while humans must die. Gilgamesh must, therefore, become either a normal man or a normal god.

In reality, Gilgamesh must become a god. For, in actual ritual practice, he is a god of the netherworld. To quote an incantation:

> Gilgamesh, supreme king, judge of the Anunnaki,
> Deliberate prince, the . . . of the peoples,
> Who surveys the regions of the world, bailiff of the underworld,
>   lord of the (peoples) beneath,
> You are a judge and have vision like a god,
> You stand in the underworld and give the final verdict,
> Your judgement is not altered, nor is your utterance neglected.
> You question, you inquire, you give judgement, you watch and you
>   put things right.
> Shamash has entrusted to you verdicts and decisions.
> In your presence kings, regents and princes bow down,
> You watch the omens about them and give the decision.[10]

10. Translation: W. G. Lambert, "Gilgamesh in Religious, Historical and Omen Texts and the Historicity of Gilgamesh," in *Gilgameš et sa légende* (ed. Paul Garelli;

Gilgamesh's place in the netherworld in Mesopotamian religion required that he become a divinity. The solution to the dilemma is provided by Tablet XII, and for this reason, Tablet XII was added to the eleven-tablet version.

Gilgamesh turned down the opportunity to assume his role as judge of the netherworld when he rejected Ishtar's offer. But all the same, he must die and be initiated into the role of netherworld judge. The passage into this new state requires that there be a change of being as well as the acquisition of new knowledge. The events precipitated by Enkidu's death and described in Tablets VII–XI result in a change in Gilgamesh's being. And Tablet XII provides the new knowledge necessary.

Tablet XII presents a vision of the netherworld and of the shades of the dead. Instruction is one of its main functions. For the essence of Enkidu's message is not a vision of glory or dread but, rather, a simple description of the norms and procedures that govern life in the netherworld. These are the rules that Gilgamesh will be obliged to administer.

With the addition of Tablet XII, the focus of the epic changed, and the emphasis is now on Gilgamesh's relationship to the netherworld. Tablets VI and XII are now the focus of the work. They deal first with the relationship between the goddess Ishtar and Gilgamesh and then provide a solution to the problem left unresolved by that relationship. The description in Tablet XII serves to teach Gilgamesh how to be a normal god and to induct him into this new identity.[11] He is now ready to assume this final normal identity.

Conclusion

Gilgamesh is presented to us as an individual who lives on a heroic plane and exists in spiritual isolation. But such a life is unbearable. Gilgamesh seeks immortality as a human being, and in all three versions of the text, he learns that this is impossible. In the Old Babylonian version, Gilgamesh finds a meaningful context within the bosom of the family, creating children who will represent him in the future, and accepts the role of builder-king. In the eleven-tablet version, he be-

Paris: C. Klincksieck, 1960) 40. For a reconstruction of this incantation, see Abusch, "Ishtar's Proposal," 150–51 nn. 13–14 [here, pp. 18–19].

11. Even if *Gilgamesh, Enkidu, and the Netherworld* did not originally serve this purpose, the use of this scene in Tablet XII of the epic does.

comes a responsible ruler who rules his community with wisdom and creates human cultural achievements that outlast his own reign and are passed down to future generations. In the twelve-tablet version, he readies himself to become a normal god who judges dead human beings for eternity.

In each version, primary instruction is given by a character who represents a different function or role in human life: in the Old Babylonian version, Siduri, the woman; in the eleven-tablet version, Utnapishtim, the elder; and in the twelve-tablet version, Enkidu, the slave turned peer and friend. Each one conveys to Gilgamesh the understanding that they possess by virtue of their own identity and present situation: the woman who has experience of human pleasures and relationships teaches him to be a man; the king turned survivor teaches him to be a king; the dead friend teaches him about the state of death.[12] When examining the three versions in turn, we are almost reminded of the stages of growth of the individual. In his youth, he is socialized and becomes a functioning member of society; in middle age, he takes on positions of leadership; and finally, in old age, he accepts death.

12. These three instructors are located outside of this world: Siduri at the shore of the cosmic sea, Utnapishtim across the sea on an island, and Enkidu in the netherworld.

The Courtesan, the Wild Man, and the Hunter

Studies in the Literary History of the Epic of Gilgamesh

This study takes up the famous episode in the *Epic of Gilgamesh* that tells first of the confrontation of the wild man Enkidu and the hunter, then of the hunter's fetching of a courtesan to neutralize Enkidu, and finally of the actual encounter and love scene between the courtesan and the wild man.[1] While first noting several general features of the story that strike me as odd and call for explanation, I shall begin the actual analysis by focusing on specific philological/exegetical difficulties at the center of the love scene itself, in the hope of making better sense of the scene. I shall then take up the question of the composition of the episode. Here, I shall work out a series of complementary, sometimes alternative, reconstructions of its development. Finally, I shall suggest a new way of looking at the composition of the epic as a whole.

This essay was composed during my sabbatical leave of 2003–2004 in Princeton and Jerusalem, while I was first a member of the School of Historical Studies of the Institute for Advanced Study, Princeton, and then a Lady Davis Visiting Professor at the Hebrew University, Jerusalem, and an NEH Fellow of the W. F. Albright Institute of Archaeological Research. I am deeply grateful to these institutions for their hospitality and support. I thank as well the École Biblique for welcoming me into its library. I acknowledge with thanks the sabbatical leave granted me by my home institution.

I am grateful to several colleagues with whom I discussed my ideas, most notably, Patricia Crone, Princeton, and Joan Westenholz, Jerusalem. I also wish to thank Robb Young, as well as the students in my seminar at the Hebrew University (Noga Ayali, Roni Goldstein, Baruch Ottervanger, and Sabena Tulbure) for their suggestions.

1. In citing the text, I have been able to make use of A. R. George's edition of the epic that has just appeared: *The Babylonian Gilgamesh Epic: Introduction, Critical Edition, and Cuneiform Texts* (2 vols.; Oxford: Oxford University Press, 2003). George's edition is fundamental and represents a major advance in the reconstruction of the text of the epic, thus enabling its further study and the pursuit of the history and interpretation of the work. George's work is careful and learned and provides much information on the text and its problems. In the main, his interpretation of the text takes the form of textual summary and paraphrase, and his study of the history of the epic is largely a description of the textual situation evident from the extant manuscripts. Unfortunately, George also seems to have an aversion to works like my own that pursue in-depth literary interpretation or literary-historical reconstruction, activities crucial for grasping the meaning and development of the epic. But just as a scholar has the right to choose the approach that suits his disposition and talents, so too must he respect the right of other scholars to strive to obtain that which they believe to be knowable. Elsewhere, I shall register my responses to George's characterizations of some of my studies of the epic.

A study of this sort is anything but definitive. It is my hope that it may solve some problems in the text and suggest possible stages of development of the work. But even if my reasoning is basically sound, both the analysis and the conclusions will surely require some correction and modification of detail. In any case, I trust that, at the very least, this study will have some heuristic value and be of interest to those who love the *Epic of Gilgamesh* as much as I do. I dedicate this study in friendship and esteem to Professor Yaʿakov Klein, a valued friend and colleague of over thirty years. Yaʿakov has devoted himself tirelessly and intelligently to the reconstruction, translation, and understanding of Mesopotamian literature and to its popularization in Israel. I hope that he finds some interest in this study of a text in which he, too, has invested his talents.

The Love Scene: An Analysis

The text is known in both Old Babylonian (OB) and Standard Babylonian (SB) versions. In gross terms, we may sketch the episode as told in the first tablet of the SB version as follows (later we shall consider the OB): In response to the complaint of the people of Uruk against Gilgamesh, the gods create Enkidu, a powerful wild man, to engage Gilgamesh and thereby provide relief to the populace. He roams with the animals and feeds with them. He frustrates a hunter's attempts to catch animals. The hunter sees him and is deeply distressed and agitated. He tells his father what he has witnessed. His father advises him to go to Uruk and to take a courtesan from there to seduce the wild man, thereby causing the animals to reject him. The hunter goes to Uruk, repeats his speech to Gilgamesh, and is given the same advice. He leads the courtesan Shamhat to the wild. Upon the appearance of Enkidu, he tells the courtesan what steps to take in order to seduce Enkidu. She successfully carries out her mission. They have intercourse for a week;[2] afterward Enkidu tries to return to the animals, but they reject him. He returns to the courtesan, who advises him to accompany her to civilization.

Before turning to the core of our analysis, the love scene itself, let us note several features of the episode that seem to require explanation. (These may serve as the framework for our study.) They are:

1. When the hunter sees Enkidu, "[He was] troubled, he grew still, he grew silent, / his mood [*was unhappy*,] his face clouded over, / There [was] sorrow in his heart, / his face was like [one who has

2. Below we shall argue that there was a sexual encounter prior to the week-long one.

travelled] distant [roads]" (SB I 118–121).[3] The hunter's response to Enkidu's appearance seems to be in the nature of an overreaction.
2. The hunter receives instruction both from his father and from Gilgamesh to fetch a courtesan and to have her seduce Enkidu so that the animals will reject him. One or the other of these instructions seems to be redundant (SB I 140–145[4] = 162–166).[5]
3. There are differences between the hunter's father's // Gilgamesh's instructions and the instructions of the hunter to the courtesan. How are we to understand these differences?
4. The love scene comprises the hunter's instructions to Shamhat and the narrator's account of the actual lovemaking. The lovemaking, especially as prescribed by the hunter, presents difficulties. The precise details of the love scene and the order of events are not clear.[6]

---

3. Translation: George, *Gilgamesh Epic*, 545. I follow George's line count throughout.

4. Note that I follow the reconstruction of line 140 found already in P. Jensen, *Assyrisch-babylonische Mythen und Epen* (Keilinschriftliche Bibliothek 6.1; Berlin: Reuther & Reichard, 1900) 122–23, and repeated with a modification by George, *Gilgamesh Epic*, 546–47: [*alik ṣayyādī* (Jensen) / *mārī* (George) *ittika ḫarimtu šamḫat*] *uruma*, ["Go, my hunter (Jensen) / son (George)], take [with you the courtesan Shamhat]." This restoration differs from that assumed by most later translators, who have tried to lessen the redundancy of the father's advice and to smooth out the connection between the father and Gilgamesh. Thus, for example, E. A. Speiser, *ANET*, 74: "[Let him give thee a harlot-lass]. Take (her) [with thee];" or A. Schott, *Das Gilgamesch-Epos* (neu herausgegeben von W. von Soden; Stuttgart: Reclam, 1988) 19: "Eine Dirne *leih' er dir*! Führ sie zur Steppe!" (in Schott's translation, italics are used for "Unsicheres oder Ergänztes"). In this tradition, see also, e.g., M. G. Kovacs, *The Epic of Gilgamesh* (Stanford, CA: Stanford University Press, 1989) 7; J. Bottéro, *L'épopée de Gilgameš* (Paris: Gallimard, 1992) 72; K. Hecker, "Das akkadische Gilgamesch-Epos," in *Mythen und Epen II* (ed. K. Hecker et al.; TUAT 3.4; Gütersloh: G. Mohn, 1994) 676; B. R. Foster in B. R. Foster et al., *The Epic of Gilgamesh* (New York: Norton, 2001) 7. R. C. Thompson's restoration takes a middle course in that he restores *iqabbima* at the beginning of a line that reads the same as Jensen's (*The Epic of Gilgamesh: Text, Transliteration, and Notes* [Oxford: Clarendon Press, 1930] 13:19).

5. After noticing the obvious redundancy, I discovered that M. Jastrow, Jr., and A. T. Clay had, in effect, already observed the same some eighty-five years ago (M. Jastrow, Jr., and A. T. Clay, *An Old Babylonian Version of the Gilgamesh Epic* [YOR 4.3; New Haven, CT: Yale University Press, 1920] 42):

> [T]he father tells his son to go to Gilgamesh to relate to him the strange appearance of the animal-man; but there is clearly no purpose in this, as is shown by the fact that when the hunter does so, Gilgamesh makes *precisely the same speech* as does the father of the hunter. . . .
>
> The artificiality of the process of introducing Gilgamesh into the episode is revealed by this awkward and entirely meaningless repetition.

Such redundancy is only partially explained by the tendency of SB literature to repetition. See below, n. 27.

6. Nor can these lines be understood simply on the basis of parallelism.

This is due in part to uncertainties that surround the translation of such crucial terms as *kuzba leqû* in lines 181–182 // 189–190.

We begin with the love scene itself, but we do so bearing in mind that any attempt at understanding this account should not treat in isolation its several sections, namely, the hunter's father's // Gilgamesh's instructions to the hunter, the hunter's instructions to the courtesan, and the description of the act itself, but analyze them in relationship to each other as well (and thus see what relationship exists between them). The passages that treat lovemaking read as follows:

Father's // Gilgamesh's Instructions

143 // 164 *šī lišḫuṭ lubūšīšama liptâ kuzubša*
144 // 165 *immaršima iṭeḫḫâ ana šâši*
145 // 166 *inakkiršu būlšu ša irbû eli ṣērišu*
....

Hunter's Instructions

180 . . . *rummî kirimmiki*
181 *ūrki pitêma kuzubki lilqe*
182 *ē tašḫutī liqê napīssu*
183 *immarkima iṭeḫḫâ ana kâši*
184 *lubūšīki muṣṣîma eliki liṣlal*
185 *epšīšuma lullâ šipir sinništi*
186 *inakkiršu būlšu ša irbû ina ṣērišu*
187 *dādūšu iḫabbubū eli ṣēriki*

Narrative

188 *urtammi šamḫat dīdāša*
189 *ūrša iptema kuzubša ilqe*
190 *ul išḫut ilteqe napīssu*
191 *lubūšīša umaṣṣima eliša iṣlal*
192 *īpussuma lullâ šipir sinništi*
193 *dādūšu iḫbubū eli ṣērīša*
194 *šeššet urrī u sebe mušâti enkidu tebima šamḫat irḫi*

I would prefer to leave the text untranslated until we have subjected it to an analysis, but a translation is necessary here to enable the reader to follow the discussion. Anticipating my results, I, therefore, provide here a somewhat unpolished translation based on the conclusions arrived at in this section.

143 // 164	Let her strip off her clothing and reveal her sex.
144 // 165	He will see her and have intercourse with her.
145 // 166	His animals that grew up on his steppe will reject him.
	....
180	. . . release your arm (thereby releasing your garment).
181	Open your loins so that he may take your sex.
182	Do not fear, take his panting.
183	(He will see you and have intercourse with you.)
184	Spread out your clothing so that he may lie on you.
185	Treat the savage-man to the skills of a woman.
186	. . . [7]
188	Shamhat released her garment.
189	She opened her loins and he took her sex.
190	She did not fear, she took his panting.
191	She spread out her clothing and he lay on her.
192	She treated the savage-man to the skills of a woman.
193	. . .
194	Six days and seven nights Enkidu was aroused and had intercourse with Shamhat.

Let us focus first on the hunter's speech rather than on the narrative, for, as we shall see, the obstacles to understanding the text derive primarily from difficulties in that passage. Lines 181–182 // 189–190 seem to refer to the sex act itself. *Kuzbu* may refer not only to sexual attractiveness and vigor but also the sexual organs themselves.[8] But in spite of the use of *kuzbu* in line 143 // 164 (*liptâ kuzubša*) as a synonym of *ūru* in line 181 // 189 (*ūrki pitêma // ūrša iptema*), translations tend to render *kuzba leqû* in line 181 // 189, an act that Enkidu performs in relation to the courtesan, as if it referred not to sexual intercourse but rather to

7. I leave line 186 // 193 untranslated because I do not yet understand it sufficiently.

8. For *kuzbu* "referring euphemistically to virility and sexual parts," see *CAD*, vol. K, pp. 614–15, (c). Also, see V. A. Hurowitz, "An Old Babylonian Bawdy Ballad," in *Solving Riddles and Untying Knots: Biblical, Epigraphic, and Semitic Studies in Honor of Jonas C. Greenfield* (ed. Z. Zevit, S. Gitin, and M. Sokoloff; Winona Lake, IN: Eisenbrauns, 1995) 551 n. 17, for a discussion of a concrete usage of *kuzbu* as "(place of) sexuality" in the phrase *kuzba lapātu*. Hurowitz shows convincingly that the phrase refers to fondling the sexual organs and is a designation of foreplay. Cf. George, *Gilgamesh Epic*, 796 on line 181 // 189: "The phrase *ūra petû* is literally 'to open the vulva' and is taken literally by some, but it also means to bare the genital area (cf. *kuzba petû* in l. 164). Similarly *kuzba leqû* may mean to possess a woman sexually but also means to take in her charms, i.e., become physically attracted to her."

being attracted by sexual charms[9]—this, in spite of the fact that Enkidu here is still an animal who is drawn to sex, but hardly to sexuality and charm, and that the text conditions the act on the immediately following statement that when he takes her *kuzbu*, she should not fear, but rather for her part accept his panting (*napīšu*).[10]

What is there about this text that causes translators to understand *kuzba leqû* as denoting Enkidu's attraction to Shamhat's charms rather than his possessing her sexually? The cause is, I suspect, the fact that line 181 is followed in 183 by a line that is understood by many as indicating that only later will Enkidu approach Shamhat, and then in 184 by a line that states that she will then spread her garment so that he may lie on her (184 //191). Hence, these translators probably surmise that *kuzba leqû* cannot refer to the act of intercourse if Enkidu only subsequently approached and lay upon Shamhat.[11] But actually, even before line 184, already line 183 states explicitly that Enkidu will have intercourse with Shamhat. For, in spite of the possible literal rendering of this line ("he will see you and approach you"), it should be translated "he will see you and have intercourse with you." *Ṭeḫû* here must refer to intercourse, as it often does, since this line also occurs in 144 // 165, where its position immediately following Shamhat's act of stripping and laying herself bare and open and immediately preceding Enkidu's rejection by the animals—a consequence of intercourse—gives it the unambiguous meaning of having intercourse. Thus, while sympathizing with those translators who desist from understanding line 181 as referring to actual intercourse, we believe that the reasons for treating line 181 as referring to this act as well as the clear meaning of line 183 are sufficiently compelling to require us to treat lines 181–182 as describing intercourse and

9. E.g., Kovacs, *Epic of Gilgamesh*, 8–9: "expose your sex so he can take in your voluptuousness. / Do not be restrained—take his energy!" Hecker, "Das akkadische Gilgamesch-Epos," 677: "öffne deinen Schoss, dass er deinen Reiz gewahr nehme! / Scheue dich nicht, seinen Atem hinzunehmen!" George, *Gilgamesh Epic*, 549: "bare your sex so he may take in your charms! / Do not show fear, take in his scent!" In contrast to Hecker and Kovacs, George is consistent in his translation of both the hunter's instructions and the actual description.

10. I thus disagree with the interpretation of line 182 // 190 given by George, *Gilgamesh Epic*, 796, who follows here a suggestion of T. Jacobsen; see below.

11. Some translations seem to render the act described in lines 181-182 as intercourse and thereby set aside the inconsistency. Cf., e.g., Schott, *Das Gilgamesch-Epos*, 21: "Deinen Schoss tu auf, dass deine Fülle er nehme! / Scheue dich nicht, nimm hin seinen Atemstoss! / Sieht er dich erst, so wird er dir nahn. / Dein Gewand entbreite, dass auf dir er sich bette"; Foster, *Epic of Gilgamesh*, 8: "Open your embrace, let him take your charms! / Be not bashful, take his vitality! / When he sees you, he will approach you, / Toss aside your clothing, let him lie upon you."

to look more closely at line 183 to see if we can explain its occurrence here in such a way as to help us out of our dilemma, a dilemma that is further aggravated by the fact that the reference of line 183 to actual intercourse creates difficulties of understanding not only for lines 181–182, but also for line 184.

How, then, are we to explain line 183? Once the question is formulated in this way, the answer is immediately evident and straightforward. As noted earlier, a line identical with 183 occurs in 144 // 165, that is, as part of the hunter's father's and Gilgamesh's instructions; on the other hand, not only does line 183 not occur in the expected place between lines 190 (// 182) and 191 (// 184) in the narrative account of lovemaking, but it is completely absent in that account. Note, moreover, that while the narrative itself (189–190) makes excellent sense: "She opened her loins[12] and he took her sex. She did not fear, she took his panting," it is the hunter's instructions (181–183) that do not. Accordingly, line 183 does not reflect lovemaking as described in the narrative, but rather derives from the hunter's father's // Gilgamesh's instructions.

Thus, we must conclude that while the hunter's instructions to Shamhat are based, in the main, on the narrative, they also draw upon the father's // Gilgamesh's instructions. The different segments of the text build on each other—not in a linear order of a single author who models later parts of his text on earlier ones, but in a redactional order. If we compare the father's // Gilgamesh's instructions with those of the hunter and with the narrative, we see that the first set of instructions is a condensation or summary of the lovemaking as found in the narrative.[13] Line 183 derives from that summary. Line 187 ("His animals that grew up on his steppe will reject him") supports this claim. Line 187 is identical with line 145 // 166, which is a condensation of lines 195–198. It, too, derives from the father's // Gilgamesh's instructions, for if that were not the case, we would expect to find lines like 195–198 (perhaps also 199–200) of the narrative in the hunter's instructions rather than the present line 187. The order and variation in manuscripts supports the notion that line 187 is an insertion or later addition to the hunter's speech,[14] for in most manuscripts it is in the wrong position (i.e., before

12. That is, she opened her thighs, thereby revealing her genitalia.

13. 140 = 162 // 167(–170); 142 = 163 // 172(-177); 143–144 = 164–165 // (178–179), 188–190; 145 = 166 // 195–198.

14. The scene of the animals' fleeing Enkidu was not part of the original narrative and was itself a later expansion. The hunter's instructions were composed on the basis of the original narrative and thus would most likely have already existed prior to the inser-

line 186), and one manuscript tried to rectify the text by rearranging the order of lines.[15]

The drawing of lines 183 and 187 from the summary is part of a process of harmonizing the hunter's speech with the advice of the hunter's father // Gilgamesh. This leveling through is intended to link the speeches even more closely. Thus, both lines 183 and 187 were drawn from the summary advice that provided a condensation of the fully developed form of the narrative. But whereas the summary instructions make sense, the hunter's instructions do not, precisely because of their secondary incorporation of material from the summary.

Accordingly, line 183 may be regarded as secondary. And once we have eliminated line 183,[16] we have no difficulty understanding the hunter's instructions in line 181 as telling Shamhat that she should open herself so Enkidu may possess her. This understanding agrees with and draws support from *liqê napissu* in line 182 if we take *napīšu* in its basic meaning of breathing or breath, rather than scent or the like, and understand *napīša leqû* as referring to Shamhat's taking of Enkidu's panting, perhaps his orgasm, thus paralleling the use of *kuzba leqû* in the preceding line. Thus, lines 181–182 of the hunter's instructions and lines 189–190 of the narrative description refer to the actual act of intercourse, and we would translate lines 181–182 as: "Open your loins so that he may take your sex. Do not fear, take his panting."

But if intercourse is being described in lines 181–182 // 189–190, how do we understand line 184 // 191? Shamhat is already unclothed (as we learn explicitly from the order of events in 143 // 164 as well as from 180–181a // 188–189a). In any case, it is difficult to imagine her

tion of the aforementioned animal scene into the narrative itself. Originally, the hunter's speech made no mention of the animals; it was updated on the basis of the summary only after the inclusion of the animal scene in the narrative. The summary found in the father's // Gilgamesh's advice was created only after the expansion of the narrative to include the rejection of the animals.

15. The manuscript that tried to create a logical order is J. J. A. van Dijk and W. R. Mayer, *Literarische Texte aus Babylon* (VAS 24; Berlin: Akademie-Verlag, 1987), no. 95, rev. iv, 15′ (= 186)–16′ (= 187). This text has been recopied by George, *Gilgamesh Epic*, vol. 2, pl. 51. That the order provided by VAS 24, no. 95 is a more logical one was already noted by van Dijk and Mayer, *Literarische Texte*, p. 13 ad no. 95: "Kol. IV 15′–16′ bietet die Verse *EG* I IV 14–15 in umgekehrter Reihenfolge, was wohl die bessere Fassung sein dürfte." So, too, George, *Gilgamesh Epic*, 797 ad lines 186–187. However, rather than being due to a transposition of lines, the illogical order (187, 186) is the result of the insertion of line 187 into a wrong position; the logical order is a later correction.

16. Beyond the desire to include all aspects of the summary in the hunter's instructions, I can find no reasonable explanation for the addition of line 183; perhaps it is due to a scribal misunderstanding.

spreading out her garment during intercourse itself or calling a halt to or interrupting intercourse (especially with Enkidu) in order to spread out her garment. In light of our understanding of lines 181–182 // 189–190, I would now suggest that Shamhat's spreading of her garment was not part of the initial act of stripping, but rather a separate act intended to humanize sex. Let us recall the fact that garments are of special significance in the *Epic of Gilgamesh.* Note the cleansing of garments (e.g., Tablet XI) and the fact that Shamhat shares her garment with Enkidu as a means of introducing him into human society and culture.

Thus, I would now suggest that we read lines 180–187 (minus lines 183 and 187) // 188–193 + 194 as referring to two sexual encounters between Enkidu and Shamhat. In the first, she draws him in and interacts with him on an animal level (180–182 // 188–190). Once Shamhat has calmed Enkidu's immediate sexual drive, she spreads out her garment and they have intercourse on it over the next seven days—intercourse that is now a human and not an animal act. For this reason, the text now states: line 185 // 192: *epšīma lullâ šipir sinništi,* for having now created a human setting or environment within nature, the courtesan is to provide Enkidu with *šipir sinništi,* the skills (not the task or work) of a human woman in contrast to the sexual behavior of a female animal. Enkidu is now humanized (and begins to be domesticated) by an act that is performed over a period of time in a manner and setting that is human.

Development of the Episode: A Minimal Reconstruction

By way of summary of our discussion thus far, let us now set out how we imagine the formation or rather redaction of the narrative and speeches that treat the encounter of the wild man and the courtesan. At this stage of our analysis, we shall take a conservative approach, that is, we will treat the episode as though all the characters were already present and will understand the redaction as affecting only their speeches.

Originally, then, a hunter saw Enkidu, he asked his father what to do, his father suggested that he go to Gilgamesh for help. Gilgamesh suggested the taking of a courtesan, and the hunter took her to the countryside, where he pointed Enkidu out to her (but did not give her detailed instructions). The text then described the love scene, the present narration.

It is not unusual for narration to be primary and to serve as the basis for the creation of speeches. Here, then, the actual narration of the encounter, lines 188ff. (as well as lines 167–179) would take precedence temporally over the speeches and would be the starting point for the development. The composer filled in the episode in order to enhance the literary force of the text but especially to emphasize the role of the hunter (and, perhaps, that of the animals). Gilgamesh's speech (162–166) is created on the basis of the narrative; it condenses and thereby summarizes the narrative (but already assumes the theme of Enkidu's rejection by the animals[17]); the speech has less detail and is more prosaic than the narrative (e.g., line 165 // 189b–194), though it does occasionally provide a lexical variation (*kuzbu*, line 164b // *ūru*, 189a). The hunter's speech was probably composed in two stages: in its earliest form, it predated Gilgamesh's summary of the narrative and drew solely upon the narrative in a verbatim fashion, but subsequently it incorporated material from the summary as well.[18] And the description of the hunter was drawn from that of Gilgamesh in Tablet X, and his father's speech was created or changed in line with Gilgamesh's.

Old Babylonian and Standard Babylonian Versions: A Major Difference

Let us now see if we can identify differences between the SB and OB texts, or rather isolate some clues that will point to changes that transpired between the OB and SB versions, and will, therefore, allow us to get a little closer to an earlier form of the text, thus providing further support for some of what we have said.

According to the SB version, Enkidu made love to Shamhat for a week; he then tried to return to his old way of life with the animals, but sexual relations between Enkidu and Shamhat had caused a rupture in relationship between Enkidu and the animals, and the animals fled from him and rejected him (I 195–200: 145 // 166 // 187). Thereupon, he turned back to the courtesan (lines 201–203); she addressed him and told him that one like him should not run with animals but should rather return with her to Uruk; she then recited the account of Gilgamesh's dreams. A segment corresponding to Enkidu's seven-day sexual marathon and Shamhat's address to Enkidu appears in the OB version P,

17. This theme was absent in the original episode. See above, n. 14, and especially the following section, "Old Babylonian and Standard Babylonian Versions: A Major Difference."

18. It is not impossible that the hunter's instructions were composed subsequent to the composition of Gilgamesh's summary instructions and that lines 165–166 of the summary were included in the hunter's speech (lines 183, 187) by the original composer of that speech, but it is far more likely that a scribe intent on harmonizing the different speeches inserted lines 183 and 187 into an already existing speech on the basis of lines 165–166, thus leveling through the material.

col. ii. Here, too, Enkidu made love to Shamhat for a week, but in contrast to the SB text, Enkidu forgot about the world of nature where he was born during their lovemaking and apparently did not attempt to rejoin the animals. Here, too, Shamhat addressed him and told him that he should not run with animals but should rather return with her to Uruk. Also this version contains the dream account, but it appears in col. i and thus precedes the narrative rather than forming the final part of Shamhat's address.

It is possible that Enkidu's pursuit of the animals was recounted at the end of the preceding, presently missing, first tablet of the OB version and that a version of what we have in OB P ii recurs in the presently broken beginning of SB II. But the strong similarities between the portions of the OB and SB versions described above suggest rather that OB P ii is the equivalent of the comparable scene in the SB version.[19] To be sure, the recital of the dreams precedes the love scene in the OB, but follows it in the SB. The divergent order is to be explained by the fact that the recital of the dreams is juxtaposed to the love scene in the OB and presented as independent if coterminous with it, while in the SB the recital has already been integrated into the episode. In the OB, the recital has been set alongside this segment of the Enkidu-Shamhat episode, whereas in the SB, it has been made part of the account by being placed into the courtesan's mouth and thus comes at the end of her speech. Though formally integrated into the episode, it is still a lengthy digression. In order to resume the story, the composer used a well-known device known as *Wiederaufnahme* or resumptive repetition.[20] Hence, the similarity of the last line of SB I with OB P ii (as well as some of the similarities of some broken lines in the beginning of SB II) does not indicate that whatever preceded the dream account in the SB also preceded it in the OB. Thus, if we are right, we have every reason to compare SB: I 194–214 and OB: P ii 45–68.

19. Cf. A. L. Oppenheim, "Mesopotamian Mythology II," *Or*, n.s., 17 (1948) 27 n. 2: "It should be stressed that the description of the seduction does not take more than one distich in the Old-Babylonian version, and the consequence of the 'Fall' of Enkidu was laconically described (Penn.-tablet II:5) as '[the pl]ace where he was born—he forgot!'" Thus, Oppenheim also took these passages as parallel to each other rather than as representing episodes that exist jointly in both versions, and he understood the OB passage as representing the seduction and the forgetting.

20. It might either be a newly created resumptive repetition or the remnant of an earlier account (e.g., the OB) that was left in this position even after the shift in order to serve as the resumptive repetition.

What, then, are the differences between the versions?[21] What is striking is the absence in the OB version of both Enkidu's attempt to return to the animals and their rejection of him. It is not the animals that reject Enkidu; rather, it is Enkidu who immediately turns his back on nature as a consequence of his experience with an urbane woman. In support of the claim that the text did not originally contain a return to and a rejection by animals is the remark by Shamhat in SB I 208 // OB P ii 54: *ammēni itti nammaššê tarappud ṣēra*, "Why do you roam the steppe with the wild animals?" This question makes perfect sense in a recension where the option of running with the animals still existed for Enkidu. But it is contrafactual and meaningless in the present SB version, for there he is in fact unable to run with the animals even if he wanted to. If we were to imagine line 196 through the first word of line 203 of the SB version as a secondary development inserted in order to develop a new theme and were to skip over these when reading the text, Shamhat's question would make perfect sense.

Thus, in the SB version, Enkidu leaves nature not by his own choice but because the animals will not have him once he has been intimate with and become related to humans. Earlier, in the OB version, on the other hand, the choice was his. And he rejected the animals/nature in favor of humans/civilization. For the equivalent of SB's rejection by the animals is OB P ii 47, where lovemaking causes him to forget the place of his birth (*ṣēram imtaši ašar iwwaldu*). Here, in the OB version the power of the prostitute is emphasized as is the inherent attractiveness of city life of which she is the representative. Animals are really unimportant in this early recension. Thus, in the OB version, after seven days of lovemaking the courtesan asks Enkidu why he wants to go back to nature. He no longer wants to, and this agrees with the double level of lovemaking: animal and then human; for it is not because of the initial act of sex but through the experience of sexuality in the context of a human relationship over the course of seven days that Enkidu forgot the place where he was born. Only at a later stage of the development of the epic was the account of Enkidu's turning back to the animals and their

21. While I arrived independently at my conclusion regarding the difference between the accounts, note that the difference between the OB and SB accounts was already noticed by Oppenheim, "Mesopotamian Mythology II," 27 n. 2 and p. 26, as well as by J. A. Bailey, "Initiation and the Primal Woman in Gilgamesh and Genesis 2–3," *JBL* 89 (1970) 138–39, repeated in idem, "Male, Female, and the Pursuit of Immortality in the Gilgamesh Epic," *La Parola del Passato Rivista di Studi Antichi* 31 (1976) 435–37.

repudiation of him introduced between the seven days of lovemaking and the speech of Shamhat to Enkidu.

The introduction of the repudiation as background for his return to the courtesan and for his readiness to accept her persuasion to become part of human culture may possibly be the result of a failure by redactors or scribes to realize that there were two stages in the lovemaking[22] and that the latter stage was intended to cause Enkidu to distance himself from the animals and join human culture. But the animals may very well also have been introduced in order to provide a background and context for the appearance of the hunter. This, too, suggests that the hunter may not have been part of the episode originally.

Development of the Scene: A More Far-Reaching Reconstruction

Earlier we sketched the development of our text by assuming that while the various speeches underwent development, that is, evolved in stages, all the characters were present in the original text. In actuality, it is perhaps more reasonable to presume that underlying the discrepancies that we have noticed are more pronounced developments and to suggest a more radical reconstruction. Neither of the scenarios precludes the other.

To be sure, the episode may have originally centered on Enkidu, a hunter, his father, and Shamhat. But, the humanization of a wild man, generally, and of Enkidu, specifically, does not require the presence of a hunter.[23] We may suggest, therefore, that originally the main character in the episode was the courtesan and that she seduced Enkidu without any involvement on the part of the hunter. The elimination of the hunter and his father also eliminates the loci of difficulties as well as the difficulties themselves. At a later stage in the development of the text, the hunter was introduced into the story. Certainly his speech to the courtesan is dependent—as we have seen—on the narration of Shamhat's

---

22. Could the insertion of line 183 have contributed to such a misunderstanding in antiquity as it has in modernity?

23. Note that there are accounts in both the Orient and Occident of the humanization of a wild man by a woman without the involvement or assistance of a hunter. See, e.g., C. A. Williams, *Oriental Affinities of the Legend of the Hairy Anchorite*, parts 1–2 (2 vols.; UISLL 10.2 and 11.4; Urbana: University of Illinois Press, 1925–26), e.g., pp. 12, 19, 25–36 (= "The Legend of Rishyasringa in India") and passim [cf. T. Jacobsen, *The Treasures of Darkness* (New Haven, CT: Yale University Press, 1976) 214]; and R. Bernheimer, *Wild Men in the Middle Ages: A Study in Art, Sentiment, and Demonology* (Cambridge, MA: Harvard University Press, 1952) 124. [For Enkidu and Ṛśyaśṛṅga, see also the essay by Abusch and West in this volume (pp. 177–218).

seduction of Enkidu, a narration that can stand on its own. There are a number of problems that are solved or phenomena explained by this suggestion. The hunter's later appearance would explain why his speech depends not only on the narration but also on Gilgamesh's advice. More important, it would explain the appearance of the hunter's father, which seems to be unnecessary to the plot of the story, and his speech (and role), which seems to be redundant. For once the hunter was introduced, he was provided with a father, in whose mouth was placed the already existing speech of Gilgamesh.

In support of the primacy of the courtesan in the account, and the later introduction of the hunter, we would point to imbalances in the episode in which Enkidu curses (and then blesses) those responsible for his imminent death. Whereas the curse upon the hunter is short, running only to some six lines (VII 94–99), and refers to the hunter in the third person, that upon the prostitute is relatively long, covering close to thirty lines (VII 102–131), and addresses her in the second person. Moreoever, at least in the SB version, Shamash, when responding to the curse, refers only to the prostitute in his address to Enkidu (VII 132ff.), and Enkidu, for his part, then, blesses only the prostitute in an attempt to neutralize his earlier curse (VII 148–162).[24] The differences between the curses and the presence of a blessing only upon the prostitute[25] support the primacy of the courtesan and our claim that the hunter was only afterward introduced into the seduction scene of Enkidu.

But we have not yet explained why the hunter was introduced, and once introduced, why he was provided with a father. The answer is suggested by the very features of the hunter's story that are most perplexing: Why is the hunter's reaction to Enkidu exaggerated and an overreaction? Why is the hunter presented as somewhat helpless and in need of an adult's advice? Why is his father's speech identical with Gilgamesh's? All these difficulties are resolved once we realize that the hunter's character and story were intended to foreshadow or anticipate those of Gilgamesh. Hence, his description is identical with that of Gilgamesh in Tablet X.

24. Note that in Shamash's response following the curses in the MB Ur text, the hunter is mentioned (though apparently not discussed) in a broken line (rev. 43 [George, *Gilgamesh Epic*, 298]) not found in SB. Even here Enkidu in response blesses only the prostitute. Perhaps this represents an abortive attempt at assimilating and expanding the treatment of the two personages.

25. An alternative explanation for the absence of a blessing of the hunter might be that such a blessing would undercut the effectiveness of the identification of Gilgamesh with a lower-class roaming/homeless hunter subsequent to Enkidu's death and his experience of the "bad" fortune associated with this way of life.

There, similar lines recur in descriptions of Gilgamesh: see, e.g., lines 8–9, 40–45, esp. 42–43;[26] Gilgamesh's reaction is appropriate to his demanding and drastic experience in the wild, whereas the hunter's behavior, on the other hand, is not appropriate and an overreaction. The hunter is presented in this way only because he is modeled on Gilgamesh, and the description of his experience in the wild taken over from a description of Gilgamesh in the wild. As part of the identification with Gilgamesh, he is presented as being in need of a parent and of a parent's advice. And just as Gilgamesh goes to his mother for help, so does the hunter go to his father when he is in difficulty. His father plays the same role as does Gilgamesh's mother. His father is, therefore, provided with a speech that has been copied from Gilgamesh's speech so that he may play his role.[27] That is, his father was given a speech in order to forge a connection with Gilgamesh and thus give the father a role similar to that of Gilgamesh's mother.[28]

That the redactor wished us to make the connection of hunter and Gilgamesh is indicated not only by the aforementioned literary usages but also by the fact that whereas the hunter is usually referred to as *ṣayyādu*, the first time he is introduced he is referred to as *ṣayyādu ḫābilu-amēlu*. This conflation provides an express link with Gilgamesh, for Gilgamesh in his speech to Siduri expressly compares himself to a *ḫābilu*: *attanaggaš kīma ḫābilim qabaltu ṣēri* (OB Meissner, ii 11′).

26. D. O. Edzard has also noted that the last two lines of the description of the hunter are found also in the descriptions of the roaming Gilgamesh ("Kleine Beiträge zum Gilgamesh-Epos," *Or*, n.s., 54 [1985] 48–49). He, too, sees this as intentional. But rather than serving primarily to create an identification of hunter and Gilgamesh by this form of foreshadowing, he interprets it as a form of parody: "Der Dichter hat also zwei Ausdrücke, die er erst später auf den verzweifelten Gilgameš anwenden wird, parodierend vorweggenommen und dies als Abschluss seiner Beschreibung des zu Tode erschrockenen Jägers. Ich halte bei der hohen literarischen Qualität des GE eine solche Deutung für näherliegend als die Annahme, der Dichter habe sich für ganz verschieden zu beurteilende Situationen mit demselben Phrasenrüstzeug versehen" (ibid., 49).

27. I certainly do not deny the existence of leveling in our text, but this term merely describes a process or mechanism and does not yet provide a full explanation for the phenomenon. The same applies to expansion and repetition.

28. Note that below, n. 45, I consider the possibility that the speech may have originated with the hunter's father and was only later carried over to Gilgamesh. But regardless of whether Gilgamesh's or the father's speech is the more original, it is clear that lines 135–139 were added in order to connect the two identical speeches and to place the father's instructions in their new context. See already Jastrow and Clay, *Old Babylonian Version*, 41.

To summarize: An earlier form of our episode existed in which a courtesan drew Enkidu from the wild.[29] This account emphasized the power and attractiveness of sex and of its purveyors. The city was defined in terms of this sexuality, and the beauty and desirability of a city with courtesans as its characteristic inhabitants were thereby emphasized: see I 226–231, esp. 230–231: "And the harlots are comely of figure, / graced with charm, full of joy";[30] cf. III 122–123 and VI 158. At a later stage, the hunter was introduced, in part in order to foreshadow Gilgamesh's later identity and activities. The balance of the episode changes with his introduction. He is set into a confrontation with Enkidu; he is provided with a father; the father takes on a speech belonging to Gilgamesh; and he himself gives a speech that mixes together the narrative description of the courtesan's actions with the speech of Gilgamesh. The detailed relative chronology of the speeches here in this reconstruction is the same as that of the more conservative reconstruction.

Moreover, in this later stage, a greater emphasis is placed upon animals, and the famous scene of the repudiation of Enkidu by the animals is introduced. The animals that belong to the world of the hunter are now given at least as much weight as is sexuality. The wild is set up as a reasonable counterpoint to the city. At this point in the evolution of the work, the writer introduced the notion that one might well prefer the wild over the city, if not permanently then at least at certain periods of one's life.

Broader Reconstruction: The Prehistory and Formation of the Epic

The identification of Gilgamesh with the hunter, or, rather, the foreshadowing of Gilgamesh by means of a hunter is not a mere happenstance or literary ploy—it is of great significance for the understanding of the epic. I shall pursue that issue elsewhere. Here, we should try to reconstruct the early history of the Enkidu episode and then to extend the discussion beyond the episode itself. Thus far, I have proceeded as if the development of the episode took place within the context of the formation of the *Epic of Gilgamesh*. Actually, it is far more likely that the

29. It is possible to construct an analysis whereby the original story began with the hunter, his father, and the wild man. Thus, the original episode would not have included the courtesan at all, and she would have been added only secondarily. However, I have preferred positing a version centering on the wild man and the courtesan as more original because it allows one to resolve more difficulties and explain more features of the text.

30. Translation: George, *Gilgamesh Epic*, 553.

episode took form independently of the story of Gilgamesh. The independence of the story would obtain whether one assumes that the tale originally centered on a wild man and hunter, or, as I have assumed, on a wild man and a woman. And, if it is the case that a version of the tale once had an independent existence, it is equally clear that while some of the internal developments in the episode took place after the tale became part of the *Epic of Gilgamesh*,[31] other developments would likely have taken place before the tale was taken over by the epic composer.

Thus, I imagine—with such early interpreters of the epic as M. Jastrow Jr. and such later ones as W. L. Moran[32]—that the tale of Enkidu and Shamhat began not with the epic but originated in a story of a primitive man[33] and his first encounter with sex. Subsequently, the female partner would have been replaced by a courtesan.[34] The tale would likely have included the bringing of the wild man to a city even before its incorporation into the epic.

In any case, some form of the tale would have developed indendently of the personage and story of Gilgamesh. But even after the linkage of the episode with the story of Gilgamesh, the woman could easily have sufficed to humanize the wild man. Subsequently, the hunter was

31. As an example of a development that took place after the episode became part of the epic, I note one development that is of some relevance for the discussion. Regardless of what developmental scheme is chosen to explain the text, it seems likely that the overt involvement of Gilgamesh in the scene, whether as an instructor to the hunter or as an immediate goal of the action, is secondary. In the early epic, Gilgamesh became aware of the coming of Enkidu only through his own dreams and his mother's interpretation of them. Their encounter was due to the gods; it was not due to an intentional act on the part of the hunter, the courtesan, or Gilgamesh himself. In support of this, note, e.g., the absence of any mention of Gilgamesh in Shamhat's speech to Enkidu in OB P ii 53ff., where she tells him of her plans to bring him to Uruk (contrast the mention of Gilgamesh in SB I 207ff., esp. 211 // 218). In the OB P text, Enkidu became aware of Gilgamesh only through the unexpected meeting with the traveler, who explained to Enkidu that he was bringing food to the city for a wedding in which Gilgamesh would be a participant. If Gilgamesh were originally involved in bringing Enkidu to the city, one would have expected Enkidu to be led to the city earlier in the story or at the command of Gilgamesh. Thus, only when the episode was linked to the story of Gilgamesh did Gilgamesh become the initiator, and the courtesan was transformed into his agent. This transformation probably did not take place immediately upon the linking of the tale to the story of Gilgamesh, but only sometime afterward.

32. Jastrow and Clay, *Old Babylonian Version*, 39–47; W. L. Moran, "Ovid's *Blanda Voluptas* and the Humanization of Enkidu," *JNES* 50 (1991) 121–27.

33. Cf. J. H. Tigay, *The Evolution of the Gilgamesh Epic* (Philadelphia: University of Pennsylvania Press, 1982) 198–213.

34. This replacement may have taken place after the incorporation of the tale into the epic, but more likely it took place before that incorporation and the designation of the wild man as Enkidu.

introduced,[35] and the humanization of Enkidu led up to his encounter with Gilgamesh and their expedition to conquer Huwawa. They succeed in killing Huwawa, and this act alone caused the gods to decree death for Enkidu, for, as I have argued elsewhere, this version did not yet include the Gilgamesh-Ishtar encounter and the battle with the Bull of Heaven of Tablet VI.[36] Subsequently, a redactor created and/or incorporated an Akkadian version of the story of *Gilgamesh, Ishtar, and the Bull of Heaven.*

Our model thus far has been that of a straightforward linear development. Thus, the epic would have developed by means of expansion and inclusion of independent Gilgamesh materials. But we may also recall that in non-Mesopotamian accounts of the capture of the wild man, occasionally either the hunter or the lady may appear alone and lead the wild man to civilization.[37] Considering the prehistory and development of the episode involving Enkidu, Shamhat, and the hunter and thinking about the implications of this evolution for the history of the epic, I begin to see another possibility and to wonder if we should not view the present epic as the result not of a linear development but rather of the conflation of two independent parallel versions. [But see now the discussion in the introduction to this volume (pp. 1–9).]

What forms might these two versions have taken?

In one version, the emphasis would have been on the conflict between the life of a city dweller and that of a hunter. The purpose or, at least, the excitement of life was to be found in the hunt. In this version, at the instigation of either Gilgamesh or the hunter's father, Enkidu was captured by a hunter who first separated him from the animals and then brought him to Gilgamesh via the sheepfold. Their friendship led to the abandonment of the city in favor of an expedition against Huwawa. This expedition resulted in the death of Enkidu. This version is male (and martial[38]) centered and does not involve an overt male/female conflict. We only find the introduction of the female in the attempt at a resolution in which Siduri is made to suggest: "Look down at the child who

35. In principle, it is possible that the hunter was introduced into the story of the wild man and the courtesan even before that story was linked with the story of Gilgamesh. My preference, however, has been to date the introduction of the hunter sometime after the linkage because of my understanding of his larger literary role in the epic.

36. T. Abusch, "Ishtar's Proposal and Gilgamesh's Refusal: An Interpretation of *The Gilgamesh Epic,* Tablet 6, Lines 1–79," *History of Religions* 26 (1986) 179ff. [here, pp. 48–52].

37. For the hunter alone, see, e.g., Bernheimer, *Wild Men in the Middle Ages,* 16–17; for the lady alone, see above, n. 23.

38. Compare, e.g., the myth of Erra, Tablet I.

holds your hand, / Let a wife ever delight in your lap."[39] (This resolution agrees with the emphasis that I have reconstructed for the OB version.[40])

In the other version, the emphasis would have been on the conflict between a rustic, traditional life and a life in an attractive cosmopolitan city, epitomized by the sexual behavior and institutions of an urbane environment. In this version, Enkidu was seduced by a courtesan. His intimate contact with her caused him to lose his interest in the natural world; he was drawn to the city[41] and to Gilgamesh perhaps by his desire to take over Gilgamesh's sexual role.[42] They became friends and distanced themselves from the sexual life of the city, for their friendship was now set up as a counterpoint to the feminine. This conflict is epitomized in Ishtar's proposal and Gilgamesh's rejection and in the subsequent killing of the Bull of Heaven of Tablet VI. As in the other version, this conquest led to the death of Enkidu. Resolution is found in the integration of the hero into a city life in which public culture is characterized not by male/female relationships, but by royal communal deeds. (This resolution agrees with the emphasis that I have reconstructed for the SB eleven-tablet version.[43])

If the suggestion of the existence of two parallel versions that were subsequently combined turns out to be correct, we may also wish to reconsider our understanding of the prehistory of the episode involving Enkidu, Shamhat, and the hunter. Earlier, we approached the episode

39. See T. Abusch, "Gilgamesh's Request and Siduri's Denial, Part I: The Meaning of the Dialogue and Its Implications for the History of the Epic," in *The Tablet and the Scroll: Near Eastern Studies in Honor of William W. Hallo* (ed. M. E. Cohen, D. C. Snell, and D. B. Weisberg; Bethesda, MD: CDL Press, 1993) 1–14 [here, pp. 58–88].

40. T. Abusch, "The Development and Meaning of the *Epic of Gilgamesh*: An Interpretive Essay," *JAOS* 121 (2001) 616–18 [here, pp. 127–143].

41. Presumably, this version did not have a section describing Enkidu's encounter with and service for the shepherds (such would have been part of the hunter version). Hence, we understand why in the scene describing the encounter between Enkidu and the traveler (OB P iv), Enkidu and Shamhat are shown sitting together as if the scene had no connection whatsoever with the shepherds and sheepfold mentioned in the preceding column. Note, also, the absence of any mention of shepherds in Shamhat's speech to Enkidu when she advises him to leave nature and proceed to the city. I do assume that the feeding scene now associated with the sheepfold probably was originally associated with Shamhat because of VII 132ff., where Shamash mentions feeding, etc., among the good deeds that Shamhat did for Enkidu.

42. This explanation of Enkidu's behavior fits the story as I imagine it; it is no more than a guess and is not stated in the text. There should, of course, be a broader social force at play here, but I cannot yet construct a more convincing personal motivation for Enkidu's desire to stop Gilgamesh. (I leave aside the possibility that the Enkidu character is simply an unmotivated puppet in the hands of the gods.)

43. Abusch, "Development and Meaning," 618–20 [here, pp. 135–39].

with a supplementary model in mind and assumed that an earlier form of the episode would have been supplemented by themes that emphasized a new *Tendenz* (original wild man–courtesan supplemented by hunter, etc., or—the approach we did not follow—wild man–hunter supplemented by courtesan) and that at some point in this development, the tale was connected to the story of Gilgamesh. In light of the possible existence of two parallel versions of the Akkadian Gilgamesh story, perhaps we should assume instead that there were two accounts of the Enkidu episode that were joined together when the parallel versions of the epic were combined.[44]

If so, we may imagine the following development: To each one of our Gilgamesh stories, a different version of the wild man account was attached. The version that was attached to the Gilgamesh story that centered on the conflict with Ishtar and the Bull of Heaven involved a wild man and a courtesan from the city who draws him away from the animals, introduces him to the human modes of sexual intercourse, eating and drinking, and leads him to the city. The version that was attached to the Gilgamesh story that centered on the conflict with Huwawa involved a wild man and a hunter who manages to trap the wild man who had been protecting the animals against him and to introduce him to the community of shepherds, where he eventually functions as a guardian of humans against the very animals that he had earlier protected.

When the two stories were joined, the various characters were brought into conjunction with each other, and either Gilgamesh suggested to the hunter that he take the courtesan to the countryside to seduce Enkidu and the hunter's father was then made to repeat the same speech, or the hunter's father was the first to make the suggestion and his speech was then repeated by Gilgamesh.[45] Finally, the activities in

44. Note that even if the more general idea of two forms of the epic is not correct, the episode itself may still have existed in two forms, and the SB version of the episode may have been created by combination rather than supplementation. In any case, there may not be a profound difference between the combination of parallel stories and supplementation because supplements also often derive from existing stories and are not free-floating, non-corporeal motifs.

45. I have assumed throughout that the instructions originated with Gilgamesh. But in a tale that included (whether originally or secondarily) the courtesan, the hunter, and the father, it is nonetheless possible that the instructions to the hunter to fetch a courtesan might have originated with the hunter's father rather than with Gilgamesh. I am not yet able to resolve the problem to my own satisfaction and decide the direction of borrowing in a definitive manner.

Let us note, therefore, some of the arguments in favor of each position. In favor of assuming that the instructions originated with Gilgamesh: (a) If the hunter and his

the sheepfold are combined with the sexual dalliance of Enkidu and the courtesan on their way to Uruk.

Perhaps, then, our epic is the consequence of the conflation of these two literary traditions. Hence, our present account. Conflation would certainly explain the occurrence of the various parallel characters such as the hunter and the courtesan or the courtesan and the alewife, as well as doublets such as the battle with Huwawa and the subsequent one with the Bull of Heaven. The one tradition would have given its imprint to the OB version, the other to the SB eleven-tablet version.

But I do not wish to press this point too hard in the absence of documentary evidence or of a detailed analysis of the lexical and stylistic features of the putative traditions. For the moment, I shall assume the correctness of the linear model and adhere to my earlier conclusion that

---

father were introduced into the epic in order to foreshadow and parallel Gilgamesh (and his mother)—as I imagine the case to be—the literary effect of this innovation would probably have been to cause further developments in the episode to center, first and foremost, on Gilgamesh, thus suggesting that the speech would have been created for him. (b) In the hypothetical version that included only the hunter, the hunter did not make use of a courtesan, and thus his father would not have had an occasion to advise him to fetch one. In favor of assuming that the instructions originated with the hunter's father: (a) If, as suggested above, n. 31, originally Gilgamesh was not actively involved in bringing Enkidu to Uruk, the speech would have more likely been created for the father and put into Gilgamesh's mouth only when he was later made into an active participant in the scene. (b) The carry-over of the speech from the father to Gilgamesh is in line with the tendency in literature for activities and accomplishments of secondary characters to be transferred to major ones (e.g., the killing of Goliath, attributed first to Elhanan and then to David), rather than the reverse. (c) Although I do not believe this to be the case, I should note that if prior to its incorporation in the epic, the tale already told a story about a courtesan, a hunter, and his father similar to that found in our present epic, then the speech would probably have originated with the hunter's father.

In both the "minimal" and the "more far-reaching" reconstruction, I have described the development of our episode on the assumption that the speech originated with Gilgamesh and was transferred to the hunter's father. I still prefer that scenario. But should the speech have originated with the father, I would stipulate the following development. The hunter was introduced into the story of Gilgamesh (or a tale that already included the hunter was linked up to the Gilgamesh account) in order to foreshadow and parallel Gilgamesh. The connection with Gilgamesh was achieved by means of the description of the hunter and the creation of a father who advised his son what to do. These were sufficient to link Gilgamesh to the episode, and an express connection was not necessary. A later redactor felt the need to introduce Gilgamesh into the action—thus distorting the thrust of the story, for as noted Gilgamesh knew of Enkidu through his dreams, and Enkidu's appearance and their encounter should have been in the nature of an unexpected event. Gilgamesh was given an overt role in the episode and was now actively involved in the solution of the problem created by Enkidu's appearance. As part of this process, he was made to repeat the hunter's father's speech (and the two speeches were connected by the insertion of I 135–139).

the Gilgamesh-Ishtar encounter and the subsequent conflict with the Bull of Heaven were incorporated into an epic that already had a developed story about Enkidu, the hunter, the courtesan, and Gilgamesh, as well as the account of the expedition against Huwawa. All the same, we should keep an open mind regarding the possibility that the present epic is a conflation of two parallel accounts.

Hunting in the Epic of Gilgamesh: *Speculations on the Education of a Prince*

Introduction

Whether originally the product of an oral tradition or of a scribal one or of a combination of the two, the *Epic of Gilgamesh* is a powerful literary composition. Perhaps we should be satisfied with just reading and appreciating the composition in its extant versions. Elsewhere, I have studied selected episodes as well as the central meaning of several recensions.[1] However, I still find myself drawn to the question of beginnings and curious to know how the earliest version of the epic was composed and what lay behind its earliest form.

We may not find fully satisfactory answers to such questions, but, even so, tackling the topic of origins can be a productive exercise, for in the process we may sometimes find answers to questions that are not

---

Professor IsraelEphᶜal is the pre-eminent scholar of warfare in the ancient Near East. It is, therefore, a particular pleasure to dedicate this study of hunting and martial training in the *Epic of Gilgamesh* to my dear friend Israel.

This essay was read before the 51st Rencontre Assyriologique Internationale, Chicago, July 2005. An early version was composed in 2003–2004 while I was first a member of the School of Historical Studies of the Institute for Advanced Study, Princeton, and then a Lady Davis Visiting Professor at the Hebrew University, Jerusalem, and an NEH Fellow of the W. F. Albright Institute of Archaeological Research. My heartfelt thanks to these institutions for their hospitality and support. I thank Stephen Geller, Kathryn Kravitz, Ellen Messer, Jeffrey Stackert, and Emily West for reading and commenting upon one or another version of this essay.

1. See my "Ishtar's Proposal and Gilgamesh's Refusal: An Interpretation of *The Gilgamesh Epic*, Tablet 6, Lines 1–79," *History of Religions* 26 (1986) 143–87 [here, pp. 11–57]; "Gilgamesh's Request and Siduri's Denial, Part 1: The Meaning of the Dialogue and Its Implications for the History of the Epic," in *The Tablet and the Scroll: Near Eastern Studies in Honor of William W. Hallo* (ed. M. E. Cohen, D. C. Snell, and D. B. Weisberg; Bethesda, MD: CDL Press, 1993) 1–14 [here, pp. 58–88]; "Gilgamesh's Request and Siduri's Denial, Part 2: An Analysis and Interpretation of an Old Babylonian Fragment about Mourning and Celebration," *JANESCU* 22 (1993) 3–17 [here, pp. 89–107]; "The Development and Meaning of the *Epic of Gilgamesh*: An Interpretive Essay," *JAOS* 121 (2001) 614–22 [here, pp. 127–43]; "The Courtesan, the Wild Man, and the Hunter: Studies in the Literary History of the *Epic of Gilgamesh*," in *"An Experienced Scribe Who Neglects Nothing": Ancient Near Eastern Studies in Honor of Jacob Klein* (ed. Y. Sefati et al.; Bethesda, MD: CDL Press, 2005) 413–33 [here, pp. 144–65].

directly related to origins, but nag at the reader of the epic all the same. For example: Why did the king initially treat his people so insensitively and immaturely when in fact he should have acted as their leader and protector? Moreover, how can a ruler simply leave his city and his responsibilities for so long a time in order to undertake a personal quest? Why does Gilgamesh's mother occupy such an important place in the work? Why is the Sumerian story of Gilgamesh and Huwawa the major Sumerian story drawn upon by the composer?

I hope to provide a few very provisional and partial answers to these questions as well as to the question of origins by setting out two suggestions regarding the prehistory of the epic. I would suggest, first, that in creating his earliest version the composer drew upon a narrative pattern that centered on hunting and, second, that this version was originally intended as a tale to educate a prince. Only later did the work turn into an account about a king.

Hunting

I would suggest that the composer started from an image of hunting and the hunter. This image provided a framework for the exploration of what would become the epic's central themes; moreover, it lent scenic and dramatic unity to the work and defined, to some extent, the composer's choice of themes and sources and his treatment of these themes and sources. The use of this image would explain why the author of the OB Akkadian version made use of certain Sumerian tales of Gilgamesh and not of others; why he introduced certain changes into those tales; and why he thought to present as his central character a king who absents himself from his normal tasks and even leaves his realm and subjects to fend for themselves.

In ancient Mesopotamia, the figure of the hunter was of no small significance.[2] More specifically, hunters appear in several guises. The

2. On hunting in Mesopotamia, see W. Heimpel, "Jagd. A. Philologisch," *RlA* 5:234–36; and L. Trümpelman, "Jagd. B. Archäologisch," *RlA* 5:236–38. Note particularly the more recent works by C. E. Watanabe, *Animal Symbolism in Mesopotamia: A Contextual Approach* (Wiener offene Orientalistik 1; Vienna: Institut für Orientalistik der Universität Wien, 2002); and E. Weissert, "Royal Hunt and Royal Triumph in a Prism Fragment of Ashurbanipal (82-5-22,2)," in *Assyria 1995: Proceedings of the 10th Anniversary Symposium of the Neo-Assyrian Text Corpus Project, Helsinki, September 7–11, 1995* (ed. S. Parpola and R. Whiting; Helsinki: Neo-Assyrian Text Corpus Project, 1997) 339–58. For hunting in the classical world, see, e.g., J. K. Anderson, *Hunting in the Ancient World* (Berkeley: University of California Press, 1985); and J. M. Barringer, *The Hunt in Ancient Greece* (Baltimore: Johns Hopkins University Press, 2001). For the hunting feats of

most dramatic and significant appearance of the hunter is that of the king fighting large animals such as lions and bulls. In the case of the royal hunt, hunting is an act of both sport and statecraft. It is closely associated with royal authority. Hunting abilities and achievements symbolize the king's strength and courage. They demonstrate his prowess as well as his ability to protect his people against enemies and to maintain order in the face of chaos. Learning to hunt, moreover, inculcates and develops various physical, personal, and military qualities and skills. As particularly good examples of royal hunting, we need only recall the self-descriptions of Shulgi and Assurbanipal as hunters[3] and the presentation of the lion hunt in the texts and art of Neo-Assyrian royalty, beginning with Tiglath-Pileser I and reaching its pinnacle with Assurbanipal. In addition to the royal hunter, we encounter a lower-class hunter; he appears in the guise of a hunter and trapper who lives on the margin of settlement.

That hunting in the wild is a major underlying theme of the work is apparent from the fact that the two largest portions of the developed text of the epic are devoted, respectively, to the expedition against powerful and evil Huwawa (SB Tablets II 184–V // OB and other versions) and to Gilgamesh's travels in the wild as a hunter (SB Tablets IX–X). In these two sections of the epic, Gilgamesh personifies, respectively, two types of hunters: the princely hunter and the socially marginal trapper. The first section, the hunting expedition against Huwawa, reflects the life of an upper-class youth: optimism, the seeking after new experiences, and the search for fame. And it focuses on the activities of a pair of warriors—Gilgamesh and Enkidu. The goal of hunting here is not survival, but rather adventure and success in the hunt. The second section, Gilgamesh's trek subsequent to Enkidu's death, shows us Gilgamesh in

the Pharaoh, see, e.g., the description of Thutmose III in *ANET*, 243–44 (trans. J. A. Wilson). [For a most recent study of the lion hunt in the ancient Near East, including Egypt, see B. A. Strawn, *What Is Stronger than a Lion? Leonine Image and Metaphor in the Hebrew Bible and the Ancient Near East* (OBO 212; Fribourg: Academic Press; Göttingen: Vandenhoeck & Ruprecht, 2005) 161–74.]

3. For Shulgi, see Shulgi B, lines 56–113, for which text, see G. R. Castellino, *Two Šulgi Hymns (B, C)* (Studi semitici 42; Rome: Istituto di studi del Vicino Oriente, 1972) 27ff., and J. A. Black et al., *The Electronic Text Corpus of Sumerian Literature*, http://etcsl.orinst.ox.ac.uk/2.4.2.02; for a summary, cf. J. Klein, *The Royal Hymns of Shulgi King of Ur: Man's Quest for Immortal Fame* (Transactions of the American Philosophical Society 71.7; Philadelphia: American Philosophical Society, 1981) 16. For Assurbanipal, see, e.g., Weissert, "Royal Hunt and Royal Triumph," passim, and esp. the references there in nn. 7–9 (p. 341) and citations in figure 1 (pp. 344–45); note esp. T. Bauer, *Das Inschriftenwerk Assurbanipals* (Leipzig: J. C. Hinrichs, 1933) 87–89.

despair, struggle, and near death. He is haggard and plays the role of a lone hunter and trapper whose survival is tenuous: as likely as not, he will starve, freeze, or be killed by predators. To survive, he must rely on his own wits and manage to kill animals and to use them for food and covering.[4]

In a study that recently appeared in a Festschrift for Jacob Klein, I examined in great detail the story of the wild man, the hunter, and the courtesan in SB Tablet I and tried to reconstruct its history.[5] There, I argued that the hunter of Tablet I was a late entry into the epic composition and was introduced into the work so that the figure of the hunter might serve to foreshadow[6] Gilgamesh. Therefore, in imitation of Gilgamesh, the hunter was made to appear in need of a parent's advice and was provided with a parent in the form of a father. The composer's description of the hunter, moreover, was modeled on that of Gilgamesh, for when the hunter sees Enkidu, "[He was] troubled, grew still, he grew silent, / his mood [*was unhappy*,] his face clouded over, / There [was] sorrow in his heart, / his face was like [one who has traveled] distant [roads]" (SB I 118–121).[7] This description reflects the description of Gilgamesh especially as he is presented in Tablet X, in the course of his

4. For parallels in Greece to these two types of hunts (collective hunt for large game; individual hunt for small game) and discussions of their relationship, see P. Vidal-Naquet, *The Black Hunter: Forms of Thought and Forms of Society in the Greek World* (trans. A. Szegedy-Maszak; Baltimore: Johns Hopkins University Press, 1986) 106–28 ("The Black Hunter and the Origin of the Athenian *Ephebia*"); Anderson, *Hunting in the Ancient World*, 17–29 (note p. 159 n. 3); and Barringer, *The Hunt in Ancient Greece*, 11–15 and 47–53.

5. Abusch, "Courtesan," 413–33 [here, pp. 144–65].

6. In foreshadowing, the composer introduces an entity in a simple, often miniature, and easily comprehensible form. This emblematic form prepares the audience so that when it later encounters the foreshadowed character, event, or situation in a larger, more complex, and possibly more amorphous form, the foreshadowing focuses the audience on the essentials of the larger scene and allows them to grasp it more easily. An excellent example of the use of this technique is found in Gen 12:10–20; there the story of Abraham and Sarah in Egypt prepares the reader for the story of Israel's subsequent descent into Egypt, enslavement, and liberation. For various types of foreshadowing, see, e.g., the several references under the entry "Foreshadowing" in the index to M. Sternberg, *The Poetics of Biblical Narrative: Ideological Literature and the Drama of Reading* (Bloomington: University of Indiana Press, 1985) 549–50.

7. I follow the line count in A. R. George, *The Babylonian Gilgamesh Epic: Introduction, Critical Edition, and Cuneiform Texts* (2 vols.; Oxford: Oxford University Press, 2003); translations are his.

wanderings in the wild subsequent to the death of Enkidu (compare, e.g., I 118–121 with X 8–9 and 42–43).[8]

At the very least, the hunter was modeled on and serves to foreshadow the identity of the lone hunter and trapper that Gilgamesh had assumed during this trek. But Gilgamesh's lifestyle was not only that of a man who hunts and traps in order to survive, but also that of a royal hunter. Even during the trek in the wilderness Gilgamesh is described as confronting lions (IX 9–18) and is said to be a slayer of wild bulls (X 13[9]), so perhaps the hunter is eventually meant to represent both trapper and large game hunter and thus to foreshadow Gilgamesh the trapper and royal lion hunter.[10]

In any case, by introducing the hunter as a foreshadowing of Gilgamesh, the composer tells us that he understood Gilgamesh, his story, and its background in a certain way. For to his mind, Gilgamesh was a hunter in addition to whatever else he was.

It is not an accident that the expedition against Huwawa overshadows the battle within the city against the Bull of Heaven, even when the account of the latter is eventually and secondarily placed at the physical center of the work.[11] The expedition against Huwawa is a hunt for a dangerous creature and is set in the wild; the battle with the Bull of Heaven is a contest or even a sport against a power that has invaded the city.[12] The desire to emphasize hunting, moreover, is consistent with—

---

8. See Abusch, "Courtesan," 425–28 [here, pp. 156–59].

9. *mindêma annû muna''ir rīmī*, "For sure this man is a slayer of wild bulls."

10. It is possible that Gilgamesh the royal lion hunter and protector of his people may be foreshadowed by Enkidu when the latter is portrayed protecting the shepherds in OB P iii 110–118. For there Enkidu is shown fighting lions and other beasts in the service of society. (Already Weissert, "Royal Hunt and Royal Triumph," 343 n. 16, noted the connection of this passage with royal lion hunting generally, that is, the similarity of Enkidu's activity here with that of a king as a lion hunter who protects his people.) Given that the hunter represents a late development in the story, it may be that originally this description of Enkidu served as a foreshadowing of Gilgamesh the royal hunter and that with the development of Gilgamesh's persona as a wanderer, the hunter was introduced in order to foreshadow that role. That the hunter of SB I may even now foreshadow both roles is perhaps suggested by the designation of the hunter by means of the hendiadys *ṣayyādu ḫābilu-amēlu* on his first appearance. Thenceforth he is simply referred to as a *ṣayyādu*.

11. In my judgment, the events of Tablet VI were not part of the original epic; see, e.g., my "Ishtar's Proposal," 179–83 [here, pp. 48–52].

12. The battle with the Bull of Heaven is not an animal hunt but a contest or even a combat sport against a power that has invaded the city of Uruk; the Bull's attack is comparable with an attack on a city by demons or an invasion of a settled area by wild animals. The battle with the Bull of Heaven seems to be in the tradition of the sport of bullfighting. Accordingly, I must disagree with Watanabe's contention (*Animal Symbolism*

and may even explain—the fact that the composer drew upon the Sumerian Gilgamesh and Huwawa tradition and utilized, or perhaps himself created, the developed form of that tradition in which the adventure had been transformed from an original expedition to cut down trees into a hunt for an evil cosmic creature.[13] D. O. Edzard has demonstrated that *Gilgamesh and Huwawa B* represents an earlier version of the Sumerian text than *Gilgamesh and Huwawa A*, and has argued convincingly that whereas in *Gilgamesh and Huwawa B* Gilgamesh perhaps even allowed Huwawa to live, *Gilgamesh and Huwawa A* has Gilgamesh defeat and

in Mesopotamia, 73–74) that the slaying of the Bull subsequent to the victory over Huwawa parallels Shalmaneser III's account of his having killed wild bulls after cutting down cedars in the Amanus mountains. (Of course, it is possible—though doubtful—that the Assyrian account was modeled on the Standard version of the epic.)

13. For the change of the purpose of the expedition from the Sumerian epic to the Akkadian, see, e.g., J. H. Tigay, *The Evolution of the Gilgamesh Epic* (Philadelphia: University of Pennsylvania Press, 1982) 79:

> It is noteworthy that the prominence of the intention to slay Huwawa in Gilgamesh and Enkidu's original discussions about the campaign is an innovation in the Old Babylonian version, and therefore deserving of attention; as we noted, in the Sumerian version Gilgamesh's intention was simply to travel to the Cedar Mountain and establish his name, with Huwawa figuring only as an obstacle who first appears when Gilgamesh and Enkidu have reached the mountain. In the Old Babylonian version, slaying Huwawa becomes the means by which Gilgamesh intends from the outset to establish his name.

There is no doubt that the defeat of Huwawa was the object of the quest in the OB Akkadian epic. But whether he had already been transformed into an embodiment of evil (*mimma lemnu*) in the OB epic is apparently open to some question. Some scholars believe that he was already treated as an evil being in the OB version; so, again, Tigay, for example:

> [A] fragmentary passage . . . can be restored on the basis of the late version: "fierce Huwawa we/I slay, and banish from the land what is baneful" (Gilg. Y. iii, 5–7, restored from *GE* III, ii, 17–18). . . . In the passage from Gilg. Y. just quoted, Huwawa appears as the personification of "what is baneful" (*mimma lemnu*). The late version characterizes "what is baneful" as "that which (Shamash) hates" (*GE* III, ii, 18). (ibid., 79)

Here Tigay and others follow the reading suggested by A. Schott, "Zu meiner Übersetzung des Gilgameš-Epos," *ZA* 42 (1934) 108; so, too, recently also, e.g., R. J. Tournay and A. Shaffer, *L'épopée de Gilgamesh* (Paris: Éditions du Cerf, 1994) 82 and n. 20, and apparently B. R. Foster in B. R. Foster et al., *The Epic of Gilgamesh* (New York: Norton, 2001) 18. On the other hand, George, *Gilgamesh Epic*, 208 ad iii 98–100, asserts that "The restorations proposed for these lines by Schott, *ZA* 42 (1934), p. 108, and followed by most translators, are too elaborate for the space available." But whether Huwawa was the embodiment of evil already in the OB version or only became so later (so III 52–54: *adi īkaššadu ana qišti erēni adi Ḫumbaba dāpinu inarru u mimma lemnu ša tazerru uḫallaq ina māti*) is of no consequence to our present discussion.

validate the killing of Huwawa.[14] In this regard, the later version, *Gilgamesh and Huwawa A,* agrees with and reflects the same tradition as the Akkadian epic.[15] Huwawa has been transformed; he has now become the object—and his defeat the objective—of the quest. Thus, perhaps, *Gilgamesh and Huwawa A* (under the influence of the Akkadian epic) and, certainly, the Akkadian Gilgamesh epic itself center upon the image of Gilgamesh as a hunter who seeks out and defeats a powerful enemy, one that is eventually transformed into a representation of evil.

The composer drew upon images, topoi, characters, and stories of hunting to create the present work, both as regards its framework and thematics. Given the place, then, of hunting in the Mesopotamian verbal and pictorial accounts of the deeds of the kings and in their self-descriptions, it comes as no surprise that an epic meant to provide the framework for the growth of a royal hero would be set in and draw upon a world of hunting—especially since hunting can provide the means to set out the various types of oppositions that characterize the epic and its main protagonist: e.g., nature vs. culture; the heroic vs. the mundane; human vs. god.

The Education of a Prince

The existence of an image of hunting, then, would explain the availability to the author of an image of the king leaving his populace and his everyday role and journeying into the wild. The composer's use of hunting imagery and his representation of Gilgamesh as a hunter may simply represent the use of a common, though certainly not trite, image of a Mesopotamian king in his presentation of Gilgamesh the king, and his account of the king's adventures.

14. D. O. Edzard, *"Gilgameš und Huwawa": Zwei Versionen der sumerischen Zedernwaldepisode nebst einer Edition von Version "B"* (Sitzungsberichte der Bayerische Akademie der Wissenschaften, Philosophisch-historische Klasse, 1993-94; Munich: C. H. Beck, 1993); see especially his discussion, pp. 11 and 53–59. Note that also J. Klein noted the existence in Šulgi O of a tradition according to which Gilgamesh spared Huwawa's life and led him before Enlil ("Šulgi and Gilgameš: Two Brother-Peers (Šulgi O)," in *Kramer Anniversary Volume: Cuneiform Studies in Honor of Samuel Noah Kramer* [ed. B. L. Eichler, J. W. Heimerdinger, and Å. W. Sjöberg; AOAT 25; Kevelaer: Butzon & Bercker, 1976], 271–92; see pp. 273, 280–81: lines 95–100; p. 291 ad lines 95–96, and p. 292 ad lines 98–99 and 100–101). In further support of Edzard's position, see A. Ganter (subsequently Zgoll), "Zum Ausgang von *Gilgameš und Huwawa* Version B," *NABU* 1995/2, no. 41 (pp. 35–36).

15. The relationship of the two is not certain. Most likely, the Akkadian epic tradition transformed Huwawa into the hunted and influenced the Sumerian tale (cf. Edzard, *"Gilgameš und Huwawa,"* 59), but it is not impossible that the development had already taken place in the Sumerian tale and the Akkadian epic derived the image therefrom.

But we may also ask whether the topos here is that of a hunter who is already a king or that of a prince who is being initiated and taught how to hunt. The education of a prince—including his education as a hunter—is a common theme in ancient and medieval literature. We need only point to Xenophon's *Cyropaedia.* To learn how to hunt is part of a prince's education, as are the goals of hunting: courage, skill, the protection of subjects, and the conquest of the other—be it in the form of undomesticated nature or foreign enemies. In this context, I recall also the remark by Xenophon in his *Cynegeticus* (*On Hunting*), I 18–II 1:

> Therefore I charge the young not to despise hunting or any other schooling. For these are the means by which men become good in war and in all things out of which must come excellence in thought and word and deed.
>
> The first pursuit, therefore, that a young man just out of his boyhood should take up is hunting, and afterwards he should go on to the other branches of education, provided he has means.[16]

Turning back to the epic, we would again emphasize not only the importance of hunting in the epic, but also the striking fact that in describing the life of a royal, the composer used not only the image of a royal hunter but also that of a marginal trapper. Gilgamesh's change and maturation come to expression in these two types of hunting experiences; that is, Gilgamesh's expedition against Huwawa in the mountain forests together with Enkidu and his trek through the wilderness subsequent to Enkidu's death provide the background and imagery for different stages in his actual and emotional growth. Thus, no less significant than the use of the image of hunting is the difference between the two major sections that deal with hunting and the pattern created when these two sections are joined.

To be sure, the presentation of the two hunting experiences serves the storyline—Gilgamesh's life before and after the demise of Enkidu. But it would not be unreasonable to imagine that a pattern of hunting underlay the literary structure that now serves to promote the growth of a hero and that this pattern reflects and was originally drawn from a real-life educational situation where a royal (and perhaps other members of the upper class) was first trained to hunt under the tutelage of a

16. Xenophon, *Scripta Minora* (trans. E. G. Marchant; LCL; London: Heinemann; Cambridge, MA: Harvard University Press, 1925) 373.

teacher and/or in the company of a companion and then sent out on his own into the wild to hunt and survive as best he could.[17]

Accordingly, I would speculate that while the epic now tells the story about the maturation of Gilgamesh the king, the use of the double pattern of hunting suggests and perhaps even supports the idea that in one of its early forms the epic may have had as one of its purposes the education of a prince, and would therefore have drawn upon materials that derive from the education of royalty. Of course, the prince need not have been Gilgamesh; this early account may have existed in oral form and would have told a story of the hunting experiences of a prince.

Thus, the story may simply have been an account of the education of a prince. But whatever its original intention, it would early have become a story of how a prince grows into the role of a king.

Moreover, my suggestion that the work was originally about the training of a prince[18] finds support in various aspects of the epic. Needless to say, it agrees with the emphasis of the epic on the expedition against Huwawa. And it explains some strange features of the work and agrees with some of the values emphasized therein. Regarding features, this suggestion that it is about a prince and not a king would explain the importance of Gilgamesh's mother in the work, and of Gilgamesh's preference for bonds of brotherhood and friendship over the hierarchical ones of ruler and subject. And the abdication by a reigning king of his responsibilities of office would come as no surprise if originally the work dealt with a crown prince and not a king. Moreover, the emphasis upon his callousness and arrogance vis-à-vis the population in Tablet I would be more than just plot motivators; they exemplify attitudes that may be characteristic of royal youngsters but which lead to failure in rulers. A similar instance occurs in Tablet II, when Gilgamesh attempts to exercise the *droit du seigneur*. Enkidu blocks the door and stops Gilgamesh, for while Gilgamesh may have had the right, it may well have been poor politics to exercise that right. Here, then, Enkidu begins to function as a tutor, a role he continues in the expedition to the Cedar Forest.

Regarding values, some of the values that are expressed in the work would agree with those appropriate to the training of a prince. Our royal protagonist is taught not only to overcome chaos but also to show

17. Though tempted, I desist from characterizing one and/or the other type of hunting experience as a reflection of rites of passage or trials and ceremonies of intiation.

18. I seem to remember Bill Moran referring many years ago in conversation to the epic as a work intended for the education of princes, but I do not recall, and probably never knew, his reasons for his belief.

respect for the citizenry and to heed the advice of his predecessors[19]—the queen mother and the elders of the community.

Further support for our argument that a story about a prince underlies the present epic is provided by the Ninurta mythology. The Ninurta epics, especially Anzu, exemplify the topos of a divine heroic warrior-prince who fights on behalf of a withdrawn or incapacitated divine king, his father, and is directly guided by a divine mother.[20] Similarities and connections between the *Epic of Gilgamesh* and Ninurta mythology have been previously noted.[21] The similarities suggest that both Ninurta and Gilgamesh operate in a similar social milieu, are at the same stage of life, and exercise similar responsibilities. Just as Ninurta was not yet king but functioned as a warrior for his father at the behest of his mother, so too the protagonist of the early form of the *Epic of Gilgamesh* was still a warrior-prince who depended upon and heeded his mother.[22]

At some point in the formation of the epic, its earlier form as an account of the education of a prince was superseded, and the hero was presented as Gilgamesh the king. As a consequence, some of the experiences, mistakes, and attributes of a prince learning to become a king were attributed to a character who is presented as if he were already king. This may be the source of some of the difficulties and tensions, but also of the drama that we find in the work.[23] By superimposing the expectations for a mature king on the behavior of a fledgling royal who is still learning his role, the topic of kingship is opened up and the composer is enabled to explore aspects and problems of kingship. Surely, this

19. I owe to Tali Ornan the observation that the epic teaches respect to the citizenry and elders.

20. Cf. M. E. Vogelzang, *Bin šar dadmē: Edition and Analysis of the Akkadian Anzu Poem* (Groningen: Styx, 1988) 170–76.

21. See, e.g., A. Annus, *The God Ninurta in the Mythology and Royal Ideology of Ancient Mesopotamia* (SAAS 14; Helsinki: Neo-Assyrian Text Corpus Project, 2002) 168–71.

22. Perhaps note, in addition, that just as the Ninurta myths are ultimately concerned with the ascension of the royal son to the throne and eventuate in Ninurta's assumption of kingship (Annus, *The God Ninurta*, passim; see, e.g., pp. 3–4, 121–23, and 171ff., and note, for example, his comments on p. 172 ["The main theme of Ninurta myths then ultimately unfolds as the royal succession"] and p. 122 ["After Ninurta returned from the battle as the avenger of his father, Enlil exalts him above himself. . . . The Ninurta narratives *Angim* and *Lugale* were undoubtedly used in the royal ceremonies celebrating the change in the status of the crown prince"]), so too the *Epic of Gilgamesh* deals with the training and experiences of a crown prince who is destined for kingship and eventuates in Gilgamesh's transformation and assumption of the identity and role of king.

23. To note the obvious: the character and story of Achilles in the *Iliad* are also driven by an internal conflict between the values and impulses of warrior and king.

dissonance contributed to the development of the tragic dimensions of the work. For the young Gilgamesh is transformed into a mature man and responsible king by means of the adventures he undertakes and the conflicts he endures as part of his education.

The Tale of the Wild Man and the Courtesan in India and Mesopotamia

The Seductions of Ṛśyaśṛṅga in the Mahābhārata *and Enkidu in the* Epic of Gilgamesh

Tzvi Abusch and
Emily West

1. *Introduction*

Elsewhere, the Akkadian account of the seduction of Enkidu by the courtesan in the *Epic of Gilgamesh* has been subjected to a detailed analysis and its stages of development traced.[1] The preserved versions, but especially a reconstructed earlier version that centered solely on the wild man and the courtesan and did not include the hunter, show strong resemblances to the Sanskrit story of the seduction of Ṛśyaśṛṅga as it is found in the *Mahābhārata* and, to a lesser degree, as it occurs in other compositions. Like Enkidu (in Tablets I–II of the Standard Babylonian version and the Pennsylvania tablet of the Old Babylonian version),[2]

Versions of this paper were read to the American Oriental Society in San Antonio in 2007, and to the Melammu conference in Sophia, Bulgaria, in 2008. The article was published in *The Ancient World in an Age of Globalization* (ed. M. J. Geller; Melammu Symposia 6; Berlin: Max-Planck-Gesellschaft zur Förderung der Wissenschaften, 2014) 69–109. Some typographical and formatting errors that impaired the readability of that version have been corrected; accordingly, we wish this version to supersede the earlier version.

1. T. Abusch, "The Courtesan, the Wild Man, and the Hunter: Studies in the Literary History of the *Epic of Gilgamesh*," in *"An Experienced Scribe Who Neglects Nothing": Ancient Near Eastern Studies in Honor of Jacob Klein* (ed. Y. Sefati et al.; Bethesda, MD: CDL Press, 2005) 413–33 [here, pp. 144–65].

2. We wish to call attention to two works that we were not able to incorporate into our argument. One is Y. V. Vas[s]ilkov, "Zemledel'českij mif v drevneindijskom epose: Skazanie o Riš'jašringe," in *Literatura i kultura drevnej i srednevekovoj Indii* (Moscow: Nauka, 1979), an article that we were unable to obtain. The other is D. E. Fleming and S. J. Milstein, *The Buried Foundation of the Gilgamesh Epic: The Akkadian Huwawa Narrative* (CM 39; Leiden: Brill, 2010), which appeared only after we submitted this paper. We should mention, however, two aspects of their discussion that are relevant to the present work: the first is their argument that a distinction be drawn between the Enkidu of the OB Penn tablet // SB Tablets I–II (who is a wild man), on the one hand, and the Enkidu of the Huwawa episode of the OB Yale tablet // SB Tablets III–IV (who is a herdsman), on the other. This distinction, which we find persuasive, does not affect our present argument, for our wild man corresponds in the main to the character of the wild man

Ṛśyaśṛṅga is an unworldly innocent with animal characteristics who, as a result of a crisis in the civilized world, must be tamed and civilized by a prostitute and brought to the city to take a position of power beside the king. The strong resemblance of the Ṛśyaśṛṅga account to the Enkidu story has been previously noticed. Some scholars have even suggested the dependence of the Indian versions upon the Near Eastern account.[3]

Throughout the last century there have been scholars who have regarded the remarkable similarity between the two episodes as ample justification for the belief in a connection between the two tales. But in some scholarly circles, parallels are viewed with skepticism, and the

found in that part of the epic that comes before the Huwawa episode. Furthermore, in composing our study we were already aware of some of the tensions between the parts (see Abusch, "Courtesan," 430–33 [here, pp. 161–65]). The second is their contention that the superimposition of the story of the wild man and prostitute (found in the Penn tablet) upon the story of the prostitute and the herdsman (found in the Yale tablet) is responsible for the creation of the first part of the OB epic. For the significance of this point for our argument, see below, n. 62.

3. This opinion was first expressed by P. Jensen in a review of A. Ungnad and H. Gressmann, *Das Gilgamesch-Epos*, *ZDMG* 67 (1913) 528:

> Edvard Lehmann hat Greßmann auf die Analogie zwischen der indischen Geschichte von *Ṛśyaśṛṅga* und der "Hierodulen"-Episode des *Gilgamesch*-Epos aufmerksam gemacht und Greßmann erwähnt dies auf S. 95 seines Buchs. Weder Lehmann noch Greßmann denken natürlich an mehr als eine bloße Analogie . . . obwohl die Analogie zwischen beiden Episoden schon allein für sich eine historische Abhängigkeit doch wohl mehr als nahelegt. Greßmann's Anmerkung mußte mich nun aber dazu veranlassen, die *Ṛśyaśṛṅga*-Geschichte ins Auge zu fassen. Und das Ergebnis war: Auch die indische *Rāmāyaṇa*-Sage, durch die *Ṛśyaśṛṅga*-Geschichte eröffnet, geht in der Hauptsache letztlich auf das *Gilgamesch*-Epos mit der "Hierodulen"-Episode in seinem Anfangsteil zurück, ebenso aber vor allem diejenigen Stücke des *Mahābhārata*, die diesem mit dem *Rāmāyaṇa* gemein sind.

See also, e.g., W. F. Albright, "Gilgames and Engidu, Mesopotamian Genii of Fecundity," *JAOS* 40 (1920) 331 ("But it is very probable that our story goes back eventually to a Mesopotamian origin; in no other case that I have seen is the likelihood so great"); C. A. Williams, *Oriental Affinities of the Legend of the Hairy Anchorite*, parts 1–2 (2 vols.; UISLL 10.2, 11.4; Urbana: University of Illinois Press, 1925–26) 1:30–31; D. Schlinghoff, "Die Einhorn-Legende," *Christiana Albertina: Forschungen und Berichte aus der Christian-Albrechts-Universität zu Kiel* (1971) 58–60 (our thanks to Oskar von Hinüber for this reference); idem, "The Unicorn: Origin and Migrations of an Indian Legend," in *German Scholars on India: Contributions to Indian Studies* (ed. Cultural Dept. of the Embassy of the Federal Republic of Germany; New Delhi: Chowkhamba Sanskrit Series Office, 1973) 303–5; A. Panaino, "Between Mesopotamia and India: Some Remarks about the Unicorn Cycle in Iran," in *Mythology and Mythologies: Methodological Approaches to Intercultural Influences. Proceedings of the Second Annual Symposium of the Assyrian and Babylonian Intellectual Heritage Project Held in Paris, October 4–7, 1999* (ed. R. M. Whiting; Melammu Symposia 2; Helsinki: Neo-Assyrian Text Corpus, 2001) 152–53, 170. Also cf. Abusch, "Courtesan," 425 n. 23 [here, p. 156 n. 23].

existence of any form of connection may even be denied. We therefore feel it is necessary to revisit the topic of the relationship of the Babylonian and the Indian accounts. To this end, we will first describe the two tales and set out a précis of our understanding of the development of the Ṛśyaśṛṅga tale. This will be followed by several detailed treatments: (1) an identification and explication of points of similarity between the Enkidu and Ṛśyaśṛṅga tales; (2) an analysis of the many variants of the Ṛśyaśṛṅga tale that may be found throughout the literature of India, evaluating the various narratives for evidence regarding the development of these variants to determine which of them may represent the earliest phase of the tale; and (3) a reconstruction of the stages of development of the *Mahābhārata* tale itself, which we believe to be the earliest recorded Indic version. Finally, we set out our understanding of the relationship of the Indian and the Mesopotamian tales. We hope to contribute to an understanding of the Sanskrit tale and its evolution and to explore the cultural and historical implications of a connection between the Near Eastern and Indian tales.

2. *The Story of Enkidu*

The *Epic of Gilgamesh* is an ancient Mesopotamian account of the deeds and struggles of Gilgamesh, a king of the city-state Uruk in the land of Sumer. This Akkadian epic was probably originally composed during (but certainly no later than) the Old Babylonian period, some time around the eighteenth century B.C.E.; the later standard version comes to us in a twelve-tablet format.[4]

The epic recounts how Gilgamesh, king of Uruk, exhausts his subjects by his unceasing demands upon them to participate in a constant round of activities. The people complain to the gods, who realize that Gilgamesh's enormous energy must find a different channel. To relieve the people, the gods create Enkidu, a wild man whose strength is equal to that of Gilgamesh, to serve as a companion who can be Gilgamesh's equal in the various activities that he is driven to undertake. Enkidu is humanized by a prostitute, who then acculturates him and leads him to Uruk. There, Enkidu prevents Gilgamesh from participating in a wedding ritual. Gilgamesh and Enkidu then do battle and, as a result, become

4. The transcriptions of the Akkadian text of the Old Babylonian (OB) and Standard Babylonian (SB) versions of the *Epic of Gilgamesh* are based upon the transliterated text in A. R. George, *The Babylonian Gilgamesh Epic: Introduction, Critical Edition, and Cuneiform Texts* (2 vols.; Oxford: Oxford University Press, 2003); the translations are his as well.

fast friends. The two friends undertake adventures (most notably, and originally, an expedition against Huwawa in the Cedar Forest) that cause them to run up against the will of the gods. The gods decide that Enkidu must bear the punishment for the friends' acts of hubris. Enkidu dies, but Gilgamesh cannot accept the death of his companion. He is devastated by Enkidu's death, both because of the grievous loss of his dearest friend and because he now fears his own death mightily. He leaves Uruk and travels the world in search of immortality. In the twelve-tablet version, Gilgamesh's quest is defined as a search for the secret of immortality held by Utnapishtim, the hero who survived the Flood and was granted immortality by the gods. When Gilgamesh reaches Utnapishtim, the latter disabuses him of his illusion, demonstrating by story (the account of the Flood) and by action (a test of Gilgamesh's ability to remain awake, a test that he fails) that immortality is no longer attainable, even by Gilgamesh. Tablet XI ends with Gilgamesh's return to Uruk, whereupon he signals his acceptance of reality by pointing out to the boatman the architectural wonders of the city that he had built.[5]

The tale of the wild man and courtesan is known in both Old Babylonian and Standard Babylonian versions.[6] The episode as told in the first tablet of the Standard Babylonian version runs as follows: In response to the complaint of the people of Uruk against Gilgamesh, the gods create Enkidu, a powerful wild man, to engage Gilgamesh and thereby provide relief to the populace. He roams with the animals and feeds with them. He frustrates a hunter's attempts to catch animals. The hunter's father advises him to go to Uruk and to take a courtesan from there to seduce the wild man, thereby causing the animals to reject him. The hunter goes to Uruk and is given the same advice by Gilgamesh. He then leads the courtesan Shamhat to the wild. Upon the appearance of Enkidu, he tells the courtesan what steps to take in order to seduce Enkidu. She successfully carries out her mission. They have intercourse for a week; afterwards Enkidu tries to return to the animals, but they reject him. He returns to the courtesan, who advises him to accompany her to civilization. She leads him to Uruk, where he and Gilgamesh meet and become fast friends.

---

5. Tablet XII contains the end of a different account of Enkidu's death. On an errand for Gilgamesh, Enkidu descends into the netherworld. He is seized by the netherworld and cannot escape death; he returns only as a shade in order to describe to Gilgamesh the state of the dead.

6. The episode is now also known from a tablet provisionally dated to the beginning of the Middle Babylonian period; see A. R. George, "The Civilizing of Ea-Enkidu: An Unusual Tablet of the Babylonian Gilgameš Epic," *RA* 101 (2007) 59–80; for the dating, see p. 63.

Unfortunately, this episode is only partially preserved in the Old Babylonian version. But even so, we can establish that in that version the wild man did not attempt to rejoin the animals after his sexual encounter with the courtesan;[7] for in that version, after their lovemaking, the courtesan asks Enkidu why he wants to go back to nature, and in fact he does not. It is not the animals that reject Enkidu; rather, it is Enkidu who immediately turns his back on nature as a consequence of his experience with an urbane woman. He rejected the natural world in favor of civilization, for lovemaking caused him to forget the place of his birth. Animals are unimportant in this early recension, as is apparently the hunter, if he even appears.[8] The absence of the hunter in the earliest forms of the tale is important and will be referred to again later.

3. The Tale of Ṛśyaśṛṅga in the Mahābhārata

We will now discuss the tale as it occurs in the *Mahābhārata*, in the epic's third section, the "Book of the Forest Teachings."[9] This book details part of the thirteen-year period of exile undergone by the heroes of the epic, the five Pāṇḍava princes and their joint wife, Draupadī. Having lost their kingdom through treachery at the dicing table, they leave their palace, allies, and children behind and resign themselves to a period of forest-dwelling asceticism. Exile is a devastating blow, but the heroes spend comparatively little time in recrimination. They turn instead to spiritual betterment, most notably in the form of a tour of various sacred bathing areas (*tīrthas*), and the epic itself turns to "the manifold narratives to which their sojourn in the forest gives occasion."[10] As the heroes make their tour, they are regaled with the stories associated with each *tīrtha*.

One of these is the "Story of Ṛśyaśṛṅga," narrated at *MBh.* 3.110–113.[11] The tale runs essentially as follows: A fearsome ascetic, Vibhāṇḍaka, is bathing in a lake when the sight of a celestial nymph causes him to

7. As far as we can see, nothing in the new "Middle Babylonian" version (cited above, n. 6) contradicts this statement.

8. Abusch, "Courtesan," 422–25 [here, pp. 153–56].

9. In regard to the *Mahābhārata*, all passages cited here are from the Critical Edition, *The Āraṇyakaparvan*, parts 1–2 = *The Mahābhārata*, vols. 3–4 (ed. V. S. Sukthankar; Poona: Bhandarkar Oriental Research Institute, 1942), and all translations are E.B.W.'s. In regard to the composition of the epic, we concur with others that the epic was assembled slowly over an extended period, roughly between 400 B.C.E. and 400 C.E.; see J. A. B. van Buitenen, *The Mahābhārata*, vols. 1–2 (Chicago: University of Chicago Press, 1973–75) 1:xxv; or J. Brockington, "The Sanskrit Epics," in *The Blackwell Companion to Hinduism* (ed. G. D. Flood; Oxford: Blackwell, 2003) 116.

10. Van Buitenen, *Mahābhārata*, 2:174.

11. A complete translation of the Ṛśyaśṛṅga episode may be found in van Buitenen, *Mahābhārata*, 2:431–441.

spontaneously ejaculate. The semen is consumed by a doe that subsequently gives birth to a human son. The boy, Ṛśyaśṛṅga, is born with an antelope horn in the middle of his forehead and is raised in the hermitage. The young ascetic's innocent life is disrupted when King Lomapāda of Aṅga commits unspecified atrocities that result in the desertion of his brahmins (including his *purohita*, the household priest) and in a subsequent falling out with the gods. On the advice of a different brahmin, Lomapāda decides to bring Ṛśyaśṛṅga to the court as his new *purohita*. Devising a plan to have the youth seduced by prostitutes, he finds a procuress willing to undertake the scheme and sends her to the hermitage on an elaborately equipped barge. When Vibhāṇḍaka leaves the hermitage to gather food, the procuress sends in an attractively dressed courtesan, who is mistaken by the boy for a fellow ascetic. Ṛśyaśṛṅga is so unworldly that he does not even understand that the prostitute is a woman but is enchanted by her very different "ascetic practices" and by the delicious food and liquor with which she plies him. The innocent boy quickly falls desperately in love with her, but she slips away to her barge before Vibhāṇḍaka comes home. Upon his return, Vibhāṇḍaka gives Ṛśyaśṛṅga stern warnings against women. But when the courtesan makes a second visit, the boy begs to go away with her. The prostitutes take Ṛśyaśṛṅga away on their barge and deliver him to the king, who installs him in the royal harem and gives him his daughter Śāntā in marriage. When the father discovers that his son has decamped to the palace, he follows the boy with the intention of burning the king and all his subjects by means of the power of his *tapas* (ascetic practices, often called "austerities"). King Lomapāda, however, is able to avert disaster by instructing the herdsmen along Vibhāṇḍaka's path to plow up the roads in order to obstruct his progress and to inform him that all the lands and herds along the way now belong to Ṛśyaśṛṅga. By the time Vibhāṇḍaka reaches the city and meets his new daughter-in-law, he is pleased and malleable, and the tale ends happily for all concerned.

The above retelling, however, only describes the central portion of the tale as it occurs in the epic. This central portion is that part found at *MBh.* 3.110.30–113.10 and is hereafter referred to as the "body" of the piece.[12] Appended to the front of the tale is a brief preamble (*MBh.* 3.110.1–10) in which the narrator, Lomaśa, attempts to loosely summa-

12. It is the narrative contained in the body of the *Mahābhārata*'s tale of Ṛśyaśṛṅga to which we refer whenever we discuss the *Mahābhārata*'s version in general terms. See below, §11, "Narrative Layers in the *Mahābhārata*," for our division and characterization of the sections of the final text.

rize the story and the eldest Pāṇḍava brother, Yudhiṣṭhira, responds with a set of leading questions. The relationship of the preamble to the rest of the *Mahābhārata*'s narrative will be discussed below in §10, "Internal Analysis of the *Mahābhārata*'s Ṛśyaśṛṅga Account."

4. *Anomalies in the Tale of Ṛśyaśṛṅga*

At the end of the nineteenth century, Heinrich Lüders attempted to explain a number of puzzling anomalies in the "Story of Ṛśyaśṛṅga," as narrated at *MBh.* 3.110–113.[13] The body of the narrative, as we have sketched it out above, is quite straightforward, but a closer study of the body in conjunction with the preamble reveals a number of irregularities and contradictions; body and preamble simply do not seem to refer to the same story. Lüders carefully analyzed various versions of the tale for comparison and concluded that the discrepancies in the *Mahābhārata* were the result of a series of editorial reworkings performed to align the *Mahābhārata*'s version with certain other variants. Though the preamble introduces a number of details or motifs that do not agree with the body of the tale, Lüders emphasized one particular issue: where the body describes Ṛśyaśṛṅga's seduction by the prostitute and subsequent marriage to a princess, the preamble states quite clearly that it was the princess who first seduced him and makes no mention of a prostitute. To solve the problem of this contradiction, Lüders envisioned a three-stage process of development in which: (1) The *Mahābhārata* originally had a version that featured princess Śāntā as the seductress; (2) the Bengali Recension of the *Padma Purāṇa* added the role of the prostitute in order to spare an innocent princess from the shame of being a seductress; (3) finally, a later redactor of the *Mahābhārata*, familiar with the *Padma Purāṇa*'s version, altered the body of the *Mahābhārata,* but neglected to change the opening verses.[14] While this solution has apparently been accepted by some,[15] others have felt that the idea is unnecessarily cumbersome and that Lüders' reasoning is unsound at a number of points.[16]

---

13. H. Lüders, "Die Sage von Ṛśyaśṛṅga," *Nachrichten der Akademie der Wissenschaften in Göttingen, Philologisch-historische Klasse* (1897) 87–135.

14. Ibid., 100–4.

15. Cf., e.g., M. Winternitz, *A History of Indian Literature* (3 vols.; Calcutta: University of Calcutta Press, 1962) 1:351–53.

16. J. Dahlmann disagreed strongly with Lüders' method for tracing the history of the story (*Die Genesis des Mahābhārata* [Berlin: Felix L. Dames, 1899] 283–87). Later scholars who present arguments against Lüders' conclusions about the nature of the original story include Panaino, "Between Mesopotamia"; E. Pauly, "The Legend of

While we concur with Lüders on the importance of the preamble/body textual problem, we do not accept his conclusions regarding the story's developmental trajectory. Lüders regarded the identity of the seductress as the primary key to understanding the evolution of the tale, a bias that, in our view, severely limited his ability to take other even more significant disparities between preamble and body into account, disparities regarding, *inter alia*, the power of Ṛśyaśṛṅga, the righteousness of King Lomapāda, the god Indra's fear of Ṛśyaśṛṅga, the nature of Ṛśyaśṛṅga's actions in ending the drought, whether Ṛśyaśṛṅga "lived as a deer," and details of his conception (each of these points will be discussed in detail below). While the preamble addresses some motifs not utterly dissimilar to those in the body of the tale, it is our contention that the preamble was initially created for a different story about a character named Ṛśyaśṛṅga.[17] This figure, Ṛśyaśṛṅga, the son of Vibhāṇḍaka, is known from quite early Hindu sources, including the *Jaiminīya Upaniṣad Brāhmaṇa* (III 40), the *Vaṃśabrāhmaṇa* (2), and the *Ārṣeyabrāhmaṇa* (VI 5).[18] In our view, the form of the Ṛśyaśṛṅga tale that originally occupied this spot in the *Mahābhārata* was a standard variation of the myriad of tales concerning the irascible *ṛṣi*s ("seers," ascetic holy men) and their conflicts with kings and gods. A vestige of this tale remains at the beginning and end of the Ṛśyaśṛṅga story that is found in the epic, in the accounts of Ṛśyaśṛṅga's conception and of Vibhāṇḍaka's appeased wrath. But the body of the tale is, in our opinion, a transplant or borrowing that derives from outside the subcontinent, and it is this possibility that we would like to explore here.

We believe that at some early point in history the Mesopotamian tale of Enkidu (or, more precisely, the Mesopotamian tale of a wild man and courtesan) passed into India and began to circulate in a Hindu milieu. Perhaps because of Enkidu's animal characteristics and his association with antelope, the story was eventually attached to the preexisting character of Ṛśyaśṛṅga and incorporated into the *Mahābhārata*, though with some contradictions remaining between the transplanted tale and the preexisting preamble to which it was attached. Eventually this new

Ṛśyaśṛṅga as a Danish Opera," *Indologica Taurinensia* 14 (1987–88) 303–12; Schlinghoff, "Unicorn"; and Williams, *Oriental Affinities*, 1:34.

17. Thus we agree with Lüders regarding the originality of the preamble; however, in contrast to Lüders, who sees the *Mahābhārata* tale as essentially a coherent whole that underwent a few contradictory revisions, we maintain that the present body of the tale (*MBh.* 3.110.30–113.10) is a later addition.

18. These are listed by Lüders as well ("Sage," 1).

composite tale, whether directly from the *Mahābhārata* or at some remove, began a second life in India, where the long-standing tradition of oral composition and verbatim preservation and recitation allowed wide circulation of stories without the use of written texts. The story was apparently able to circulate widely and underwent various modifications as it was taken up by different religious and cultural communities. Thus, in later versions, numerous variations were introduced regarding the number of seductions in the tale, the nature of the crisis at the center of the plot, the name and nature of Ṛśyaśṛṅga himself, and the nature of the transformation that seduction effects in him.[19]

Our solution to the mystery of the mismatched preamble differs, therefore, from that of Lüders. Whereas we believe that the present tale of Ṛśyaśṛṅga was created by the superimposition of a Near Eastern borrowing upon an earlier Indian story with native subcontinental or Indo-European roots, he envisioned a multistep process of revision and redaction. First, we do not think that his line of argumentation takes account of the dramatic similarity of the *Mahābhārata* to the Enkidu tale, which similarity others have found so compelling as well.[20] Moreover, it seems to us that a redactor setting out to harmonize the *Mahābhārata* with the *Padma Purāṇa* would also have rewritten our preamble to bring it in line with the body of the tale. Lüders' redactor is mainly concerned with harmonizing; our redactor, on the other hand, is mainly concerned with bringing in new material—for him, harmonization would have been a secondary goal. Furthermore, while we agree with Lüders that a princess was probably the love interest in the earliest tale to occupy this spot in the *Mahābhārata*, we do not subscribe to the view that the original princess played a role functionally equivalent to that of the prostitute in the *Mahābhārata*'s tale; rather, in that tale she was simply a young woman with whom Ṛśyaśṛṅga fell in love. This and other more detailed pieces

19. The Ṛśyaśṛṅga tale as it occurs in the *Mahābhārata* may not be the direct progenitor of other variants of the tale in India, but we believe it to be the earliest version of the tale of the seduction of the wild man in India for two reasons: (1) because the other tales all contain elements that appear to be alterations of the *Mahābhārata*'s version, and (2) the *Mahābhārata* contains the evidence of superimposition. For further analysis of the variations in the tales, see E. B. West, "The Transformation of Ṛśyaśṛṅga: Toward a Comparative Approach," in *Gazing on the Deep: Ancient Near Eastern and Other Studies in Honor of Tzvi Abusch* (ed. J. Stackert, B. N. Porter, and D. P. Wright; Bethesda, MD: CDL Press, 2010) 637–62.

20. In 1897, when Lüders published "Die Sage von Ṛśyaśṛṅga," the story of Enkidu and the prostitute might not yet have been widely known, but the story had been translated and retold, for example, in A. Jeremias, *Izdubar-Nimrod: Eine altbabylonische Heldensage, nach den Keilschriftfragmenten Darstellt* (Leipzig: B. G. Teubner, 1891) 16–18.

of evidence will be examined below in context, beginning with our assessment of the shared features of the Indian and Mesopotamian tales.

5. Parallel Elements in the Stories of Enkidu and Ṛśyaśṛṅga

We note the following fourteen parallel elements in the two texts. These elements suggest the existence of a relationship between the two episodes. While many tales may share common elements and themes, these stories are composed of nearly identical sets of motifs that form the fundamental building blocks of both tales. Even more significant is the fact that this set of motifs is a heterogeneous collection in that the individual motifs generally do not lead inevitably to the ones that follow them. Thus, their appearance *en masse* in two otherwise unrelated traditions strains the likelihood of coincidence.

A. The Wild Man's Miraculous Birth. Both wild men are the product of miraculous births, and both births are "typical" within their respective canons. Enkidu is created by Aruru from a pinch of clay, just as the first humans were created. Ṛśyaśṛṅga is conceived when the hermit Vibhāṇḍaka has a spontaneous ejaculation at the sight of Urvaśī, a prominent celestial nymph (*apsaras*), and the ejaculate is consumed by a doe that becomes pregnant with Vibhāṇḍaka's child. These two types of birth are thus functionally equivalent, for in Indian literature an ascetic's spontaneous ejaculation is a common mechanism employed to mark out a birth as unusual or auspicious[21] and would be a natural substitution for a motif of birth by divine creation imported from another tradition.

B. The Wild Man Has an Animal Appearance. Both wild men are represented as being a combination of animal and human and as having a connection to wild deer.[22] Enkidu's animal nature is reflected in his hairiness and in the fact that he lives with the gazelle herds and protects them. Using excessive hairiness as the defining characteristic of a wild man would be problematic within the *Mahābhārata* tradition, at least as a distinguishing trait, for long matted hair is a standard characteristic of

21. See, for example, the similar conceptions of Satyavatī (*MBh.* 1.57), Agastya and Vasiṣṭha (*Matsya Purāṇa* 61, 20–32), Droṇa (*MBh.* 1.121), and Kṛpa (*MBh.* 1.120).

22. In this section, we refer to Ṛśyaśṛṅga's animal characteristics as they are portrayed in the body of the tale, not to the use of *mṛgabhūtasya* in the preamble at 3.110.8. As stated in §10.E, "Ṛśyaśṛṅga's Life as a Deer," we believe the use of *mṛgabhūtasya* in the preamble relates to the class of tales within the *Mahābhārata* in which an *ṛṣi* assumes, or appears to assume, the form of a deer. *Ṛṣi*s with animal characteristics such as those exhibited by Ṛśyaśṛṅga in the body of his tale are not a standard type in the epic (cf. *MBh.* 1.109), supporting the idea that his animal-*ṛṣi* character is largely a borrowing from elsewhere.

many holy men,[23] as is suggested by the name of the ascetic who escorts them around the sacred fords and narrates the story to them (Lomaśa, "Hairy") and by the description of Vibhāṇḍaka at *MBh.* 3.111.19 as "covered with hair to his nail-tips" (*praveṣṭito romabhirā nakhāgrāt*).[24] Instead, Ṛśyaśṛṅga's animal origin is exhibited by the antelope horn he wears on his head, *tasya ṛśyaśṛṅgam śirasi* (*MBh.* 3.110.17).[25]

C. The Plot Precipitated by the Actions of a Hubristic King. Though they are a part of the natural world, the wild men are actually linked to the human social order. In both narratives, the wild man's very existence, certainly his role, is necessitated by a crisis brought about by offenses on the part of the king. Both stories preserve a similar ambiguity regarding the king's character and manner of rule. The significance of this parallel is deepened by the fact that both kings are eventually rehabilitated.

D. The King's Offenses Are Unclear and Possibly Sexual. In both narratives, the nature of the king's misdeeds is obscure. As noted above, in the Sanskrit we are told that *tena kāmaḥ kṛto mithyā brāhmaṇebhya iti śrutiḥ*, "the report is that [Lomapāda] improperly forced his desires on the brahmins" (*MBh.* 3.110.20), an ambiguous statement that could be understood to have sexual overtones. *Kāma*, 'desire', has obvious and well-known sexual overtones, but it is also frequently used in more innocent contexts, especially with the verbal root *kṛ*-. Similarly, the adverb *mithyā*, 'wrongly, improperly', in itself is not necessarily sexual, but the *mith*- root from which it is derived carries a wide variety of aggressive and sexual connotations. The combination of the *mith*- root and *kāma* in such proximity suggests that the two may (at least at one point) have added up to more than the sum of their parts, with the implication that the king may have sexually mistreated his priests. Such an action would be close to unthinkable within the *Mahābhārata*. The text is willing to discuss many questionable acts, but male rape is outside its pale. We suggest that *MBh.* 3.110.20 either attempts to blur or gloss over a piece of

---

23. Cf., e.g., the terrifying matted hair of Vyāsa at *MBh.* 1.100.5.

24. Williams also finds Vibhāṇḍaka's hairiness provocative, and reaches conclusions similar to ours: "That there should be *two* beast-men, father and son, in this legend seems at first peculiar. They may indicate a coalescing of two traditions, or rather the development of an original story of the seduction of a partly beast-like hero of fertility into a legend containing two hermits" (*Oriental Affinities*, 1:33).

25. Remnants of the motif of hairiness may exist elsewhere in the tale, however. The name of the Sanskrit story's king, Lomapāda, "he whose feet are covered in body hair," is somewhat suggestive, though certainly not definitive. We observe here, in anticipation of later discussion, that nearly all of these references to animal characteristics are lost in other versions of the tale.

the story that the editors felt they were unable to report fully but were reluctant to omit entirely, or, more likely, preserves a faint linguistic vestige of the story's past.

The account of Gilgamesh's offense is equally cloudy. Is it simply that he is demanding of his subjects that they devote themselves completely to his athletic or building activities, or is he making excessive sexual demands on them? It is likely that this ambiguity reflects a development in the text: apparently the description of Gilgamesh's "oppression" of his people in the epic is modeled on the Sumerian *Gilgamesh, Enkidu, and the Netherworld*, where Gilgamesh and his people seem to be fully engaged in athletic activities;[26] subsequently, in the epic the situation was changed to one where Gilgamesh's demands were no longer athletic but seem to have been sexual. But this new orientation—at least in our presently fragmented text—has not yet been articulated clearly.

E. The King's Offenses Require the Intervention of the Gods. In both tales, the king's actions have cosmic repercussions. Lomapāda's misbehavior angers the gods and causes them to withhold the rains, leading to the suffering of his people. As for Gilgamesh, his tyranny becomes oppressive to the point that his people cry out to the gods; thus, the gods become involved and ask Aruru to create Enkidu.

F. The Wild Man Is an Innocent. In direct contrast to the king, the wild man is innocence personified. Not only is he ignorant of sexual matters, he is entirely without political consciousness. Enkidu lives among the animal herds and is completely unfamiliar with fundamental characteristics of human life:

> *[š]u''ur šārta kalu zumrišu*
> *uppuš pēretu kīma sinništi*
> *itqī*[!27] *pērtišu uḫtannabā kīma* ᵈ*Nissaba*
> *lā īde nišī u mātamma*
> *lubušti labiš kīma* ᵈ*Šakkan*
> *itti ṣabâtimma ikkala šammī*

26. For the athletic activities in *Gilgamesh, Enkidu, and the Netherworld*, see, e.g., J. Klein, "A New Look at the 'Oppression of Uruk' Episode in the Gilgameš Epic," in *Riches Hidden in Secret Places: Ancient Near Eastern Studies in Memory of Thorkild Jacobsen* (ed. T. Abusch; Winona Lake, IN: Eisenbrauns, 2002) 187–201. These activities are no longer evident in the Akkadian, where instead such lines as SB Tablet I 76–77 suggest that his demands are sexual. This would agree with the nature of the situation that occasioned the encounter and battle of Gilgamesh and Enkidu (SB Tablet II 100–115, OB P cols. iv–vi).

27. Text: *itiq*; cf. I 60.

itti būli mašqâ itepper
itti nammaššê mê iṭâb[28] *libbašu*
Gilgamesh SB Tablet I 105–112

All his body is matted with hair,
he is adorned with tresses like a woman:
The locks of his hair grow as thickly as Nissaba's,
he knows not at all a people nor even a country.
He was clad in a garment like Šakkan's,
feeding on grass with the very gazelles.
Jostling at the water-hole with the herd,
he enjoys the water with the animals.[29]

Similarly, Ṛśyaśṛṅga lives a simple existence in the forest. The text mainly emphasizes his state of perfect and uncompromised celibacy:

na tena dṛṣṭapūrvo 'nyaḥ pitur anyatra mānuṣaḥ
tasmāt tasya mano nityaṃ brahmacarye 'bhavan nṛpa.
MBh. 3.110.18

He had never before seen any other person than his father
and because of this, his mind was always that of a *brahmacārin*,
Oh King.

Ṛśyaśṛṅga's innocence is so profound that he is not even aware that the courtesan is female: his subsequent lengthy description of her to Vibhāṇḍaka presumes, to comic effect, that she is male:

dvau cāsya piṇḍāvadhareṇa kaṇṭham
majātaromau sumanoharau ca.
vilagnamadhyaśca sa nābhideśe
kaṭiśca tasyātikṛtapramāṇā.
MBh. 3.112.3–4

And he had two round globes below his throat,
hairless and charming.

28. Others *iṭīb*. W. von Soden and W. Röllig retracted the value *ṭàb* for DAB, which von Soden had earlier based on our text (*Das akkadische Syllabar* [4th ed.; Rome: Pontificio Istituto Biblico, 1991] 18* s. 293); however, because of the durative forms in the preceding lines, we believe that von Soden was right to have read *iṭâb* in our passage ("Beiträge zum Verständnis des babylonischen Gilgameš-Epos," *ZA* 53 [1959] 222, and p. 58, s. 293 of the original *Syllabar*), in spite of the variant *i-ṭi-bu* in the parallel lines of SB Tablet I 173 and 177. Note that in the translation we have replaced George's "enjoyed" with "enjoys."

29. Cf. George, *Gilgamesh Epic*, 545.

And he was slender-waisted in the region of his navel,
 and his hips were exaggerated in size.

G. *The King Arranges for a Courtesan to Seduce the Wild Man.* The hallmark of both tales, the sexual seduction of the wild man by the courtesan, is carried out at the suggestion of the beleaguered kings. In both cases, the creature's transformation from animal to human is accomplished by means of arousing his sexual interest. In the Ṛśyaśṛṅga story, the courtesan knows her task is accomplished when she sees that he has been *vikṛtam*, 'transfigured, changed', by her attentions (*MBh.* 3.111.17). In the *Epic of Gilgamesh*, the wild man is dramatically changed by the sexual encounter—in the SB version, the change is both physical and mental: "Enkidu was diminished, his running was not as before, but he had *reason*, he [was] wide of understanding";[30] in the OB version, his definition of his place in the world has changed: "The two of them were making love together, he forgot the wild where he was born."[31]

H. *The Seduction Occurs Adjacent to Water.* Both seduction scenes take place beside a body of water. Enkidu is first spotted by the hunter, and later seduced by Shamhat, at the water hole to which he accompanies the herds. In the *Mahābhārata*, Vibhāṇḍaka's hermitage is on the shore of a great lake (*mahāhrada*, possibly the lake's proper name, 3.110.12, 13), in which he is bathing when Ṛśyaśṛṅga is conceived. The seduction of Ṛśyaśṛṅga by the prostitute (*veśyā*) takes place there. Moreover, a barge specially equipped for the prostitutes serves as a blind from which the *veśyā* approaches her quarry and on which she carries him off.

I. *The Transformation Is Cultural as Well as Sexual.* Once existentially transformed, Enkidu is then led to a camp of shepherds where he is introduced to the ways of human society:

akalam iškunū maḫaršu
iptēqma inaṭṭal u ippallas
ul īde ^{d}Enkidu akalam ana akālim
šikaram ana šatêm lā lummud
ḫarīmtum pīša īpušamma
issaqqaram ana ^{d}Enkidu
akul aklam ^{d}Enkidu simat balāṭim
šikaram šiti šīmti māti

30. SB Tablet I 201–202: *umtaṭṭu ^{d}Enk[idu u]l kī ša pāni lasānšu / u šū īši ṭ[ēma r]apaš ḫasīsa* (Translation: George, *Gilgamesh Epic*, 551).

31. OB P col. ii 46–47: *ur[ta'']amū kilallūn / ṣēram imtaši ašar iwwaldu* (Translation: George, *Gilgamesh Epic*, 175).

īkul aklam ^d^*Enkidu adi šebêšu*
šikaram ištiam sebe assammī⟨⟨m⟩⟩
ittapšar kabtatum inangu
īliṣ libbašuma pānūšu ittamrū
ultappit gallābum šu''uram pagaršu
šamnam iptašašma awīliš īwi
ilbaš libšam kīma muti ibašši
ilqe kakkašu lābī ugerre

Gilg. OB P col. iii 87–112

They put bread before him,
he *watched intently*, gazing and staring.
Enkidu did not know how to eat bread,
how to drink ale he had never been shown.
The harlot opened her mouth,
saying to Enkidu:
"Eat the bread, Enkidu, the thing proper to life;
drink the ale, the lot of the land."
Enkidu ate the bread until he was sated,
he drank the ale, seven jugs (full).
His mood became free, he was singing,
his heart became merry and his face shone bright.
The barber treated his body so hairy,
he anointed himself with oil and became a man.
He put on a garment, becoming like a warrior,
he took up his weapon to do battle with the lions.[32]

Just as Shamhat cares for Enkidu, so the prostitute offers Ṛśyaśṛṅga food (*bhakṣān mahārhān, MBh.* 3.111.13), alcohol (*pānāni cāgryāṇi, MBh.* 3.111.14), and fine clothing (*citrāṇi vasāṃsi ca bhānumanti, MBh.* 3.11.14),[33] as well as sex, completing his transformation from animal to

32. Cf. George, *Gilgamesh Epic,* 177.

33. Shamhat provides clothing for Enkidu by dividing her garments in two and sharing them with Enkidu. The greater preparations made for the capture of Ṛśyaśṛṅga obviate the need for a similar action on the part of the *veśyā*, as the barge has been equipped to provide for him. We do, however, find the motif of the divided garment elsewhere in the *Mahābhārata,* and in close textual proximity to the story of Ṛśyaśṛṅga. Immediately preceding the Pāṇḍavas' decision to tour the sacred bathing areas, they listen to a recitation of the story of Nala, another king who lost his kingdom through addiction to dicing. Eventually, reduced to nakedness, Nala must share the single garment of his wife, Damayantī (*MBh.* 3.59.1–5). Initially, the two wrap themselves in it together. But Nala's story takes an even more tragic turn when he secretly cuts the garment in two after Damayantī falls asleep and then abandons her in the forest (*MBh.* 3.59.12–26).

human. But while the Gilgamesh story makes the culture/nature contrast explicit—Enkidu does not even know *how* to eat bread or drink ale—Ṛśyaśṛṅga's story conveys this through a stylized exchange which is part of the seduction. In Gilgamesh the food is a symbol of transformation and acculturation but not a part of the seduction itself. But in both cases, the action is not merely seduction and entrapment; it is the awakening of a human consciousness within an animal.

J. The Wild Man Is Taken Willingly. Though the purpose of the mission in both texts is to capture the wild man, in both stories the creature himself is more than willing to be taken away to the city following his consciousness-raising encounter with the woman. So Enkidu in SB Tablet I 205ff. // OB P col. ii 51ff.; Ṛśyaśṛṅga begs the *veśyā* to take him away with her when she returns after her three-day absence (*MBh.* 3.113.7). Both wild men express enthusiasm for the human life to which they have been exposed, and both are eager to learn more.

K. The Wild Man's Transformation Sparks Alienation from His Former Life. After his awakening to human consciousness, Enkidu is rejected by the herd he lived with, at least in the SB version. Ṛśyaśṛṅga's interest in the prostitute ignites the wrath of his father, Vibhāṇḍaka, who lectures his son on the dangers of succumbing to feminine wiles (*MBh.* 3.113.1–4).

L. Interaction with Herdsmen Marks the Transition from Country to City. Enkidu and Shamhat spend time with herdsmen after his seduction but before his departure for Uruk. Ṛśyaśṛṅga himself does not do so, for he is taken straight to the city on the barge and installed in the harem. However, Vibhāṇḍaka does interact with the herdsmen when he himself goes to the city looking for his son. Instead of Ṛśyaśṛṅga, it is the father, Vibhāṇḍaka, who is fed and housed by the herdsmen (*MBh.* 113.16–18). The simple reassignment of a motif or action from one character to another is a common practice within the evolution of narrative. In the tale of Ṛśyaśṛṅga, the herdsmen have been carefully coached by King Lomapāda to inform the angry father that all their lands and herds belong to his son, a ruse designed, as used in "Puss-in-Boots," to induce good humor and pliability in the character being so deceived. This portion of the tale has a decidedly Indo-European flavor, and there is no equivalent section in the story of Enkidu. It is our reading, therefore, that while the visit to the herdsmen probably originated with the Near Eastern tale, the coaching of the herdsmen either originated with the preexisting tale, or was a modification made to the borrowed Near Eastern story after it was included in the epic.

M. City/Country Dichotomy Echoes King/Wild Man Dichotomy, and Other Oppositions. At its heart, the tale of the wild man and courtesan is about the union of opposites: male and female, animal and human, rural and urban, wild man and king, natural innocence and royal misconduct. In the *Epic of Gilgamesh* the dichotomies are made explicit; in the case of the Sanskrit version, less so, though of course the union of opposites is a mainstay of Hindu thought. The Ṛśyaśṛṅga story is not as overtly pious in theme or content as many of the other tales from the sacred fords section, but perhaps its inclusion in this section indicates that it may have been these themes of dichotomy that resonated with the composers and compilers of the Indian epic.

N. The Wild Man and the King Complete One Another. Enkidu becomes Gilgamesh's dearest companion and counterpart, and Ṛśyaśṛṅga becomes Lomapāda's *purohita*, his household priest and intercessor to the gods, a more formal, but equally indispensable role.[34]

As Ṛśyaśṛṅga's story comes to a close, its similarity to Enkidu's decreases. The narrative reverts to the earlier story, roughly as introduced in the preamble: Ṛśyaśṛṅga is married to Śāntā, forgiven by his father, and ordered to return to the hermitage with his bride when he has "granted the king all the favors he asks" (*MBh.* 3.113.21). The tale closes with references to six iconic mythological marriages (*MBh.* 3.113.22–24).

6. *Summary of the Comparison of the Two Narratives*

In view of the overwhelming number of shared motifs, there can be little doubt that the two stories are related.[35] Furthermore, in our view, acceptance of the relationship leads inexorably to the conclusion that the Near Eastern tale is the older. Certainly the age of the Gilgamesh epic suggests this initially, but other factors support it as well. The idea that the tale of the wild man and the courtesan is an Indo-European story that made its way to the Near East seems unlikely, as there are no other identifiable Indo-European reflexes of the tale (at least, none that are known to us). Thus, while it is not reasonable to suppose that the shared tale originated in India and was carried over to Mesopotamia, it does seem more than reasonable to assume that the shared tale originated in Mesopotamia.

34. Schlinghoff identifies a Jain reflex of the tale in which the wild man is actually the king's long-lost brother ("Unicorn," 302–5).

35. See above, n. 3, for a selected list of scholars who support this conclusion.

Our case is strengthened by a recent analysis of the Enkidu episode, for that analysis suggests that earlier versions of the Enkidu story may have resembled the story of a seduced Indian hermit even more closely than do the later versions.[36] Although a hunter plays a role in the present episode in the *Epic of Gilgamesh*, it is likely that a form of the episode of the wild man and courtesan existed independently of the epic and did not contain the hunter. Critical analysis suggests that originally the main characters in the episode were the courtesan and the wild man and that the courtesan seduced Enkidu without any involvement on the part of the hunter; the hunter was not part of the original tale but was added to the text at a later stage of its development.[37] The reconstructed version involving only the wild man and the courtesan almost certainly took a form separate from and independent of the larger Gilgamesh epic and would likely have been the form of the episode when it was first incorporated into the Gilgamesh epic.[38] Only after that episode was introduced into the Akkadian epic would the hunter have been added. Given the form of the Indian story, the present Ṛśyaśṛṅga story would agree even more with a Mesopotamian version without a hunter than with the standard version of the epic.[39] Certainly, the putative existence of a version without the hunter strengthens the evidence from parallelism and our contention of relationship. But, all the same, we should reiterate that even if the reconstruction of a version without a hunter turns out to be mistaken, the agreements with the standard version suffice for our argument.

36. Abusch, "Courtesan" [here, pp. 144–65].

37. Ibid., 425–28 [here, pp. 156–59]; T. Abusch, "Hunting in the *Epic of Gilgamesh:* Speculations on the Education of a Prince," in *Treasures on Camels' Humps: Literary and Historical Studies from the Ancient Near East Presented to Israel Ephʿal* (ed. M. Cogan and D. Kahn; Jerusalem: Magnes, 2008) 11–20 [here, pp. 166–76].

38. Abusch, "Courtesan," 428–29 [here, pp. 159–61].

39. As an aside, we may mention that the dependence of the secondary layer of the Ṛśyaśṛṅga story on a Mesopotamian prototype thus also provides further—though perhaps circular—proof of the existence of a form of the wild man–courtesan account without a hunter in Mesopotamia. Here, we may also note that the fact that the capture of the wild man by the courtesan is carried out at the suggestion of the king in both stories further supports the notion that the hunter was not part of the original Near Eastern story and that the hunter's father's suggestion was a duplication of Gilgamesh's idea that he take along a courtesan and not the original source of the plan. (That the suggestion originated with Gilgamesh and was then carried over to the hunter's father is explained in Abusch, "Courtesan," 425–28 [here, pp. 156–59], but see also pp. 432–33 n. 45 [here, pp. 163–64 n. 45].)

7. *Description of the Various Indic Versions of the Tale*

There is, however, one obstacle to this otherwise straightforward identification of a parallel: the *Mahābhārata*'s version of the story is only one of many Indian variants, and other versions of the tale are far less similar to the story of Enkidu. The compositional date for these variants cannot be conclusively determined, for the texts were composed within broad and overlapping time periods (see n. 9, above) and endlessly revised and edited. Generations of retellings of various tales resulted in a complex web of borrowings, influences, and counter-influences among various pieces of Indian literature. The oral preservation of narratives and the eventual commission of narratives to text are processes governed by the need to employ those narratives for new religious or ideological purposes; every retelling will preserve hallmarks of the tale, but it will also update the story in ways that serve the narrator's own ends. In the case of the tale of Ṛśyaśṛṅga, we believe that analysis of the differences among the various versions offers a number of clues to each one's place in the tale's developmental trajectory, and we will now proceed to discuss these variants.

The story has been productive in India, and variants are found in both Hindu and Buddhist sources. In Hindu versions a prostitute seduces the innocent youth, while in the Buddhist sources princesses and a celestial nymph play the role of seductress. Extant versions of the tale in Sanskrit and Pali include the following:[40]

a. *Mahābhārata*, 3.110–113. As related above. At just over one hundred verses, this is the longest of the Sanskrit versions; in this Hindu version of the tale, a prostitute figures as the primary seductress in the body of the tale.
b. Rāmāyaṇa, I, 8–10. This Hindu version, also in Sanskrit, is roughly equivalent to that found in the *Mahābhārata*, though much abbreviated. Its sole deviation from the *Mahābhārata*, other than minor omissions, is that a group of prostitutes carries out the seduction. The interest value of this version is minimal since it is only told in order to establish the *bona fides* of Ṛśyaśṛṅga, who is called in to officiate at a horse sacrifice for Rāma's father, Daśaratha. It is quite short, just under fifty verses.

40. Two additional sources make brief mention of Ṛśyaśṛṅga, placing him as one element in a list of unusual births: the *Skanda Purāṇa* (III iii 19.65) and the *Buddhacarita* of Aśvaghoṣa (IV 19).

c. The Bengali Recension of the *Padma Purāṇa*. This third Sanskrit Hindu version differs from the *Mahābhārata* at only a few points: Ṛśyaśṛṅga's mother is an enchanted princess in the form of a deer; the ruse of the herdsmen is not employed; instead, Ṛśyaśṛṅga himself goes out to implore his father not to destroy the city. At 78 verses, this is not quite as rich and detailed as the *Mahābhārata*'s version but is longer than the *Rāmāyaṇa*'s.
d. The *Mahāvastu's Jātaka of Nalinī*. In this Sanskrit Buddhist version, the king's dilemma is the lack of an heir, rather than a conflict involving his priests. Accordingly, he sends his daughter Nalinī to "Ekaśṛiṅga" to entice the boy into love and marriage; afterward, it is revealed that the two have been married for a thousand previous lives. However, they have no sexual contact before the solemnizing of the union. In spite of his name, Ekaśṛiṅga lacks a corresponding animal characteristic, though this is the only Sanskrit version in which the character interacts with animals after his birth, and it even contains a speaking role for Ekaśṛiṅga's mother, the doe.
e. The *Naḷinikā Jātaka* (no. 526, Bk. XVIII of the *Jātakas*). In this Pali Buddhist version, it is the innocent king who has been unwittingly embroiled in conflict between the gods and the holy man (the exact opposite of the *Mahābhārata*'s version). The holy man is now called Isisiṅga, and the god Sakka, threatened by his powerful meditations, causes a drought. When the king prays for a means of resolution to ease the suffering of his people, he is told that the boy must be seduced by the king's daughter Naḷinikā. She accomplishes this by impersonating another type of ascetic. When Isisiṅga's father discovers that he has been compromised, he explains to the boy how to resume the path of righteousness. There is no departure for the city, no anger of the father, and no marriage.
f. The *Alambusā Jātaka* (no. 523, Bk. XVII of the *Jātakas*). This second Pali Buddhist version contains a second story in which the powerful ascetic practices of Isisiṅga have again caused celestial havoc. This time Sakka himself sends the nymph Alambusā to disrupt his *tapas*, but the seduction, though a short-term success in that it puts Isisiṅga into a coma-like sleep for three years, ultimately fails when he wakes and recalls his father's advice about women. The nymph departs, chastened, and reports back to Sakka who thanks her graciously. The story is similar to the *Mahābhārata*'s tale of Viśvāmitra and Menakā,[41] and may well owe more to that tradition than to the Ṛśyaśṛṅga story.

41. As told to Duḥṣanta by Śakuntalā at *MBh.* 1.65.20–66.10.

The variants, though diverging widely in some respects, conform to certain observable trends of type and presentation, many of which involve motifs found elsewhere in Indian literature. It is therefore necessary to address the variants with an eye to understanding their relationship to one another and establishing a possible chronology of the story's evolution. The transformations, and therefore the versions which contain them, can be plotted along a gradient which moves from the unusual (in an Indic context) to the typical; in our estimation, the nature of the alterations provides valuable clues as to the direction of change.

8. *Assessment of the Relative Ages of the Variants of the Tale*

The issue of priority among the versions was, of course, the primary focus of Lüders' 1897 study, which study has stood as the flashpoint of the discussion on chronology for some time. Lüders concluded, as discussed above, that the *Mahābhārata*'s story originally employed a princess as the seductress,[42] but was revised to reflect the Bengali Recension of the *Padma Purāṇa*, which was, in his view, the originator of the prostitute-variation. Moreover, though he considered the existing Buddhist versions to have a "jüngere und schlechtere Form" of the tale than the Hindu versions,[43] Lüders thought that they preserved an earlier element of the story, specifically: the princess as seductress. It is our contention that the prostitute is the original seductress in the tale, and that the character of the seductress is only one among a number of important factors in determining the priority of the versions. We will now address some of the transformations observable in the versions and their implications regarding the history and development of the narrative in India, with reference to Lüders' arguments where applicable.

A. The Nature of the Seductress. The seduction of the youth is performed by one or more prostitutes in the *Rāmāyaṇa,* in the Bengali Recension of the *Padma Purana*, and in the *Mahābhārata,*[44] but by the

42. Others who disagree about the nature of the original seductress include Pauly, "Legend," 304–5 ("Though Lüders has shown that two of the brahmanical versions of the legend [in the *Mahābhārata* and the *Rāmāyaṇa*] have substituted a courtesan for the princess of their own earlier versions, it cannot be taken for granted that a courtesan was not originally the seductress in the story. The two versions existed along with each other for a long time, and our texts do not permit us to decide which of the two versions is original in this respect"); Panaino, "Between Mesopotamia," 151 n. 20; Schlinghoff, "Unicorn," 302–3; and Williams, *Oriental Affinities*, 1:34.

43. Lüders, "Sage," 126.

44. We remind the reader once again that when we talk of the tale of Ṛśyaśṛṅga in the *Mahābhārata* in our comparison of the Indian variants, we are referring to the body of the *Mahābhārata* tale at *MBh.* 110.30–113.10.

princess Naḷinikā in the *Naḷinikā Jātaka* and in the *Mahāvastu*'s *Nalinīka Jātaka*. In Lüders' analysis, as noted above, the princess is the original seductress, and the prostitute a later revision first introduced by the Bengali Recension of the *Padma Purāṇa* and subsequently copied by the epic tales. Even if this sequence were not militated against by numerous other points to be discussed below, Lüders' reading, in and of itself, would still be untenable. On the basis of our reading of the tale in the *Mahābhārata* and the other variants, we feel that a prostitute must have been the original seductress. The alteration of a common motif (princesses abound in the *Mahābhārata*) to one less common (prostitutes) is simply not consonant with the standard trends of oral literature. The addition of a prostitute, in particular, is also in no way in character with the *Mahābhārata* as a whole; there is, in fact, only one other use of the word (*veśyā*) in the entire epic.[45] The use of a prostitute as the seductress thus seems to be a motif equally foreign to both Hindu and Buddhist traditions and unlikely to have been a later revision. Logically, the idea of a story independently evolving away from culturally accepted norms to become nearly identical with a foreign story (without the direct influence of that story) is not credible; the reverse is far more likely. Lüders' analysis also does not take account of (and even fails to allude to) the nymph-as-seductress of the *Alambusā Jātaka*, whose very existence provides strong evidence that the Buddhist versions were willing to tolerate more flexibility than the Hindu. Finally, the several name changes that the female protagonist undergoes (Śāntā, Nalinī, Naḷinikā, Alambusā) support the idea that her role was very much in flux.

B. The Number of Seductions in the Tale. Lüders regarded the identity of the seductress as the key to understanding the evolution of the tale, a bias which, in our view, severely limits his ability to take other even more significant variations (such as the number of seductions) into account. There are three distinct acts which might be termed "seductions" in the *Mahābhārata* and *Padma Purāṇa*: (1) Vibhāṇḍaka is seduced by the sight of the celestial nymph; (2) Ṛśyaśṛṅga is seduced by the prostitute; and (3) Princess Śāntā marries Ṛśyaśṛṅga (this will be discussed at length under §10, "Internal Analysis of the *Mahābhārata*'s Ṛśyaśṛṅga Account"). This multiplicity of seductions contrasts sharply with the presence of only one seduction in the other versions, a seduction structurally equivalent to Ṛśyaśṛṅga's seduction by the prostitute. This super-

45. This occurs at *MBh.* 3.231.10: *śakaṭāpaṇaveśyāś ca yānayugyaṃ ca sarvaśaḥ*, a description of the camp-followers of an army.

abundance suggests that the tale is a compound, the product (as we believe) of the combination, via borrowing, of two tales into one story, a combination created by the superimposition of one upon the other.

The first of the *Mahābhārata* and *Padma Purāṇa*'s seductions is brought about by Vibhāṇḍaka's arousal and ejaculation at the sight of the celestial nymph Urvaśī. This version of the conception of the boy has been omitted in the *Rāmāyaṇa*, and carefully desexualized in the three Buddhist versions: the production of the father's semen is either explained away as the result of a rich meal, as in the *Mahāvastu*, or not explained at all, as in the *Jātakas*. Significantly, this form of seduction (arousal at the sight of a nymph) is not so very different from the seduction of Isisiṅga in the *Alambusā Jātaka*, in which Alambusā is sent by the god Sakka to disrupt Isisiṅga's meditations.

The tale's second seduction, the primary narrative element of the tale, is that performed in the Hindu versions by the prostitute (*Mahābhārata* and *Padma Purāṇa*) or prostitutes (*Rāmāyaṇa*). In the Buddhist versions, the prostitute has been removed: in the *Mahāvastu*, her role is taken over by the princess who marries Ṛśyaśṛṅga; the *Naḷinikā* and *Alambusā Jātakas* go one step further and omit the marriage entirely and replace the seducing prostitute with, respectively, a princess and a nymph.

Our assessment of the *Alambusā* and *Naḷinikā Jātaka* versions, therefore, is that the *Mahābhārata*'s seductions of father (by nymph) and son (by prostitute/princess) were first conflated, and then split into separate stories. The two *Jātaka* tales clearly reference one another without providing any evidence of a shared temporal sequence, essentially acknowledging that they are two halves of a previous whole, with no attempt made to reconcile the different versions. This reinforces the idea that during the period of the composition of the *Jātakas* the tale was being revised for a new milieu and changing mores.

C. The Name of the Wild Man. The changing name of the wild man (Ṛśyaśṛṅga, Ekaśṛnga, Isisiṅga) should be taken into account in the evaluation of priority. It is true that inexplicable name changes are not that uncommon in Indian literature, but, in this instance, the change in the wild man's name is, in our estimation, a critical issue in determining the time sequence of the tales. The name of Ṛśyaśṛṅga (lit., "antelope-horn"), son of Vibhāṇḍaka, appears (though not in association with the specific narrative we have here) in quite early Hindu sources—the *Jaiminīya Upaniṣad Brāhmaṇa* (III 40), the *Vaṃśabrāhmaṇa* (2), and the *Ārṣeyabrāhmaṇa* (VI 5)—which almost certainly predate the earliest Buddhist occurrences of the character. Thus, it is likely that "Ṛśyaśṛṅga" was the earliest name of the character to whom the story was attached in India, and accordingly that the versions of the story in which the character's name is Ṛśyaśṛṅga have the greater claim on being the original versions as well.

Further evidence that the Buddhist versions reflect later developments lies in the fact that the main character's name does not remain static, but alters over time, becoming "Ekaśṛnga" (lit., "one-horn") in the *Mahāvastu*, and "Isisiṅga" (lit., "seer-horn") in the *Naḷinikā* and *Alambusā Jātakas*. Finally, in the *Digha Nikāya* Commentary (ii 370) and the Bharhut Tope, we find yet another version of the name: "Migasiṅgi," the Pali version of Mṛgaśṛnga, "deer-horn."

The "Isisiṅga" form is of particular interest to us, as it actually reflects a misunderstanding of the meaning of the original Sanskrit name, no doubt arising from the similarity of the words for "seer" (*ṛṣi*) and "antelope" (*ṛśya*). In Pali, Sanskrit's vocalic *ṛ* becomes *i* in word-initial position, both *ś* and *ṣ* become *s*, and *sy* goes to *ss*. Thus, the expected result from *Ṛśyaśṛṅga* would be *Issasiṅga*, but the tales give us "Isisiṅga"; that is, *ṛśya* (antelope) is changed to *ṛṣi*, and his name is no longer "antelope-horn" but "seer-horn." While it is within the realm of possibility that the reverse of this proposed sequence occurred, namely, that the names Ekaśṛnga and/or Isisiṅga arose in legend or folktale earlier than the name Ṛśyaśṛṅga, and that it is Ṛśyaśṛṅga that is therefore either the corrupted form of the name or an unrelated character assimilated to the others on the basis of similarity in the names, our proposed sequence seems to be a better reading of the evidence.

D. The Nature of the Crisis. In the *Mahābhārata,* the *Padma Purāṇa,* and the *Rāmāyaṇa*, as in the Gilgamesh epic, it is offenses on the part of the king that require that the wild man be seduced and brought to the town. The Buddhist versions, however, have transformed the crisis in such a way as to exonerate the king. In the *Mahāvastu*, for example, the problem is the king's lack of a son, and the king himself has committed no wrong. In the *Naḷinikā Jātaka*, the king is a benevolent character, and the adversarial role has been transferred to the god Sakka, who, intimidated by Isisiṅga's flawless virtue, conceives of a plan to disrupt the *ṛṣi*'s asceticism. The jealous god causes a three-year drought, and when the people suffer, the king arranges the seduction of the ascetic to appease the god. The *Alambusā Jātaka* eliminates both the king and the conflict; Sakka alone arranges the disruption of Isisiṅga's meditations.

E. The Wild Man's Animal Characteristics. The texts' attention to the wild man's animal characteristics also varies. The three versions which utilize prostitutes also mention that Ṛśyaśṛṅga possesses the horn that gives him his name, while the horn goes unmentioned in the three Buddhist versions (though it seems to be present in some of the relevant Buddhist art depicting the tale[46]). The epic and puranic versions also contain a reference to hairiness through the king's name, Lomapāda or Romapada, "He whose feet are covered in body hair," though only the *Mahābhārata* describes Vibhāṇḍaka as hairy as well.

F. The Nature of the Wild Man's Transformation. Perhaps the most compelling evidence for the direction of the tales' evolution lies in the shifting presentation of the transformation that the boy undergoes as a result of the seduction. In the *Mahābhārata*, the seductive powers of women may be an unwelcome distraction from the acquisition of spiritual potency, but they do not cause spiritual corruption. Ṛśyaśṛṅga's awakening is not a fall from grace: ignorance is changed to understanding, not to bitterness or regret. In the *Mahābhārata, Rāmāyaṇa,* and *Padma Purāṇa*, the only negative consequence of Ṛśyaśṛṅga's awakening is a sort of generational conflict with his father, and the seduction does absolutely nothing to compromise Ṛśyaśṛṅga's virtue. In the *Mahāvastu*, we are in something of a middle ground: the piece is primarily a love story, the *ṛṣi*'s spiritual powers are of no importance because he is merely being recruited as a son and heir, and while the seduction causes him no spiritual setbacks, it is also not a physical seduction. In the *Jātaka*s, on the other hand, consonant with a greater emphasis on the ascetic lifestyle as more rule-bound and result-oriented, the seduction has become an act of deliberate corruption and damaging sabotage.[47] This is particularly true in the *Alambusā Jātaka*, while in the *Naḷinikā Jātaka* the overall effect is softened somewhat by the altruistic motives of the princess. If the tale had originated in a Buddhist milieu, it seems unreasonable to imagine that a redactor would have replaced the harsh moral lessons of the *Jātaka*s with the spiritually positive outcomes of the seduction of Ṛśyaśṛṅga found in the *Mahābhārata*.

46. For examples, see Schlinghoff, "Unicorn," 305–6.

47. Albright also asserts that the corruptive power of the seduction is a Buddhist contribution to the tale: "The hermit relates the experience to his father, who admonishes him, and draws him back to his ascetic career; the last is naturally a Buddhistic modification, quite foreign to the original tale" ("Gilgames and Engidu," 330).

9. Summary and Conclusions regarding the Chronology of the Ṛśyaśṛṅga Story

The motif of the tempted or besotted ascetic occurs in many forms in Indian literature,[48] and clearly commanded considerable interest from audiences and composers alike, making this tale a magnet for revisions and variations on this theme. On the basis of our assessment of the variations noted above, but especially the form of the name, we conclude that the existing Ṛśyaśṛṅga story in the *Mahābhārata* is the oldest Indic version of the tale and the others are later variations. The Buddhist versions appear to have evolved by reverting to stereotypical story patterns, especially regarding the king's character, the seductress, and the nature of the change wrought in Ṛśyaśṛṅga. What we have attempted to demonstrate by means of this analysis of the variations in the tale is that the tale in the *Mahābhārata* is the closest one to an "original" Indic version and that the other versions are derivative. Accordingly we believe that the Ṛśyaśṛṅga tale presently found in the *Mahābhārata* is the oldest Indic version of the tale of the wild man and the courtesan.

10. Internal Analysis of the Mahābhārata*'s Ṛśyaśṛṅga Account*

Finally, we must turn to one more issue with which Lüders' analysis was also concerned, that is, the issue of the preamble-body disconnect, and then to an analysis of the relationship between *Mahābhārata*'s preamble and the versions of the story. Thus far, in discussing the *Mahābhārata*'s narrative, we have treated only the central portion of the tale as it is found there (essentially that part found at *MBh.* 3.110.30–113.10, and referred to in this article as the "body" of the piece[49]). As stated above, appended to the front of the tale is a brief preamble (*MBh.* 3.110.1–10) in which the narrator, Lomaśa, loosely summarizes the story and the eldest Pāṇḍava brother, Yudhiṣṭhira, responds with a set of leading questions. The body of the narrative, as we have discussed it above, is quite straightforward, but a closer study of the body in conjunction with the preamble indicates that the body and preamble do not match and points to the existence of a number of irregularities and contradictions.

---

48. In the *Mahābhārata* alone we have Viśvāmitra (1.65–66), Cyavana (3.122), Sunda and Upasunda (1.201–204), and Triśiras (5.9). In the *Rāmāyaṇa*, cf. Māṇḍakarṇi 3,11. The motif is particularly fascinating because it can be associated with a variety of positive or negative outcomes for ascetic, temptress, and any potential offspring.

49. See §11, "Narrative Layers in the *Mahābhārata*," for an explanation of our terminology.

Whereas Lüders saw these discrepancies as the result of a series of editorial reworkings designed to harmonize an original *Mahābhārata* version featuring a princess with the Bengali recension of the *Padma Purāṇa*, we consider them to be the result of a borrowing from an external source. Thus we do not agree with Lüders' conclusions; moreover, while we concur with Lüders on the importance of several of the textual problems he identified,[50] we feel that he did not take account of several significant issues. Let us now examine the preamble itself. It runs as follows:

lomaśa uvāca

1. *eṣā devanadī puṇyā kauśikī bharatarṣabha*
   viśvāmitrāśramo ramyo eṣa cātra prakāśate
2. *āśramaś caiva puṇyāravyaḥ kāśyapasya mahātmanaḥ*
   ṛśyaśṛṅgaḥ suto yasya tapasvī saṃyatendriyaḥ
3. *tapaso yaḥ prabhāvena varṣyāmāsa vāsavam*
   anāvṛṣṭaryāṃ bhayādyasya vavarṣa balavṛtrahā.
4. *mṛgyāṃ jātaḥ sa tejasvī kāśyapasya sutaḥ prabhuḥ*
   viṣaye lomapādasya yaś cakārādbhutaṃ mahat.
5. *nivartiteṣu sasyeṣu yasmai śāntāṃ dadau nṛpaḥ*
   lomapādo duhitaraṃ sāvitrīṃ savitā yathā.

yudhiṣṭhīra uvāca

6. *ṛśyaśṛṅgaḥ kathaṃ mṛgyām utpannaḥ kāśyapātmajaḥ*
   viruddhe yonisaṃsarge kathaṃ ca tapasā yutaḥ.
7. *kimarthaṃ ca bhayāc chakras tasya bālasya dhīmataḥ*
   anāvṛṣṭaryāṃ pravṛttāyāṃ vavarṣa balavṛtrahā.
8. *kathaṃ rupā ca śāntābhūd rājaputrī yatavratā*
   lobhayāmāsa yā ceto mṛgabhūtasya tasya vai.
9. *lomapādaś ca rājarṣir yadāśrūyata dhārmikaḥ*
   kathaṃ vai viṣaye tasya nāvarṣatpākaśāsanaḥ.
10. *etan me bhagavan sarvaṃ vistareṇa yathātatham*
    vaktum arhasi śuśrūṣor ṛśyaśṛṅgasya ceṣṭitam.

MBh. 3.110.1–10

Lomaśa said:

1. This, O Bull of the Bhāratas is the divine sacred river Kauśikī; and here shines forth the charming hermitage of Viśvāmitra,

50. Lüders, "Sage," 88–92.

2. And also, O Great-Souled One, the hermitage called Puṇyā, of Kāśyapa's son, Ṛśyaśṛṅga, powerful, and of controlled senses,
3. Who, by the power of his *tapas*, caused Vāsava to rain in a drought; from fear of him the slayer of Bala and Vṛtra rained.
4. That *ṛṣi* was conceived upon a deer, the powerful son of Kāsyapa.
   He performed this great wonder in the kingdom of Lomapāda.
5. When the crops had been restored, the king gave Śāntā to him—
   Lomapāda [gave] his daughter as Savitṛ did Sāvitri.

Yudhiṣṭhīra said:

6. How was Ṛśyaśṛṅga, the son of Kāśyapa, born from the deer in prohibited sexual congress, and how was he engaged with *tapas*?
7. Why, out of fear of the boy, endowed with wisdom, did Śakra,
   the slayer of Bala and Vṛtra, rain in the ongoing drought?
8. How great was the beauty of the strict-vowed princess Śāntā, she who seduced his consciousness, when indeed he was living as a deer?
9. It has been heard that Lomapāda was a dharmic royal *ṛṣi*—
   Why indeed did the Chastiser of Pāka not rain in his kingdom?
10. Lord, all of this to me carefully as it happened
    you ought to tell; I want to hear the ways of Ṛśyaśṛṅga.

In contrast to the body of the story, the tale anticipated by this preamble is one in which Lomapāda is a law-abiding king, both Ṛśyaśṛṅga and Śāntā play active roles, the gods involve themselves, and fear generated by Ṛśyaśṛṅga's powers is a critical element. All of the above hallmarks of the preamble are absent from the body of the story in the *Mahābhārata*. Introductory question-and-answer exchanges are not uncommon in the beginning of an embedded narrative, but they are typically restricted to a few pertinent (and accurate) questions about the nature of the tale to come or about some background information not handled in the body of the story.[51] In this case, the exchange in the preamble is not only espe-

51. Cf. the various other preambular statements attached to the front of stories in this section: *Agastya* 3.94.2–3; *The Meeting of the Vṛṣṇis and Pāṇḍavas* 3.119.1–2; *Cyavana* 3.121.20–25; *Māndhātar* 3.125.23, 126.1–4; *Jantu* 3.127.1; *Aṣṭāvakra* 3.132.1–5; *Bhar-*

cially long and detailed, but is also unusual in that it contains material that inaccurately represents, or even contradicts, the storyline of the body.

Elements found in the preamble that do not agree with the story are as follows:

A. Ṛśyaśṛṅga was extremely powerful (*śl.* 2, 3). The body of the tale contains no suggestion of Ṛśyaśṛṅga's power whatsoever. If anyone in the tale generates fear, it is Vibhāṇḍaka, not the harmless and gentle Ṛśyaśṛṅga. *Śl.* 6 of the preamble also asks, "How was he engaged with *tapas*?," another issue that is never really adequately addressed by the tale.

B. Indra was afraid of Ṛśyaśṛṅga. Indra's fear is expressed twice in the preamble, in *śl.* 3 (Indra rained "out of fear of [Ṛśyaśṛṅga]") and *śl.* 7, Yudhiṣṭhira's second question ("Why did Śakra, slayer of Bala and Vṛtra, out of fear of the wise boy, rain in the ongoing drought?").[52] These statements anticipate a tale that describes some form of interaction or an ongoing relationship between Ṛśyaśṛṅga and Indra. However, no mention is made of Indra's fear of the boy in the body of the tale, where Indra's role is nearly nonexistent (only one verse at *MBh.* 3.113.10).

C. Ṛśyaśṛṅga's power ended the drought. *Śloka* 3 of the preamble specifically says that Ṛśyaśṛṅga "by the power of his *tapas* caused Vāsava [Indra] to rain." This does not accord with *MBh.* 3.113.10, in the body of the tale, where there is no further mention of Indra's fear, and no actions on the boy's part are ever narrated. Indra simply sends the rain as soon as Ṛśyaśṛṅga has been installed in the women's quarters. Similarly, the preamble's assertion in *śl.* 4 that Ṛśyaśṛṅga "performed a great wonder" also suggests more activity on the boy's part than merely being abducted and locked up as a kind of talisman.

Ṛśyaśṛṅga's apparently passive role in the bringing of the rains also ties in with a general imbalance in the import of the drought as it is presented in the preamble and in the body. Though the drought is the central issue of the preamble and looms large in the opening of the tale, by the conclusion of the narrative it has been largely replaced by the issue of the pacification of the irate *ṛṣi*, and the actual account of its resolution at *MBh.* 3.113.10 occupies only half a verse.[53]

---

advāja 3.135.9–11. None of these exceeds five verses, and none contains material that contradicts the story about to be told.

52. Note also that Indra's relationship to the drought and rain is constructed differently in the *MBh.* preamble than it is in the Buddhist versions that contain a drought; in the Buddhist tales the drought, not the rain, is caused by Indra's fear of the ascetic's powers, whereas the *MBh.* preamble claims that Indra sends the drought as punishment for the king's lack of sacrifices and the rains out of fear of Ṛśyaśṛṅga.

53. Schlinghoff, too, felt that the drought and its resolution seem extraneous to the tale; in order to provide a motivation for the abduction, he adduces the Jain tale of

D. Antelope/deer alteration. Ṛśyaśṛṅga's name, "Antelope-Horn," raises an interesting issue in respect to a slight irregularity regarding the narrative's use of the words *mṛga*, "deer," and *ṛsya*, "male antelope." The terms are to some degree interchangeable in Sanskrit (i.e., all *ṛśya*s are *mṛga*s, but not all *mṛga*s are *ṛśya*s), but their use in this story is sharply delineated. *Ṛśya*, the more specific term, is used only in the character's name and in the explanation of the name at *MBh.* 3.110.17: *tasya ṛśyaśṛṅgam sirasi*, "on his head was an antelope horn." Every reference to the doe that bore him understandably employs the far more common *mṛga* (3.110.4, 6, 14, 16). Thus far, the irregularity may simply be an issue of venery and reflect the alteration of the terms for buck and doe. Less clear, however, is 3.110.8 in the opening summary, where Ṛśyaśṛṅga himself is referred to as a *mṛga*:

> *kathaṃ rupā ca śāntābhūd rājaputrī yatavratā.*
> *lobhayāmāsa yā ceto mṛgabhūtasya tasya vai.*
> *MBh.* 3.110.8

> How great was the beauty of the strict-vowed princess Śāntā,
> she who seduced his consciousness when indeed he was living as a *mṛga*?

But the alteration of terms is only one facet of the difficulties we encounter in 3.110.8, and below we continue a discussion of this problematic verse.

E. Ṛśyaśṛṅga's life as a deer. While the body of the Sanskrit tale reports in detail that Ṛśyaśṛṅga, though horned, lives in the style of an ascetic, *MBh.* 3.110.8 claims that Ṛśyaśṛṅga was seduced, literally, "while his being was that of a deer" (*mṛgabhūtasya*[54] *tasya vai*), in apparent contradiction to the rest of the narrative. Elsewhere, the story never indicates that Ṛśyaśṛṅga lived in either the form or the manner of a deer; rather, it emphatically states that he lived as an ascetic, though possessed of an antelope's horn. Thus, we read this reference to his life "while his being was that of a deer" as an indication that these opening questions were originally intended to accompany either a story in which an ascetic lives in the *manner* of a deer (*mṛgacāriṇī*), as Yayāti's daughter Mādhavī does at *MBh.* 5.118.7 and 5.119.20, 24, or, perhaps, in the *form* of a deer

---

Valkalacīrin, which he believes to be cognate with the Ṛśyaśṛṅga story and which features a wild man seduced and brought to the city by prostitutes because he is the king's long-lost brother ("Unicorn," 304–5).

54. Mss $Ś_1$, K_1, and K_2 read *mṛgarūpasya*, "in the form of a deer," a variant equally far removed from the actual content of the body of the tale.

(*mṛgo bhūtvā,* "having become a deer"), like the *ṛṣi* who curses Pāṇḍu for killing him as he mates with his doe at *MBh.* 1.109.[55] The suggestion that Ṛśyaśṛṅga lived in deer form grounds the preamble of the tale in story patterns found elsewhere in the epic, heightening the contrast between preamble and body.

F. Princess Śāntā was the seductress. Another crux to be found in the introduction to the story regards the seduction of Ṛśyaśṛṅga. *MBh.* 3.110.8 suggests that it was the princess Śāntā who first lured the ascetic: "she who seduced his consciousness."[56] This is, of course, the line that led Lüders to his conclusion that the *Mahābhārata* had originally contained a version closer to that of the *Mahāvastu* or the *Naḷinikā Jātaka.* However, the rest of the tale is emphatic in its assertion that the seduction was performed by the nameless *veśyā* ("courtesan") who first appears when she is selected by the procuress:

> *tato duhitaraṃ veśyā samādhāyetikṛtyatām*
> *dṛṣṭvāntaraṃ kāśyapasya prāhiṇodbuddhisaṃmatām*
> *sā tatra gatvā kuśalā taponityasya saṃnidhau*
> *āshramaṃ taṃ samāsādya dadarśa tam ṛṣeḥ sutam*
> *MBh.* 3.111.5–6

> Then the [chief] *veśyā*, having considered what needed to be done,
> seeing the departure of Kāśyapa, dispatched her daughter known for her intelligence.
> The clever girl, having gone there, to the vicinity of the ascetic,
> having entered the hermitage, she saw the *ṛsi*'s son.

The contradiction between 3.110.8 and 3.111.5–6 cannot be resolved. It forms a significant crux and provides clear evidence of a disconnect

55. In a similar passage at *MBh.* 3.139.1–10, an unwitting son sees his ascetic father wrapped in a black antelope skin walking at night in the hermitage and, mistaking him for an actual antelope, kills him with an arrow. There are profound and widespread associations between *ṛṣis* and antelope/deer, from their propensity to assume deer form to the black antelope skins that formed part of the standard accoutrements of a *ṛṣi* (as in *Śatapatha Brāhmaṇa* 1:1:4:11: "He now takes the black antelope skin, for completeness of the sacrifice. For once upon a time the sacrifice escaped the gods, and having become a black antelope roamed about. The gods having thereupon found it and stripped it of its skin, they brought it [the skin] away with them"). This issue of *ṛṣis* living as deer may perhaps even be one of the details that precipitated the adoption and modification of the tale; the transplanted wild man character may very well have fallen into the role of a *ṛṣi* because of this long-standing association between *ṛṣis* and antelopes.

56. Van Buitenen renders *cetas* here with the more contextually conventional "heart," but "consciousness" is the more common meaning (*Mahābhārata,* 2:443).

between the preamble and the body of the episode.[57] The seduction by the prostitute takes up the bulk of the story and is, in fact, the entire point of the tale. The preamble's attribution of the seduction to Princess Śāntā cannot be reconciled with the rest of the text. Indeed, within the context of the *Mahābhārata* as a whole, the seduction by the *veśyā* is a glaring anomaly. However, the *Mahābhārata* does have many stories of princesses who take an active role in finding husbands or who cause men to fall in love with them through more demure behavior. It may well be that in an earlier phase of the development of this tale, Princess Śāntā seduces his heart in a manner not unlike that in which Śakuntalā seduces Duhṣanta's (*MBh.* 1.65–66), Sukanyā Cyavana's (*MBh.* 3.122–123), or Sāvitrī Satyavan's (*MBh.* 3.277–283), making the alleged seduction simply another slightly unusual *svayamvara* (bridegroom-choice).

G. Lomapāda was a just king (śl. 9). Though Lomapāda has apparently redeemed himself by the end of the tale, disrespectful treatment of brahmins is a serious crime. As discussed above in §5, "Parallel Elements in the Stories of Enkidu and Ṛśyaśṛṅga," the body of the narrative even contains a faint suggestion that the king's mistreatment of his priests was of a sexual nature.

H. Vibhāṇḍaka had intercourse with the deer. *Śloka* 6 has Yuddhiṣṭhira ask, "How was Ṛśyaśṛṅga, the son of Kāśyapa, born from the deer in prohibited sexual congress?" Every other version of the tale is scrupulous in eliminating any possible suggestion of sexual contact between Vibhāṇḍaka and the deer; and in the body of this version the deer is impregnated by the accidental ingestion of semen, rather than via sexual contact. However, the phenomenon of ascetics in deer form engaging in sexual activity is far from unknown (as described above in §10.E) and may well have been a part of the *Mahābhārata*'s tale in an earlier phase of this narrative's development.

I. The Desertion of the Brahmins. The Sanskrit story contains an interesting crux at the point of the narrative when the king's problem is discussed. At *MBh.* 3.110.20, the brahmins desert Lomapāda in response to his behavior. Among those who have deserted the king, so the next verse reveals, is the royal *purohita*, the absence of whose sacrifices angers the gods and causes them to withhold the monsoon so that the people suffer. Lomapāda's reaction to the brahmins' abandonment is to consult (other) brahmins, and this second group of priests assists him in formu-

57. As noted earlier, Lüders recognized the difficulties presented by this verse ("Sage," 100).

lating a plan. One of their number advises him to capture Ṛśyaśṛṅga, and the king accepts the suggestion and begins to make amends for his previous misdeeds:

etacchrutvā vaco rājan kṛtvā niṣkṛtim ātmanaḥ
sa gatvā punar āgacchat prasanneṣu dvijātiṣu
rājānam āgatam dṛṣṭvā pratisaṃjagṛhuḥ prajāḥ
MBh. 3.110.27

Upon hearing these words the king performed expiation for himself,
Having gone away again, he returned when the brahmins were satisfied,
Having seen the king returned, the subjects took him back.

The presence of two sets of brahmins seems excessive. Where does the second group of brahmins come from? To be sure, nothing in the narrative is irresolvable, but it is unnecessarily cumbersome as it stands.[58] Moreover, though *MBh.* 110.21 refers to the subjects' misery, it does not anticipate the suggestion at *MBh.* 3.110.27f. that the subjects may actually have been on the brink of rebellion as well.

Prominent among the above irregularities are a number of elements that are portrayed differently in the preamble and in the body of the story (dharmic Lomapāda/unjust Lomapāda, dynamic Ṛśyaśṛṅga/passive Ṛśyaśṛṅga, *mṛga/ṛśya*, living as a deer/living as a *brahmacārin*, Princess Śāntā/nameless courtesan), with the result that the summary not only fails to accurately foreshadow the contents of the narrative, but actually contradicts them.

In our opinion, the issue of the preamble's difficulties is also connected to a similar awkwardness at the ending of the tale. While the body forms a seamless whole with no internal contradictions, after *MBh.* 3.113.11 the ending of the episode undergoes another puzzling shift. Ṛśyaśṛṅga is whisked off to the harem, and the focus shifts to Vibhāṇḍaka's journey to the city and the abatement of his wrath. We are never given any particulars about the resolution of the drought or Ṛśyaśṛṅga's role in stopping it, issues that are rather important in the Buddhist versions.

58. As Lüders remarks, "Wie kann der König die Brahmanen um Rat fragen, von denen eben gesagt ist, daß sie ihn im Zorn verlassen haben!" ("Sage," 90).

11. *Narrative Layers in the* Mahābhārata

We believe that the best way to explain these discrepancies is to assume that the present text is made up of two accounts, the latter superimposed upon the earlier. In our reconstruction, the story of a wild man seduced by a prostitute at the command of a scandal-embroiled king has been grafted onto a preexisting tale, whose remnants we see in the preamble: the story of a powerful ascetic and his conflict with Indra. From the conclusion of the current story, we may also infer that this ascetic, or his son, marries a princess and produces a male child. We therefore analyze the structure of the existing story in the *Mahābhārata* as follows:

110.1–15	*Preamble and Opening.* This section includes the opening questions plus the establishment of the locus of the tale and is a vestige of the original Indian tale in the *Mahābhārata.* It contains no reference to any of the motifs found in the wild man/prostitute story that we identify with the body of the tale. The converse of this is also true: aside from the necessary details of Ṛśyaśṛṅga's parentage, the only parts of the story that the preamble anticipates correctly are those that occur at the ending of the tale.
110.16–29	*First Transitional Area.* Here, the two narrative layers are spliced together, resulting in minor redundancies: the two sets of brahmins, as well as the uncertainty as to whether the subjects are also in revolt.
110.30–113.10	*Body.* Here, the story of a wild man who is seduced by a prostitute has been incorporated and adapted to its new cultural milieu. This adaptation includes, for example, a more stylized scene of seduction, and the conversion of the wild man into an ascetic, as well as the humorous presentation of Ṛśyaśṛṅga as charmingly ignorant of human gender.
113.11–113.18	*Second Transitional Area.* Here, the visit to the herdsmen (which originated in the body) and the father's wrath (which came from the original underlying tale) are combined, and the father visits the herdsmen instead of his son.
113.19–113.24	*Ending.* Here, the text retains the climax and resolution of the original underlying tale—the marriage to the princess—now attached to the story of the wild man and the courtesan.

The suggestion that the body of the Ṛśyaśṛṅga story is a borrowing is also generally supported by the context in which the tale is found, the *Mahābhārata*'s *Tīrthayātrāparvan*, a guided tour of sacred bathing areas (often referred to as the *Tour of the Sacred Fords*). A number of the tales found in this section are Vedic in origin;[59] others appear to be folktales or local legends.[60] The opportunity for the exchange of stories and information has always been an attractive feature of pilgrimage sites; the *Tour* is thus a logical clearinghouse for a wide variety of borrowings or accretions. Situating the tales among these is likely a tacit acknowledgement of their varying provenances; we shall later revisit the issue of what might constitute acceptable sources for borrowing.

12. *The Relationship of the Preamble to Other Versions of the Tale*

We cannot leave this part of our discussion of the Ṛśyaśṛṅga tale and take up the question of borrowing before raising and discussing the issue of whether or not the preamble might simply reflect other versions of the Ṛśyaśṛṅga story, which, as we have seen, in some cases stray quite profoundly from the tale as it is found in the body of the *Mahābhārata*'s version. If so, this might contradict our results and suggest that these other versions are earlier.

In fact, some of the elements in the preamble are quite reminiscent of those in the other tales. For example, the assertions in *śl.* 2–3 that Ṛśyaśṛṅga was extremely powerful would be an accurate description of the character as he appears in the *Naḷinikā* and *Alambusā Jātakas*. The preamble's statement that the princess was the seductress is appropriate to both the *Mahāvastu* and the *Naḷinikā Jātaka*, excepting that her name in the other versions is not Śāntā, but Naḷinī or Naḷinikā. Also, the assertion that Lomapāda was a just king, in *śl.* 9, is far more descriptive of the kings in the Buddhist versions (the *Mahāvastu* and the *Naḷinikā Jātaka*) than it is of Lomapāda.

However, other elements featured in the preamble are equally out of place in the other versions, including the idea that Ṛśyaśṛṅga's power was somehow directly instrumental in ending the drought: *śl.* 3 declares that "from fear of him the slayer of Bala and Vṛtra rained," which is at odds with the *Naḷinikā Jātaka*'s account, in which it is the *breaking*

59. E.g., Agastya (*MBh.* 3.94–108), Sukanyā (*MBh.* 3.121–125).
60. E.g., the irascibility of Mount Ṛṣabha (*MBh.* 3.109).

of Ṛśyaśṛṅga's power that satisfies the god; and the *Mahāvastu* and the *Alambusā Jātaka* contain no drought at all. The statement that Ṛśyaśṛṅga was seduced "while his being was that of a deer" is also not found in any of the other versions of the tale, nor is the idea that Vibhāṇḍaka may have had intercourse with the deer; in fact, every other version of the tale is careful to explain away any possibility of sexual contact between ascetic and deer (both these issues were discussed in greater detail above under §10, "Internal Analysis of the *Mahābhārata*'s Ṛśyaśṛṅga Account").

Therefore, in view of the fact that every narrative element shared between the Buddhist versions and the preamble is a fairly common and typical motif of Indic literature, we feel that the resemblances are best explained as a consequence of the assimilation by the Buddhist derivatives to other typical Indian tales and the absorption of those typical features. That is, their evolution caused them to become less, rather than more, unique: the Buddhist versions of the tale took on a semblance of uniformity with the typical Indian tale that formed the original preamble version.

13. Origins and Transmission of the Tale

Especially in view of the absence (as far as we know) of an Indo-European or earlier Indic version of a wild man–prostitute story, the composite nature of the Ṛśyaśṛṅga story and its present location in the *Mahābhārata* (a tale-within-a-tale in the storehouse of disconnected material) suggest that the body of the present Ṛśyaśṛṅga story is a borrowing. In view of (1) our conclusion that the Ṛśyaśṛṅga story drew its wild man–courtesan layer from elsewhere and (2) the obvious relationship of the accounts in the *Mahābhārata* and the *Epic of Gilgamesh*, it is evident that the wild man account in the *Mahābhārata* derives—though perhaps at some remove—from a Mesopotamian source. In fact, there are other episodes in the "Tour of the Sacred Fords" with possible Near Eastern relations,[61] and it may be that their proximity to one another is evidence of their common Near Eastern background.

The Mesopotamian source of the Ṛśyaśṛṅga tale is probably some form of the Enkidu story known from the *Epic of Gilgamesh*. But the form is not yet certain, for while it is possible that both the Ṛśyaśṛṅga and the Enkidu stories derive from a common Near Eastern ancestor,

61. "Matsya" (*MBh.* 3.185), which has pronounced similarities to the Mesopotamian Flood story, and the "Colloquy of the Brahmin and the Hunter" (*MBh.* 3.198–206), which resembles a great deal of Near Eastern wisdom literature.

the Indian tale may derive from a form of the *Epic of Gilgamesh* itself. But given the absence of a hunter both in the Ṛśyaśṛṅga tale and in the original form of the Mesopotamian wild man tale, it is likely that the Ṛśyaśṛṅga story derives from an independent story of the Wild Man and the Prostitute that existed either prior to the latter's incorporation into the *Epic of Gilgamesh* or that continued to circulate alongside the epic after the incorporation. Of course, there is no objection to assuming that it derived from the epic itself after the tale was incorporated into it, but then this derivation would likely have taken place before the hunter became part of the epic.

Two final questions remain to be addressed: first, when was the story incorporated into the *Mahābhārata*, and second, how and when was the story transmitted from the Near East to India? The following sections will treat these issues separately.

14. *The Tale's Incorporation into the* Mahābhārata

We have already discussed at length the evidence that we perceive for the existence of "layers" in the Indian tale. Whatever the time period of the tale's introduction to India, our reconstruction of the story's layering supports the idea of a late addition of the Near Eastern overlay onto the preexisting story in the *Mahābhārata*.[62]

62. See below under §15, "Mode and Time of Transmission" for chronological parameters.

Fleming and Milstein (*Buried Foundation*) contend that the story of Gilgamesh, Enkidu, and Huwawa is the nucleus around which the OB epic of Gilgamesh was created. They think that the prostitute was used in the original Huwawa narrative to bring Enkidu to Gilgamesh in Uruk; but this Enkidu was a herdsman and not a wild man, and therefore no process of humanization and acculturation was involved. Upon this earlier narrative was imposed the new construction that we find in the OB epic. This new construction that highlighted Enkidu the wild man and Shamhat the prostitute who humanizes him involved (among other things) the introduction of the tale of seduction and acculturation presently preserved in the OB Penn tablet. As for the harlot, though she originally served in the Akkadian Huwawa narrative to bring Enkidu to Gilgamesh, her role underwent a major expansion with the creation of the OB epic and the imposition of the new Enkidu character upon the older one. We find Fleming and Milstein's argument convincing. More to the point, we believe that their argument supports our argument, and ours theirs, for we have argued that the *Mahābhārata* version underwent a similar transformation and that the wild man and prostitute were superimposed upon an earlier tale of a sage, king, and princess. Accordingly, parallel developments seem to have taken place in both the Mesopotamian and Indian spheres. While this may be only an interesting coincidence, the fact that literary developments along the same lines took place in this story in both Mesopotamia and India is generally supportive of the developments we have posited.

As was noted earlier, in §11, "Narrative Layers in the *Mahābhārata*," a number of the tales found in this section of the *Mahābhārata* are Vedic, though others appear to be folktales or local legends; by situating the tales at a pilgrimage site, the compilers may have been acknowledging the varied sources of their material. But, though the tales may range widely in origin, it seems likely that at the time of their adoption all of them must have already circulated in Hindu society for quite some time; inclusion in the epic supports this, and a conceit of the *Tīrthayātrāparvan* is that its stories are equivalent to the Vedas in merit. The populist-yet-conservative ethos of the book is expressed in repeated assertions that the merit of bathing at the sacred *tīrtha*s and of hearing their associated tales is accessible to those unable to afford expensive sacrifices. Thus, folktales would be a logical and acceptable vehicle for relaying the merit that can be awarded to a pilgrim, but obvious borrowings from abroad would seem unlikely to have been deemed acceptable to the compilers of the section. This suggests that a Near Eastern tale would have had to have circulated in India for some time before it would have been considered eligible for inclusion in the epic. On the face of it, this supports an earlier date for the borrowing, but whether this process of being absorbed and accepted by Hindu culture would have been the work of decades or of centuries remains unclear.[63]

15. *Mode and Time of Transmission*

The matter of the tale's arrival on the subcontinent is a thorny one. While it is possible that a folktale version simply diffused from west to east in a slow overland crawl, more direct contact may also be suggested. Two broad possible periods for transmission between Mesopotamia and India suggest themselves, the first sometime roughly between 2400 and 1700 B.C.E., and the second from 500 B.C.E. to 200 C.E.[64] We will explore both scenarios, beginning with the later one.

---

63. It is the hope of the authors that closer examination of the other possible Near Eastern borrowings from the "Tour of the Sacred Fords" (as described in n. 61) may shed further light on this matter.

64. As noted above (n. 9), the *Mahābhārata* seems to have been assembled and edited between the fourth century B.C.E. and the fourth century C.E. Here, we have chosen the date 200 C.E. as a *terminus ante quem* for the entry of the tale into India, on the basis of the evidence of the *Physiologus* (cf. Schlinghoff, "Unicorn," 301), for that Greek text was composed circa 200 C.E., and it already incorporates elements borrowed from our Indian story. Hence, the last date for the entry of the tale into India cannot be later than 200 C.E., though of course the tale could have entered the *Mahābhārata* even later than it was taken up by the *Physiologus*.

A. Later Scenario: Approximately 500 B.C.E.–*200* C.E.

This scenario carries the advantage of allowing ample opportunity for the story to move from the Near East to India; for the period from the Achaemenid domination of Gandhara to the final phases of the assemblage of the *Mahābhārata* provides a generous span of time during which there was plenty of documented contact and political interaction between the two cultural areas.[65] On the surface, this appears to be the more reasonable choice, though the specifics of the transmission must then remain at the level of broad and rough conjecture. But we should note that this scenario carries hidden pitfalls. As discussed above in the section treating the story's incorporation into the *Mahābhārata*, one difficulty is the identification of a path and timetable that might bring the story to India early enough for it to become properly Hinduized.

To our minds, however, a more serious obstacle to transmission within this time period is the issue of the figure of the hunter in the *Epic of Gilgamesh*. As discussed above (§6, "Summary of the Comparison of the Two Narratives"), we believe the absence of a hunter in the Indian version strongly suggests that the Indian tale was drawn either from a free-standing folktale without a hunter or from the Gilgamesh epic prior to the inclusion of the hunter. Therefore, we are somewhat uneasy about deriving the Indian tale directly from the Near Eastern epic during this later period.

Written versions of the *Epic of Gilgamesh* are known from numerous first-millennium B.C.E. copies, but there is no reason to believe that a version of the epic without the hunter existed during that millennium. There remains the possibility that the tale of the wild man and the courtesan may have been transmitted even during the first millenium B.C.E. as an independent tale, for, in order to be passed to India sometime after the middle of the sixth century B.C.E., the tale of the wild man and the courtesan would have had to continue to circulate in the Near East. Unfortunately, we have no direct evidence that such an independent tale circulated either orally or in writing during the first millenium B.C.E. Perhaps it did not, for had the story remained in circulation during the first millenium B.C.E., it seems probable that it would have resurfaced at some point in Near Eastern literature, if not in a Greek or Latin

65. For contact and borrowing during the first millennium B.C.E., see, e.g., D. Pingree, "Legacies in Astronomy and Celestial Omens," in *The Legacy of Mesopotamia* (ed. S. Dalley; Oxford: Oxford University Press, 1998) 127–28, 130–32.

borrowing or in an aggregative source such as Herodotus or Athenaeus.[66] It is therefore possible that the tale passed out of circulation at all points west of the Indus Valley, at least until the Indic variant resurfaced in the West as the unicorn legend.[67]

These two factors (the absence of a hunter figure in the Indian version and the lack of evidence that the tale without a hunter was still in circulation in the Near East) make us wonder about this later time frame for transmission. However, given the speculative nature of this part of our reconstruction, these difficulties are not of such a magnitude as to invalidate this later time frame. But these difficulties do exist, and there is also an argument to be made for an earlier transmission of the tale.

B. Earlier Scenario: 2400–1700 B.C.E.

Contact between Mesopotamia and the civilizations of the Indus Valley at Harappa, Mohenjo-daro, and similar sites is well documented during the latter part of the third millennium and into the Old Babylonian period.[68] Since an early form of the Mesopotamian tale of the wild man and the courtesan would have existed prior to the composition of the

66. But note that W. L. Moran makes a case that a passage in Ovid may reflect the ancient Near Eastern tale's central philosophical idea of sexual love as a civilizing/humanizing force ("Ovid's *Blanda Voluptas* and the Humanization of Enkidu," *JNES* 50 [1991] 121–27). According to Moran, Ovid's description of primitive man and his humanization derives from an earlier tradition of acculturation through sex in which the participants are a man and his wife, rather than a man or wild man and a prostitute. The tale of Enkidu and the prostitute may well have had its roots in similar Near Eastern tales of the civilizing of early man (cf. Abusch, "Courtesan," 429 [here, p. 160]).

67. See, e.g., van Buitenen, *Mahābhārata*, 2:188–93; Schlinghoff, "Einhorn-Legende," 51–64; and Panaino, "Between Mesopotamia."

68. See, e.g., S. Parpola, "Cultural Parallels between India and Mesopotamia: Preliminary Considerations," *Studia Orientalia* 70 (1993) 57–64, who gives a general survey of comparable elements in the two societies; cf. also S. Dalley, "Occasions and Opportunities, I & II," in *The Legacy of Mesopotamia* (ed. S. Dalley; Oxford: Oxford University Press, 1998) 14–15:

> Contact deduced from goods found within Mesopotamia has been traced in the form of etched carnelian beads, stamp and cylinder seals featuring elephants and characteristically Indian cattle. There are no *bullae* of clay impressed with cylinder seals from the Indus, or terra-cotta cone mosaics, and it appears as if the contact between the two regions was both later in time and of a kind different from that which is traceable in Egypt and along the upper Euphrates. It seems to have lasted from around 2500 B.C. until the Indus cities were destroyed after some 700 years of splendour, with textual evidence from the cities of lower Mesopotamia in particular revealing that textiles and foodstuffs flowed eastwards.
>
> Just as happened earlier, some of the ideas and skills of Mesopotamian society were adopted in an area which had already become quite cultured, but the resulting development looked very different from the form it took elsewhere.

Epic of Gilgamesh in the Old Babylonian period, the borrowing may have occurred while the Indus Valley civilization still flourished, sometime between 2400 and 1700 B.C.E., thus perhaps even prior to the composition of the Old Babylonian version of the epic. Merchants, or even traveling storytellers, could have introduced the story into the Indus Valley, and the fact that the two cultures seem to have been receptive to one another's influence on at least some levels[69] increases the likelihood that the tale would have been embraced and preserved.[70]

Though the advanced level of society represented at Harappa and Mohenjo-daro eventually went into decline, folktale is known for its remarkable durability in the face of cultural and political upheaval. The tale of the wild man and the courtesan may well have enjoyed its own life on Indian soil for well over a millennium before being incorporated into the great epic.

16. *Conclusion*

In summary: the tale of the wild man seduced by the courtesan originated in the ancient Near East and eventually became an integral part of the *Epic of Gilgamesh*. Through contact between the Near East and India,

69. For example, Akkadian-style cylinder seals with Akkadian-style carving have been found in the Indus Valley, and the two cultures were avid trade partners. The archaeologist W. A. Fairservis believed that a seal showing a male figure overpowering two tigers reflected a Gilgamesh motif imported from Mesopotamia (*The Roots of Ancient India: The Archaeology of Early Indian Civilization* [New York: Macmillan, 1971] 275). Note again the quotation from Dalley, n. 68 above.

70. This hypothesis may even be supported by material evidence. It is difficult to resist the temptation to connect the tale's theme of the horned *brahmacārin* with the famous Indus Valley seals depicting horned and ithyphallic figures seated as if in meditation (such as DK 12050 from Mohenjo-daro, currently in the Islamabad Museum, NMP 50.296). Another seal depicts the meditating figure surrounded by an assortment of wild beasts, much as Enkidu was prior to his awakening to human consciousness (the "Proto-Shiva Seal," M-304A, National Museum, New Delhi). A similar figure, and another with a similar headdress but bearing the body of a tiger, appears in several other contexts as well. (All the above seals are discussed and pictured in J. Aruz, ed., *Art of the First Cities: The Third Millenium B.C. from the Mediterranean to the Indus* [New Haven, CT: Yale University Press, 2003] 402–8.) Although these figures all have what appear to be two or more horns, the "unicorn," a single-horned, bull-like animal is also popular, appearing on a total of 1,156 seals, more than half of all seals found. Our single-horned *ṛṣi* may represent a later conflation of these two distinctive motifs of the Indus civilization.

It is important to acknowledge here that if the presence of such motifs in the Indus Valley can be used in support of the hypothesis that Indus Valley culture was the conduit of transmission from West to East, then it is equally possible that the tale originated in the Indus Valley and the role of the traveling merchants was to transmit it from East to West. Nevertheless, the only argument in favor of this is logical deduction. In the absence of evidence to the contrary, we continue to favor the theory that the tale originated in the ancient Near East on the basis of its entrenched position in the *Epic of Gilgamesh*.

the story passed into the Indian subcontinent. Once established as oral narrative, the story circulated in India, perhaps even for centuries. As a folktale, it might easily resurface at a pilgrimage site and thereafter be deemed worthy of inclusion in the subcontinent's great epic within the corpus of legends that makes up the "Tour of the Sacred Fords." Having been thoroughly adapted to an Indian cultural and literary milieu, it was taken up by the *Mahābhārata*; but, rather than taking an independent place in the epic, it was introduced as a sort of overlay upon another story about an ascetic who lives as a deer, this one culminating in marriage to a princess and a mollified father. However, the combined version retained the structure of the tale of the wild man and his seduction by the prostitute. Of course, the integration of the two tales was not entirely seamless, but passable enough to escape further revision.

Our explanation for the similarities between the wild man tale in the *Epic of Gilgamesh* and the *Mahābhārata* is speculative, but it is in fact the simplest explanation of the evidence that we have. Hypotheses based upon the contact of civilizations are tricky, but such contact, where discernible, is of enormous significance for the history of cultural development. And it is surely edifying, especially for scholars like ourselves who specialize in the study of individual cultures, to witness the transformations that may take place when cultures borrow and adapt materials from each other.

Abbreviations

AB	Anchor Bible
AHw	*Akkadisches Handwörterbuch.* W. von Soden. 3 vols. Wiesbaden, 1965–81
ANET	*Ancient Near Eastern Texts Relating to the Old Testament.* Edited by J. B. Pritchard. 3rd ed. Princeton, NJ: Princeton University Press, 1969
AOAT	Alter Orient und Altes Testament
AOS	American Oriental Series
ASOR	American Schools of Oriental Research
BKP	Beiträge zur klassischen Philologie
BJS	Brown Judaic Studies
BO	*Bibliotheca Orientalis*
CAD	*The Assyrian Dictionary of the Oriental Institute of the University of Chicago.* Chicago: Oriental Institute, 1956–2011
CM	Cuneiform Monographs
GE	*The Epic of Gilgamesh*
GEN	*Gilgamesh, Enkidu, and the Netherworld*
HSM	Harvard Semitic Monographs
HSS	Harvard Semitic Studies
JANESCU	*Journal of the Ancient Near Eastern Society of Columbia University*
JAOS	*Journal of the American Oriental Society*
JBL	*Journal of Biblical Literature*
JCS	*Journal of Cuneiform Studies*
JNES	*Journal of Near Eastern Studies*
JSOTSup	Journal for the Study of the Old Testament: Supplement Series
KAR	*Keilschrifttexte aus Assur religiösen Inhalts*
LCL	Loeb Classical Library
LKA	*Literarische Keilschrifttexte aus Assur*
MB	Middle Babylonian
MVAG	Mitteilungen der Vorderasiatischen Gesellschaft
NABU	*Nouvelles Assyriologiques Brèves et Utilitaires*
OB	Old Babylonian
OBO	Orbis biblicus et orientalis
OIP	Oriental Institute Publications
Or	*Orientalia*
RA	*Revue d'assyriologie et d'archéologie orientale*
RIME	Royal Inscriptions of Mesopotamia, Early Periods
RlA	*Reallexikon der Assyriologie und vorderasiatischen Archäologie.* Edited by E. Ebeling et al. Berlin, 1928–
SAAS	State Archives of Assyria Studies
SANE	Sources from the Ancient Near East
SB	Standard Babylonian
ScrHie	Scripta Hierosolymitana

SpBTU	Spätbabylonische Texte aus Uruk
TCS	Texts from Cuneiform Sources
TUAT	*Texte aus der Umwelt des Alten Testaments.* Edited by Otto Kaiser. Gütersloh, 1984–
UE	Ur Excavations
UISLL	University of Illinois Studies in Language and Literature
VAS	Vorderasiatische Schriftdenkmäler
YOR	Yale Oriental Series, Researches
ZA	*Zeitschrift für Assyriologie*
ZDMG	*Zeitschrift des Deutsche Morgenländische Gesellschaft*

Bibliography

Abrahams, I. *Jewish Life in the Middle Ages*. New York: Macmillan, 1896. Repr., New York: Meridian; Philadelphia: Jewish Publication Society, 1958.

Abusch, T. "The Courtesan, the Wild Man, and the Hunter: Studies in the Literary History of the *Epic of Gilgamesh*." Pp. 413–33 in *"An Experienced Scribe Who Neglects Nothing": Ancient Near Eastern Studies in Honor of Jacob Klein*. Edited by Y. Sefati et al. Bethesda, MD: CDL Press, 2005.

______. "The Demonic Image of the Witch in Standard Babylonian Literature: The Reworking of Popular Conceptions by Learned Exorcists." Pp. 27–58 in *Religion, Science, and Magic: In Concert and in Conflict*. Edited by J. Neusner, E. S. Frerichs, and P. V. Mc. Flesher. Oxford: Oxford University Press, 1989.

______. "The Development and Meaning of the *Epic of Gilgamesh*: An Interpretive Essay." *JAOS* 121 (2001) 614–22.

______. "Gilgamesh: Hero, King, God and Striving Man." *Archaeology Odyssey* 3, no. 4 (July/August 2000) 32–42, 58–59.

______. "The Epic of Gilgamesh and the Homeric Epics." Pp. 1–6 in *Mythology and Mythologies: Methodological Approaches to Intercultural Influences. Proceedings of the Second Annual Symposium of the Assyrian and Babylonian Intellectual Heritage Project Held in Paris, October 4–7, 1999*. Edited by R. M. Whiting. Melammu Symposia 2. Helsinki: Neo-Assyrian Text Corpus, 2001.

______. "Gilgamesh's Request and Siduri's Denial, Part I: The Meaning of the Dialogue and Its Implications for the History of the Epic." Pp. 1–14 in *The Tablet and the Scroll: Near Eastern Studies in Honor of William W. Hallo*. Edited by M. E. Cohen, D. C. Snell, and D. B. Weisberg. Bethesda, MD: CDL Press, 1993.

______. "Gilgamesh's Request and Siduri's Denial, Part II: An Analysis and Interpretation of an Old Babylonian Fragment about Mourning and Celebration." In *Comparative Studies in Honor of Yohanan Muffs* = *JANESCU* 22 (1993) 3–17.

______. "Hunting in the *Epic of Gilgamesh*: Speculations on the Education of a Prince." Pp. 11–20 in *Treasures on Camels' Humps: Historical and Literary Studies from the Ancient Near East Presented to Israel Ephʿal*. Edited by M. Cogan and D. Kahn. Jerusalem: Magnes, 2008.

______. "Ishtar's Proposal and Gilgamesh's Refusal: An Interpretation of *The Gilgamesh Epic*, Tablet 6, Lines 1–79." *History of Religions* 26 (1986) 143–87. Repr. (in abbreviated form), pp. 365–74 in vol. 3 of *Classical and Medieval Literature Criticism*, edited by J. Krstovic et al. Detroit: Gale, 1989.

______. "Mesopotamian Anti-Witchcraft Literature: Texts and Studies. Part 1: The Nature of *Maqlû*: Its Character, Divisions, and Calendrical Setting." *JNES* 33 (1974) 259–61.

______. "Mourning the Death of a Friend: Some Assyriological Notes." Pp. 53–62 in *The Frank Talmage Memorial Volume, Part I*. Edited by B. Walfish. Haifa: University of Haifa Press, 1993. Repr., pp. 109–21 in *Gilgamesh: A Reader*. Edited by J. Maier. Wauconda, IL: Bolchazy-Carducci, 1997.

Abusch, T., and E. B. West, "The Tale of the Wild Man and the Courtesan in India and Mesopotamia: The Seduction of Ṛśyaśṛṅga in the *Mahābhārata* and Enkidu in the *Epic of Gilgamesh*." Pp. 69–109 in *The Ancient World in an Age of Globalization*. Edited by M. J. Geller. Melammu Symposia 6. Berlin: Max-Planck-Gesellschaft zur Förderung der Wissenschaften, 2014.

Ackerman, R. *The Myth and Ritual School: J. G. Frazer and the Cambridge Ritualists*. London: Routledge, 2002.

Albright, W. F. "Gilgames and Engidu, Mesopotamian Genii of Fecundity." *JAOS* 40 (1920) 307–35.

Algazi, G. "Private Houses and Burials in the 'Y' Trench Area of Ingharra: Kish." M.A. thesis, University of Chicago, 1980.

Allotte de la Fuÿe, F.-M. *Documents présargoniques*. Paris: E. Leroux, 1909.

Andersen, F. I., and D. N. Freedman. *Hosea: A New Translation with Introduction and Commentary*. AB 24. Garden City, NY: Doubleday, 1980.

Anderson, G. A. *A Time to Mourn, A Time to Dance: The Expression of Grief and Joy in Israelite Religion*. University Park: Pennsylvania State University Press, 1991.

Anderson, J. K. *Hunting in the Ancient World*. Berkeley: University of California Press, 1985.

Annus, A. *The God Ninurta in the Mythology and Royal Ideology of Ancient Mesopotamia*. SAAS 14. Helsinki: Neo-Assyrian Text Corpus Project, 2002.

Aruz, J., ed. *Art of the First Cities: The Third Millenium* B.C. *from the Mediterranean to the Indus*. New Haven, CT: Yale University Press, 2003.

Assmann, J. "Der schöne Tag—Sinnlichkeit und Vergänglichkeit im altägyptischen Fest." Pp. 3–28 in *Das Fest*. Edited by W. Haug and R. Warning. Poetik und Hermeneutik 14. Munich: Fink, 1989.

Ataç, M.-A. "'Angelology' in *The Epic of Gilgamesh*." *Journal of Ancient Near Eastern Religions* 4 (2004) 3–27.

Bailey, J. A. "Initiation and the Primal Woman in Gilgamesh and Genesis 2–3." *JBL* 89 (1970) 137–50.

______. "Male, Female, and the Pursuit of Immortality in the Gilgamesh Epic." *La Parola del Passato Rivista di Studi Antichi* 31 (1976) 435–37.

Barringer, J. M. *The Hunt in Ancient Greece*. Baltimore: Johns Hopkins University Press, 2001.

Bauer, T. *Das Inschriftenwerk Assurbanipals*. Leipzig: J. C. Hinrichs, 1933.

Bernheimer, R. *Wild Men in the Middle Ages: A Study in Art, Sentiment, and Demonology*. Cambridge, MA: Harvard University Press, 1952.

Beye, C. R. "The Epic of Gilgamesh, the Bible, and Homer: Some Narrative Parallels." Pp. 7–19 in *Mnemai: Classical Studies in Memory of Karl K. Hulley*. Edited by H. D. Evjen. Chico, CA: Scholars Press, 1984.

Biggs, R. D. *ŠÀ.ZI.GA. Ancient Mesopotamian Potency Incantations*. TCS 2. Locust Valley, NY: J. J. Augustin, 1967.

Borger, R. "Das Tempelbau-Ritual K 48+." *ZA* 61 (1971) 72–80.

______. *Handbuch der Keilschriftliteratur*. 3 vols. Berlin: De Gruyter, 1962–75.

Bottéro, J. *L'épopée de Gilgameš*. Paris: Gallimard, 1992.

Bowra, C. M. *Heroic Poetry*. London: Macmillan, 1952. Repr., London: Macmillan, 1964.

Brockington, J. "The Sanskrit Epics." Pp. 116–28 in *The Blackwell Companion to Hinduism*. Edited by G. D. Flood. Oxford: Blackwell, 2003.

Buitenen, J. A. B. van. *The Mahābhārata*, vols. 1–2. Chicago: University of Chicago Press, 1973–75.
Burkert, W. *Greek Religion*. Translated by John Raffan. Cambridge, MA: Harvard University Press, 1985.
———. *The Orientalizing Revolution: Near Eastern Influence on Greek Culture in the Early Archaic Age*. Cambridge, MA: Harvard University Press, 1992.
______. *Structure and History in Greek Mythology and Ritual*. Berkeley: University of California Press, 1979.
Caplice, R. I. *The Akkadian Namburbi Texts: An Introduction*. SANE 1.1. Los Angeles: Undena, 1974.
______. "The Akkadian Text Genre Namburbi." Ph.D. diss., University of Chicago, 1963.
Cassuto, M. D. *A Commentary on the Book of Exodus* [Hebrew]. Jerusalem: Magnes, 1951.
Castellino, G. R. *Two Šulgi Hymns (B, C)*. Studi semitici 42. Rome: Istituto di studi del Vicino Oriente, 1972.
Cavigneaux, A., and F. N. H. Al-Rawi. *Gilgameš et la mort: Textes de Tell Haddad VI*. CM 19. Groningen: Styx, 2000.
Childs, B. S. *The Book of Exodus*. Philadelphia: Westminster, 1974.
Civil, M. "Notes on Sumerian Lexicography, I." *JCS* 20 (1966) 119–24.
Cohen, M. E. "Another Utu Hymn." *ZA* 67 (1977) 1–19.
Cooper, J. S. *The Curse of Agade*. Baltimore: Johns Hopkins University Press, 1983.
Cornford, F. M. *The Origin of Attic Comedy*. London: Arnold, 1914.
Crane, G. *Calypso: Backgrounds and Conventions of the Odyssey*. BKP 191. Frankfurt am Main: Athenäum, 1988.
Dahlmann, J. *Die Genesis des Mahābhārata*. Berlin: Felix L. Dames, 1899.
Daiches, D. *A Study of Literature: For Readers and Critics*. Ithaca, NY: Cornell University Press, 1948.
Dalley, S. *Myths from Mesopotamia: Creation, The Flood, Gilgamesh and Others*. Oxford: Oxford University Press, 1989.
______. "Occasions and Opportunities, I & II." Pp. 1–35 in *The Legacy of Mesopotamia*. Edited by S. Dalley. Oxford: Oxford University Press, 1998.
Davila, J. R. "The Flood Hero as King and Priest." *JNES* 54 (1995) 199–214.
Dhorme, E. "Rituel funéraire assyrien." *RA* 38 (1941) 57–66.
Diakonoff, I. M. Review of F. M. T. de Liagre Böhl, *Het Gilgamesj Epos*, and L. Matouš, *Epos o Gilgamešovi*. *BO* 18 (1961) 63.
Diakonoff, I. M., and N. B. Jankowska. "An Elamite Gilgameš Text from Argištihenele, Urartu (Armavir-blur, 8th century, B.C.)." *ZA* 80 (1990) 102–24.
Dijk, J. J. A. van. "La fête du nouvel an dans une texte de Šulgi." *BO* 11 (1954) 83–88.
Dijk, J. J. A. van, and W. R. Mayer. *Literarische Texte aus Babylon*. Berlin: Akademie-Verlag, 1987.
Durand, J.-M. "Un commentaire à *TDP* I, AO 17661." *RA* 73 (1979) 153–70.
Dyson, R. H., Jr. "A Note on Queen Shub-Ad's 'Onagers.'" *Iraq* 22 (1960) 102–4.
Ebeling, E. *Keilschrifttexte aus Assur religiösen Inhalts*. Leipzig: J. C. Hinrichs, 1915–23.
______. *Tod und Leben nach den Vorstellungen der Babylonier*. Berlin: Walter de Gruyter, 1931.
Ebeling, E., et al. *Literarische Keilschrifttexte aus Assur*. Berlin: Akademie-Verlag, 1953.

Edzard, D. O. *"Gilgameš und Huwawa": Zwei Versionen der sumerischen Zedernwaldepisode nebst einer Edition von Version "B."* Sitzungsberichte der Bayerische Akademie der Wissenschaften, Philosophisch-historische Klasse, 1993–94. Munich: C. H. Beck, 1993.

______. "Kleine Beiträge zum Gilgamesh-Epos." *Or,* n.s., 54 (1985) 46–55.

______. "Mesopotamien: Die Mythologie der Sumerer und Akkader." Pp. 19–139 in vol. 1 of *Wörterbuch der Mythologie.* Edited by H. W. Haussig. Stuttgart: E. Klett, 1965.

Fairservis, W. A. *The Roots of Ancient India: The Archaeology of Early Indian Civilization.* New York: Macmillan, 1971.

Falkenstein, A. "Gilgameš. Nach sumerischen Texten." *RlA* 3:357–63.

Firth, R. *Symbols: Public and Private.* Ithaca, NY: Cornell University Press, 1973.

Fleming, D. E., and S. J. Milstein. *The Buried Foundation of the Gilgamesh Epic: The Akkadian Huwawa Narrative.* CM 39. Leiden: Brill, 2010.

Foster, B. R., ed. *The Epic of Gilgamesh.* New York: Norton, 2001.

Fox, M. V. "The Entertainment Song Genre in Egyptian Literature." Pp. 268–316 in *Egyptological Studies.* Edited by S. Israelit-Groll. ScrHie 28. Jerusalem: Magnes, 1982.

______. "A Study of Antef." *Or,* n.s., 46 (1977) 393–423.

Foxvog, D. A. "Funerary Furnishings in an Early Sumerian Text from Adab." Pp. 67–75 in *Death in Mesopotamia: Papers Read at the XXVIe Rencontre assyriologique internationale.* Edited by B. Alster. Mesopotamia 8. Copenhagen: Akademisk Forlag, 1980.

Frankena, R. "Nouveaux fragments de la sixième tablette de l'épopée de Gilgameš." Pp. 113–22 in *Gilgameš et sa légende.* Edited by P. Garelli. Paris: C. Klincksieck, 1960.

Frayne, D. *Old Babylonian Period (2003–1595* BC*).* RIME 4. Toronto: University of Toronto Press, 1990.

Friedman, M. A. "Israel's Response in Hosea 2:17b: 'You are my husband.'" *JBL* 99 (1980) 199–204.

Gadd, C. J. "The Harran Inscriptions of Nabonidus." *Anatolian Studies* 8 (1958) 35–92.

______. "Some Contributions to the Gilgamesh Epic." *Iraq* 28 (1966) 105–21.

Ganter (Zgoll), A. "Zum Ausgang von *Gilgameš und Huwawa* Version B." *NABU* 1995/2, no. 41.

Gaster, T. H. *The Holy and the Profane: Evolution of Jewish Folkways.* 2nd ed. New York: W. Morrow, 1980.

Gennep, A. van. *The Rites of Passage.* Chicago: University of Chicago Press, 1960.

George, A. R. *The Babylonian Gilgamesh Epic: Introduction, Critical Edition, and Cuneiform Texts.* 2 vols. Oxford: Oxford University Press, 2003.

______. "The Civilizing of Ea-Enkidu: An Unusual Tablet of the Babylonian Gilgameš Epic." *RA* 101 (2007) 59–80.

______. *The Epic of Gilgamesh: A New Translation.* New York: Penguin, 1999.

Gibson, Mc., ed. *Uch Tepe I: Tell Razuk, Tell Ahmed al-Mughir, Tell Ajamat.* Chicago: Oriental Institute of the University of Chicago, 1981.

Graves, R. *The Greek Myths.* 2 vols. Baltimore: Penguin, 1955.

Grayson, A. K., trans. "The Epic of Gilgamesh: Additions to Tablets V–VIII and X." Pp. 503–7 in *ANET.*

Greengus, S. "Old Babylonian Marriage Ceremonies and Rites." *JCS* 20 (1966) 55–72.

______ . "The Old Babylonian Marriage Contract." *JAOS* 89 (1969) 505–32.

Gresseth, G. K. "The Gilgamesh Epic and Homer." *The Classical Journal* 70, no. 4 (1975) 1–18.

Gurney, O. R. "Two Fragments of the Epic of Gilgamesh from Sultantepe." *JCS* 8 (1954) 87–95.

Gurney, O. R., and P. Hulin, eds. *The Sultantepe Tablets*, vol. 2. London: British Institute of Archaeology at Ankara, 1964.

Hallo, W. W. "The Death of Kings: Traditional Historiography in Contextual Perspective." Pp. 148–65 in *Ah, Assyria . . . : Studies in Assyrian History and Ancient Near Eastern Historiography Presented to Hayim Tadmor*. Edited by M. Cogan and I. Ephᶜal. ScrHie 33. Jerusalem: Magnes, 1991.

______ . "Šullanu." *RA* 74 (1980) 94.

Hallo, W. W., and J. J. A. van Dijk. *The Exaltation of Inanna*. Yale Near Eastern Researches 3. New Haven, CT: Yale University Press, 1968.

Harris, R. "Images of Women in the Gilgamesh Epic." Pp. 219–30 in *Lingering over Words: Studies in Ancient Near Eastern Literature in Honor of William L. Moran*. Edited by T. Abusch, J. Huehnergard, and P. Steinkeller. HSS 37. Atlanta: Scholars Press, 1990.

______ . "Independent Women in Ancient Mesopotamia?" Pp. 145–56 in *Women's Earliest Records: From Ancient Egypt and Western Asia*. Ed. B. S. Lesko. BJS 166. Atlanta: Scholars Press, 1989.

______ . "The *Naditu* Woman." Pp. 106–35 in *Studies Presented to A. Leo Oppenheim*. Edited by R. D. Biggs and J. A. Brinkman. Chicago: Oriental Institute of the University of Chicago, 1964.

Haupt, P. *Das babylonische Nimrodepos*. Assyriologische Bibliothek 3. Leipzig: J. C. Hinrichs, 1884–91.

Hecker, K. "Das akkadische Gilgamesch-Epos." Pp. 646–744 in *Mythen und Epen II*. Edited by K. Hecker et al. *TUAT* 3.4. Gütersloh: G. Mohn, 1994.

______ . *Untersuchungen zur akkadischen Epik*. AOAT, Sonderreihe 8. Kevelaer: Butzon und Bercker; Neukirchen-Vluyn: Neukirchener Verlag, 1974.

Heimpel, W. "Jagd. A. Philologisch." *RlA* 5:234–36.

Hesiod. *The Works and Days*. Pp. 15–118 in *Hesiod: The Works and Days, Theogony, The Shield of Herakles*. Translated by R. Lattimore. Ann Arbor: University of Michigan Press, 1959.

Heubeck, A., and A. Hoekstra. *A Commentary on Homer's Odyssey*. 3 vols. Oxford: Clarendon Press, 1988–92.

Hoffner, H. "The Arzana House." Pp. 113–22 in *Anatolian Studies Presented to Hans Gustav Güterbock*. Edited by K. Bittel, P. H. J. Houwink ten Cate, and E. Reiner. Istanbul: Nederlands Historisch-Archaeologisch Institut in Het Nabije Oosten, 1974.

Homer. *The Iliad*. Translated by R. Fitzgerald. Garden City, NY: Anchor, 1974.

______ . *The Odyssey*. Translated by R. Lattimore. New York: Harper & Row, 1975.

Huntington, R., and P. Metcalf. *Celebrations of Death: The Anthropology of Mortuary Ritual*. Cambridge: Cambridge University Press, 1979.

Hurowitz, V. A. "An Old Babylonian Bawdy Ballad." Pp. 543–58 in *Solving Riddles and Untying Knots: Biblical, Epigraphic, and Semitic Studies in Honor of Jonas C. Greenfield.* Edited by Z. Zevit, S. Gitin, and M. Sokoloff. Winona Lake, IN: Eisenbrauns, 1995.

Jacobsen, T. "The Gilgamesh Epic: Romantic and Tragic Vision." Pp. 231–49 in *Lingering over Words: Studies in Ancient Near Eastern Literature in Honor of William L. Moran.* Edited by T. Abusch, J. Huehnergard, and P. Steinkeller. HSS 37. Atlanta: Scholars Press, 1990.

______. *The Treasures of Darkness: A History of Mesopotamian Religion.* New Haven, CT: Yale University Press, 1976.

Jastrow, M., Jr., and A. T. Clay. *An Old Babylonian Version of the Gilgamesh Epic.* YOR 4.3. New Haven, CT: Yale University Press, 1920.

Jensen, P. *Assyrisch-babylonische Mythen und Epen.* Keilinschriftliche Bibliothek 6.1. Berlin: Reuther & Reichard, 1900.

______. Review of A. Ungnad and H. Gressmann, *Das Gilgamesch-Epos. ZDMG* 67 (1913) 503–29.

Jeremias, A. *Izdubar-Nimrod: Eine altbabylonische Heldensage, nach den Keilschriftfragmenten Dargestellt.* Leipzig: B. G. Teubner, 1891.

Kilmer, A. Draffkorn. "A Note on an Overlooked Word-Play in the Akkadian Gilgamesh." Pp. 128–32 in *Zikir Šumim: Assyriological Studies Presented to F. R. Kraus on the Occasion of his Seventieth Birthday.* Edited by G. van Driel et al. Leiden: Brill, 1982.

Kirk, G. S. *Myth: Its Meaning and Functions in Ancient and Other Cultures.* Cambridge: Cambridge University Press; Berkeley: University of California Press, 1970.

Klein, J. "The Assumed Human Origin of Divine Dumuzi: A Reconsideration." Pp. 1121–34 in part 2 of *Language in the Ancient Near East,* vol. 1 of *Proceedings of the 53e Rencontre Assyriologique Internationale.* Edited by L. Kogan et al. Winona Lake, IN: Eisenbrauns, 2010.

______. "A New Look at the 'Oppression of Uruk' Episode in the Gilgameš Epic." Pp. 187–201 in *Riches Hidden in Secret Places: Ancient Near Eastern Studies in Memory of Thorkild Jacobsen.* Edited by T. Abusch. Winona Lake, IN: Eisenbrauns, 2002.

______. *The Royal Hymns of Shulgi King of Ur: Man's Quest for Immortal Fame.* Transactions of the American Philosophical Society 71.7. Philadelphia: American Philosophical Society, 1981.

______. "Šulgi and Gilgameš: Two Brother-Peers (Šulgi O)." Pp. 271–92 in *Kramer Anniversary Volume: Cuneiform Studies in Honor of Samuel Noah Kramer.* Edited by B. L. Eichler, J. W. Heimerdinger, and Å. W. Sjöberg. AOAT 25. Kevelaer: Butzon & Bercker, 1976.

______. *Three Šulgi Hymns: Sumerian Royal Hymns Glorifying King Šulgi of Ur.* Ramat-Gan: Bar-Ilan University Press, 1981.

Köcher, F. *Die babylonisch-assyrische Medizin in Texten und Untersuchungen.* Berlin: De Gruyter, 1963–.

Komoróczy, G. "Akkadian Epic Poetry and Its Sumerian Sources." *Acta Antiqua Academiae Scientiarum Hungaricae* 23 (1975) 41–63.

Kovacs, M. G., trans. *The Epic of Gilgamesh.* Stanford, CA: Stanford University Press, 1989.

Kramer, S. N. "The Death of Ur-Nammu and His Descent to the Netherworld." *JCS* 21 (1967 [1969]) 104–22.

______ . *From the Poetry of Sumer: Creation, Glorification, Adoration.* Berkeley: University of California Press, 1979.

______ . *History Begins at Sumer.* 3rd rev. ed. Philadelphia: University of Pennsylvania Press, 1981.

Kübler-Ross, E., ed. *Death: The Final Stage of Growth.* Englewood Cliffs, NJ: Prentice-Hall, 1975.

Labat, R., et al. *Les religions du Proche-Orient asiatique: Textes babyloniens, ougaritiques, hittites.* Paris: Fayard-Denoël, 1970.

Lackenbacher, S. "Note sur l'*ardat-lilî*." *RA* 65 (1971) 119–54.

Lambert, W. G. *Babylonian Wisdom Literature.* Oxford: Clarendon Press, 1960. Repr., Winona Lake, IN: Eisenbrauns, 1996.

______ . "Gilgamesh in Religious, Historical and Omen Texts and the Historicity of Gilgamesh." Pp. 39–56 in *Gilgameš et sa légende.* Edited by P. Garelli. Paris: Klincksieck, 1960.

______ . "The Hymn to the Queen of Nippur." Pp. 173–218 in *Zikir Šumim: Assyriological Studies Presented to F. R. Kraus on the Occasion of his Seventieth Birthday.* Edited by G. van Driel et al. Leiden: Brill, 1982.

______ . "The Theology of Death." Pp. 53–66 in *Death in Mesopotamia: Papers Read at the XXVIe Rencontre assyriologique internationale.* Edited by B. Alster. Mesopotamia 8. Copenhagen: Akademisk Forlag, 1980.

Le Breton, L. "The Early Periods at Susa, Mesopotamian Relations." *Iraq* 19 (1957) 79–124.

Levy, G. R. *The Sword from the Rock: An Investigation into the Origins of Epic Literature and the Development of the Hero.* London: Faber and Faber, 1953.

Lewis, B. *The Sargon Legend.* ASOR Dissertation Series 4. Cambridge, MA: American Schools of Oriental Research, 1980.

Lewis, T. J. *Cults of the Dead in Ancient Israel and Ugarit.* HSM 39. Atlanta: Scholars Press, 1989.

Lichtheim, M. *The New Kingdom.* Vol. 2 of *Ancient Egyptian Literature.* Berkeley: University of California Press, 1976.

______ . *The Old and Middle Kingdoms.* Vol. 1 of *Ancient Egyptian Literature.* Berkeley: University of California Press, 1973.

______ . "The Songs of the Harpers." *JNES* 4 (1945) 178–212.

Liverani, M. "The Ideology of the Assyrian Empire." Pp. 297–317 in *Power and Propaganda: A Symposium on Ancient Empires.* Edited by M. T. Larsen. Mesopotamia 7. Copenhagen: Akademisk Forlag, 1979.

Lord, A. B. "Gilgamesh and Other Epics." Pp. 371–80 in *Lingering over Words: Studies in Ancient Near Eastern Literature in Honor of William L. Moran.* Edited by T. Abusch, J. Huehnergard, and P. Steinkeller. HSS 37. Atlanta: Scholars Press, 1990.

Luckenbill, D. D. *The Annals of Sennacherib.* OIP 2. Chicago: University of Chicago Press, 1924.

Lüders, H. "Die Sage von Ṛśyaśṛṅga." *Nachrichten der Akademie der Wissenschaften in Göttingen, Philologisch-historiche Klasse* (1897) 87–135.

Mallowan, M. E. L. "The Early Dynastic Period in Mesopotamia." Pp. 238–314 in *The Early History of the Ancient Near East.* Edited by I. E. S. Edwards, C. J. Gadd, and N. G. L. Hammond. Vol. 1, pt. 2, of *The Cambridge Ancient History.* 3rd ed. Cambridge: Cambridge University Press, 1971.

Maul, S. M. "Der Kneipenbesuch als Heilverfahren." Paper presented at the 38th Rencontre assyriologique internationale. Paris, 1991.

Mayer, W. R. *Untersuchungen zur Formensprache der babylonischen "Gebetsbeschwörungen."* Studia Pohl, Series Maior 5. Rome: Biblical Institute, 1976.

McCarter, P. K., Jr. *II Samuel: A New Translation with Introduction, Notes, and Commentary.* AB 9. Garden City, NY: Doubleday, 1984.

Meissner, B. *Ein altbabylonisches Fragment des Gilgamosepos.* MVAG 7.1. Berlin: Peiser, 1902.

Mekilta de-Rabbi Ishmael. Edited by J. Z. Lauterbach. 3 vols. Philadelphia: Jewish Publication Society of America, 1933–35.

Mekhilta d'Rabbi Šimʿon b. Jochai. Edited by J. N. Epstein and E. Z. Melamed. Jerusalem: Meqitse Nirdamim, 1955.

Millard, A. R. "Gilgamesh X: A New Fragment." *Iraq* 26 (1964) 99–105.

Moorey, P. R. S. "Cemetery A at Kish: Grave Groups and Chronology." *Iraq* 32 (1970) 86–128.

______ . *Kish Excavations, 1923–1933.* Oxford: Clarendon Press, 1978.

______ . "A Re-consideration of the Excavations on Tell Ingharra (East Kish), 1923–33." *Iraq* 28 (1966) 18–51.

______ . *Ur 'of the Chaldees': A Revised and Updated Edition of Sir Leonard Woolley's "Excavations at Ur."* Ithaca, NY: Cornell University Press; London: The Herbert Press, 1982.

Moran, W. L. "The Gilgamesh Epic: A Masterpiece from Ancient Mesopotamia." Pp. 2327–36 in vol. 4 of *Civilizations of the Ancient Near East.* Edited by J. M. Sasson. New York: Scribner, 1995.

______ . "Ovid's *Blanda Voluptas* and the Humanization of Enkidu." *JNES* 50 (1991) 121–27.

______ . "Ut-napishtim Revisited." *New York Times Book Review*, November 11, 1984, 13–14.

Nagy, G. *The Best of the Achaeans: Concepts of the Hero in Archaic Greek Poetry.* Baltimore: Johns Hopkins University Press, 1979.

Nilsson, M. P. *The Mycenaean Origin of Greek Mythology.* Berkeley: University of California Press, 1932. Repr., New York: Norton, 1963.

Ong, W. J. *Orality and Literacy: The Technologizing of the Word.* London: Methuen, 1982. Repr., London: Routledge, 2002.

Oppenheim, A. L. "Mesopotamian Mythology II." *Or*, n.s., 17 (1948) 17–58.

———, trans. "The Mother of Nabonidus." Pp. 560–62 in *ANET.*

Page, D. *Folktales in Homer's Odyssey.* Cambridge, MA: Harvard University Press, 1973.

______ . *The Homeric Odyssey.* Oxford: Clarendon Press, 1955.

Panaino, A. "Between Mesopotamia and India: Some Remarks about the Unicorn Cycle in Iran." Pp. 149–79 in *Mythology and Mythologies: Methodological Approaches to Intercultural Influences. Proceedings of the Second Annual Symposium of the Assyrian and Babylonian Intellectual Heritage Project Held in Paris, October 4–7, 1999.* Edited by R. M. Whiting. Melammu Symposia 2. Helsinki: Neo-Assyrian Text Corpus, 2001.

Parpola, S. "The Assyrian Tree of Life: Tracing the Origins of Jewish Monotheism and Greek Philosophy." *JNES* 52 (1993) 161–208.

______ . "Cultural Parallels between India and Mesopotamia: Preliminary Considerations." *Studia Orientalia* 70 (1993) 57–64.

Paul, S. M. *Studies in the Book of the Covenant*. Leiden: Brill, 1970.

Pauly, E. "The Legend of Ṛśyaśṛṅga as a Danish Opera." *Indologica Taurinensia* 14 (1987–88) 303–12.

Pingree, D. "Legacies in Astronomy and Celestial Omens." Pp. 125–38 in *The Legacy of Mesopotamia*. Edited by S. Dalley. Oxford: Oxford University Press, 1998.

Pope, M. H. "The Cult of the Dead at Ugarit." Pp. 159–79 in *Ugarit in Retrospect: Fifty Years of Ugarit and Ugaritic*. Edited by G. D. Young. Winona Lake, IN: Eisenbrauns, 1981.

______ . *Song of Songs: A New Translation with Introduction and Commentary*. AB 7C. Garden City, NY: Doubleday, 1977.

Postgate, J. N., and P. J. Watson. "Excavations in Iraq, 1977–78." *Iraq* 41 (1979) 141–81.

"A Praise Poem of Šulgi (Šulgi B)." *The Electronic Text Corpus of Sumerian Literature*, 2.4.2.02. http://etcsl.orinst.ox.ac.uk/.

Renger, J. "Gilg. P ii 32 [PBS 10/3]." *RA* 66 (1972) 190.

Rohde, E. *Psyche: The Cult of Souls and Belief in Immortality among the Greeks*. Translated by W. B. Hillis from the 8th German edition. London: K. Paul, Trench, Trubner; New York: Harcourt, Brace, 1925.

Sallaberger, W. *Das Gilgamesch-Epos: Mythos, Werk und Tradition*. Munich: Beck, 2008.

Schauss, H. *The Lifetime of a Jew throughout the Ages of Jewish History*. New York: Union of American Hebrew Congregations, 1950.

Scheindlin, R. P. *Wine, Women, and Death: Medieval Hebrew Poems on the Good Life*. Philadelphia: Jewish Publication Society, 1986.

Schlinghoff, D. "Die Einhorn-Legende." *Christiana Albertina: Forschungen und Berichte aus der Christian-Albrechts-Universität zu Kiel* 11 (1971) 51–64.

______ . "The Unicorn: Origin and Migrations of an Indian Legend." Pp. 292–307 in *German Scholars on India: Contributions to Indian Studies*. Edited by the Cultural Dept. of the Embassy of the Federal Republic of Germany. New Delhi: Chowkhamba Sanskrit Series Office, 1973.

Schott, A. *Das Gilgamesch-Epos*. Neu herausgegeben von W. von Soden. Stuttgart: Reclam, 1988.

______ . "Zu meiner Übersetzung des Gilgameš-Epos." *ZA* 42 (1934) 92–143.

Schott, A., and W. von Soden. *Das Gilgamesch Epos*. Stuttgart: Reclam, 1970.

Seux, M.-J. *Hymnes et prières aux dieux de Babylonie et d'Assyrie*. Paris: Éditions du Cerf, 1976.

Shaffer, A. *Sumerian Sources of Tablet XII of the Epic of Gilgameš*. Ann Arbor, MI: University Microfilms, 1963.

Smith, B. Herrnstein. *Poetic Closure: A Study of How Poems End*. Chicago: University of Chicago Press, 1968.

Soden, W. von. *Akkadisches Handwörterbuch*. 3 vols. Wiesbaden: Harrassowitz, 1959–81.

______ . "Aus einen Ersatzopferritual für den assyrischen Hof." *ZA* 45 (1939) 42–61.

______ . "Beiträge zum Verständnis des babylonischen Gilgameš-Epos." *ZA* 53 (1959) 209–35.

______. "Bemerkungen zu den von Ebeling in *Tod und Leben* Band I bearbeiteten Texten." *ZA* 43 (1936) 251–76.

Soden, W. von, and W. Röllig. *Das akkadische Syllabar*. 4th ed. Rome: Pontificio Istituto Biblico, 1991.

Sommer, B. "Reflecting on Moses: The Redaction of Numbers 11." *JBL* 118 (1999) 601–24.

Sourvinou-Inwood, C. *"Reading" Greek Death: To the End of the Classical Period*. Oxford: Clarendon Press, 1995.

Speiser, E. A., trans. "The Epic of Gilgamesh." Pp. 60–99 in *ANET*.

______. "Gilgamesh VI 40." *JCS* 12 (1958) 41.

Spronk, K. *Beatific Afterlife in Ancient Israel and in the Ancient Near East*. AOAT 219. Kevelaer: Butzon & Bercker; Neukirchen-Vluyn: Neukirchener Verlag, 1986.

Steinkeller, P. "Early Dynastic Burial Offerings in Light of the Textual Evidence." Paper presented at the annual meeting of the American Oriental Society. San Francisco, 1980.

Sternberg, M. *The Poetics of Biblical Narrative: Ideological Literature and the Drama of Reading*. Bloomington: University of Indiana Press, 1985.

Strawn, B. A. *What Is Stronger than a Lion? Leonine Image and Metaphor in the Hebrew Bible and the Ancient Near East*. OBO 212. Fribourg: Academic Press; Göttingen: Vandenhoeck & Ruprecht, 2005.

Sukthankar, V. S., ed. *The Āraṇyakaparvan*, parts 1–2. Vols. 3–4 of *The Mahābhārata*. Poona: Bhandarkar Oriental Research Institute, 1942.

Tanakh: A New Translation of the Holy Scriptures according to the Traditional Hebrew Text. Philadelphia: Jewish Publication Society, 1985.

Thompson, R. Campbell. *The Epic of Gilgamesh: Text, Transliteration, and Notes*. Oxford: Clarendon Press, 1930.

Tigay, J. H. *The Evolution of the Gilgamesh Epic*. Philadelphia: University of Pennsylvania Press, 1982.

Tournay, R. J., and A. Shaffer. *L'épopée de Gilgamesh*. Paris: Éditions du Cerf, 1994.

Trümpelman, L. "Jagd. B. Archäologisch." *RlA* 5:236–38.

Turner, V. *The Forest of Symbols: Aspects of Ndembu Ritual*. Ithaca, NY: Cornell University Press, 1967.

Vas[s]ilkov, Y. V. "Zemledel'českij mif v drevneindijskom epose: Skazanie o Riš'jašringe." Pp. 99–133 in *Literatura i kultura drevnej i srednevekovoj Indii*. Moscow: Nauka, 1979.

Veldhuis, N. "The Solution of the Dream: A New Interpretation of Bilgames' Death." *JCS* 53 (2001) 133–48.

Vidal-Naquet, P. "The Black Hunter and the Origin of the Athenian *Ephebia*." Pp. 106–28 in *The Black Hunter: Forms of Thought and Forms of Society in the Greek World*. Translated by A. Szegedy-Maszak. Baltimore: Johns Hopkins University Press, 1986.

Vogelzang, M. E. *Bin šar dadmē: Edition and Analysis of the Akkadian Anzu Poem*. Groningen: Styx, 1988.

Wallace, A. F. C. *Religion: An Anthropological View*. New York: Random House, 1966.

Watanabe, C. E. *Animal Symbolism in Mesopotamia: A Contextual Approach*. Wiener offene Orientalistik 1. Vienna: Institut für Orientalistik der Universität Wien, 2002.

Watson, W. G. E. *Classical Hebrew Poetry: A Guide to Its Techniques*. JSOTSup 26. Sheffield, UK: JSOT Press, 1984.

Webster, T. B. L. *From Mycenae to Homer*. London: Methuen, 1964.

Weidner, E. *Bilinguen, mythologische Texte, medizinische Texte, Omina*. Keilschrifturkunden aus Boghazköi 4. Berlin: Akademie-Verlag, 1922.

Weiher, E. von. "Ein Fragment des Gilgameš-Epos aus Uruk." *ZA* 62 (1972) 222–29.

Weissert, E. "Royal Hunt and Royal Triumph in a Prism Fragment of Ashurbanipal (82–5-22,2)." Pp. 339–58 in *Assyria 1995: Proceedings of the 10th Anniversary Symposium of the Neo-Assyrian Text Corpus Project, Helsinki, September 7–11, 1995*. Edited by S. Parpola and R. Whiting. Helsinki: Neo-Assyrian Text Corpus Project, 1997.

Wente, E. F. "Egyptian 'Make Merry' Songs Reconsidered." *JNES* 21 (1962) 118–28.

West, E. B. "The Transformation of Ṛśyaśṛṅga: Toward a Comparative Approach." Pp. 637–62 in *Gazing on the Deep: Ancient Near Eastern and Other Studies in Honor of Tzvi Abusch*. Edited by J. Stackert, B. N. Porter, and D. P. Wright. Bethesda, MD: CDL Press, 2010.

West, M. L. *The East Face of Helicon: West Asiatic Elements in Greek Poetry and Myth*. Oxford: Clarendon Press, 1997.

Westenholz, J. G. "A Forgotten Love Song." Pp. 415–25 in *Language, Literature, and History: Philological and Historical Studies Presented to Erica Reiner*. Edited by F. Rochberg-Halton. AOS 67. New Haven, CT: American Oriental Society, 1987.

Whitman, C. H. *Homer and the Heroic Tradition*. Cambridge, MA: Harvard University Press, 1958.

Wilcke, C. "Politische Opposition nach sumerischen Quellen: Der Konflict zwischen Königtum und Ratsversammlung: Literaturwerke als politische Tendenzschriften." Pp. 37–65 in *La voix de l'opposition en Mesopotamie: Colloque organisé par l'Institut des Hautes Études de Belgique, 19 et 20 mars 1973*. Edited by A. Finet. Brussels: Institut des Hautes Études, 1975.

Wilhelm, G. "Neue akkadische Gilgameš-Fragmente aus Ḫattusa." *ZA* 78 (1988) 99–121.

Williams, C. A. *Oriental Affinities of the Legend of the Hairy Anchorite*, parts 1–2. 2 vols. UISLL 10.2 and 11.4. Urbana: University of Illinois Press, 1925–26.

Wilson, J. A., trans. "Pharaoh as a Sportsman." Pp. 243–45 in *ANET*.

Wilson, J. R. "The Gilgamesh Epic and the Iliad." *Echos du Monde Classique / Classical Views* 30, n.s. 5, no. 1 (1986) 25–41.

Winternitz, M. *A History of Indian Literature*. 3 vols. Calcutta: University of Calcutta Press, 1962.

Woolley, C. L., et al. *The Royal Cemetery: A Report on the Predynastic and Sargonid Graves Excavated between 1926 and 1931*. UE 2. London: Trustees of the British Museum and the Museum of the University of Pennsylvania, 1934.

Xenophon, *Scripta Minora*. Translated by E. G. Marchant. LCL. London: Heinemann; Cambridge, MA: Harvard University Press, 1925.

Zarins, J. "The Domesticated Equidae of Third Millennium B.C. Mesopotamia." *JCS* 30 (1978) 3–17.

Index of Citations

The Old Babylonian tablets are cited according to the line numbering used in my original publications, with George's numbering, when it differs, added in brackets. Citations of the Standard Babylonian version follow George's numbering.

1. Old Babylonian Version

Sippar tablet = Meissner fragment + Millard fragment

Meissner fragment

i 7′–8′	78 n. 46
i 8′	81 n. 48
ii	70
ii–iii	58–88, 89–107, 108–118
ii 1′ff.	65
ii 1′–13′	8
ii 4′–9′	87
ii 5′	102
ii 5′–8′	106
ii 5′–9′	62 n. 8, 91, 92, 93–100, 116
ii 10′	78, 78 n. 42, 78 n. 44, 81 n. 48, 114
ii 10′–13′	67
ii 11′	158
ii 12′–13′	67, 81 n. 48, 84 n. 54, 87, 107
ii 14′–iii 13	133–34
iii 1–2	78 n. 46, 80
iii 1–5	72, 113
iii 2	81 n. 48
iii 2–5	106
iii 2–14	63
iii 3–5	80
iii 6–9	62 n. 8, 72, 91, 92, 100–106, 113, 115–16
iii 6–13	87
iii 10	66
iii 10–11	103 n. 16
iii 10–13	61, 61 n. 4, 72, 113
iii 11	66
iii 12	66, 72, 75, 75 n. 37, 105
iii 13	66, 75 n. 38, 76, 76 n. 38, 103, 105
iii 14	66 n. 16
iii 14–16	61 n. 2, 61 n. 4, 90–91 n. 2, 110 n. 3
iii 18–21	81 n. 48
iv 6	82 n. 50
iv 12–13	79
iv 13	82 n. 50

Millard fragment

iv 1′ [= Sippar iv 16] 82 n. 50

Pennsylvania Tablet

passim	177, 177–78 n. 2, 213 n. 62
i	154
i 20	76 n. 39
i 32–34	76 n. 39
ii	153, 154

ii 5 [= ii 47] 154 n. 19
ii 8 [= ii 50] 76
ii 31–32 [= ii 73–74] 75, 75 n. 37
ii 32 [= ii 74] 75 n. 37
ii 45–68 154
ii 46–47 190 n. 31
ii 47 155
ii 51ff. 192
ii 53ff. 160 n. 31
ii 54 155
iii 22–27 [= iii 106–111] 62
iii 87–112 190–91
iii 110–118 170 n. 10
iv 162 n. 41
iv–vi 188 n. 26
v 196–199 140
v 200–203 140

Yale Tablet

passim 177–78 n. 2
iii 5–7 [= iii 97–99] 171 n. 13
iv 5ff. [= iv 140ff.] 50
iv 138–150 133

2. Standard Babylonian Version

I 3, 43, 154, 169, 170 n. 10, 174
I–II 177, 177 n. 2
I–XI 54
I 1–28 131, 138
I 5–10 135
I 11 134 n. 7
I 11–23 50, 135
I 12 134 n. 7
I 24–28 139
I 29–34 136
I 29–36 132
I 45–50 140
I 63–74 136
I 76–77 188 n. 26
I 105–112 188–89
I 118–121 145–46, 169, 170
I 135–139 158 n. 28, 164 n. 45
I 140 146 n. 4, 150 n. 13
I 140–145 146
I 142 150 n. 13
I 143 148, 151
I 143–144 150 n. 13
I 143–145 147–148
I 144 149, 150
I 145 150, 153
I 162 150 n. 13
I 162–166 146, 153
I 163 150 n. 13
I 164 148, 148 n. 8, 151
I 164–165 150 n. 13
I 164–166 147–148
I 164b 153
I 165 149, 150, 153
I 165–166 153 n. 18
I 166 150, 153
I 167–170 150 n. 13
I 167–179 152
I 172–177 150 n. 13
I 173 189 n. 28
I 177 189 n. 28
I 178–179 150 n. 13
I 180–194 148–152
I 181–182 147
I 183 153 n. 18, 156
I 187 153, 153 n. 18
I 188–194 152
I 189–190 147
I 189a 153
I 189b–194 153
I 194 76
I 195–198 150
I 195–200 153
I 196–203 155
I 199–200 150
I 201–202 190 n. 30
I 201–203 153
I 205ff. 192
I 207ff. 160 n. 31
I 208 155

I 211	160 n. 31
I 218	160 n. 31
I 226–231	159
I 230–231	159
II	154bis, 174
II 100–115	188 n. 26
II 184–V	168
III 122–123	159
III–V	177 n. 2
IV 140ff.	50
VI	25 n. 35, 29, 29 n. 48, 39 n. 66, 42 n. 68, 43, 44, 46 n. 69, 47, 47 n. 71, 48–50, 51bis, 52, 52 n. 80, 53, 54, 54–55 n. 85, 55, 56, 68 n. 19, 71, 72, 85, 85–86, 86 n. 58, 115, 123, 124, 125, 128 n. 3, 131, 135, 142, 161, 162, 170 n. 11
VI–VII	54 n. 85
VI 1–5	13, 28, 38
VI 1–6	86 n. 58
VI 1–79	11–57
VI 6	13, 36, 38
VI 6–9	141
VI 7–9	21, 27
VI 7–21	13
VI 8	36, 36 n. 62, 38, 44
VI 8–21	21
VI 9–21	38
VI 10–12	21, 21–23
VI 10–17	27
VI 12	16, 21
VI 13	21, 23, 24 n. 33, 27
VI 13–14	24 n. 32, 38 n. 65
VI 13–17	28
VI 13ff.	21
VI 14–17	23–25
VI 15	24 n. 32
VI 15–16	24 n. 33
VI 16	12, 17, 18 n. 13, 20
VI 17	24 n. 33, 25
VI 18–21	25, 27, 28, 45
VI 22–23	13, 38
VI 24–32	13, 13 n. 4, 36bis, 37, 38, 39
VI 24–79	13
VI 24ff.	31 n. 50
VI 26–27	36
VI 27–28	14 n. 6
VI 27–30	14 n. 5
VI 33	37
VI 33–41	13, 13 n. 4, 37bis, 38, 39
VI 34	37 n. 63
VI 35	14, 37 n. 63
VI 36	37, 37 n. 63
VI 37	37 n. 63
VI 38	37 n. 63
VI 39	37 n. 63
VI 40	13 n. 4, 37 n. 63
VI 41	37 n. 63
VI 42	14 n. 7, 32
VI 42–43	14
VI 42–44	13 n. 4
VI 42–79	13, 39
VI 43	14 n. 7
VI 44–45	13 n. 4
VI 45–50	13 n. 4
VI 45ff.	31 n. 50
VI 46	35
VI 46–47	14 n. 7, 141
VI 47	32, 33bis
VI 48	32
VI 48–50	14 n. 7
VI 48–63	45
VI 49	32, 33, 33 n. 56
VI 50	32
VI 51	32
VI 52	32, 33
VI 53	32
VI 54	33
VI 55	32, 33
VI 56	33
VI 57	33bis
VI 58	32
VI 61	32, 33
VI 62–63	32

VI 64 32
VI 64–66 38, 45
VI 67 33, 33 n. 59, 36bis, 38
VI 68 36bis, 36 n. 62, 38
VI 68–69 36
VI 69 38, 38 n. 65
VI 70 38
VI 71–73 36, 38
VI 71–74 36
VI 74 37bis, 38
VI 75 38, 41
VI 76 32, 33
VI 76–78 38
VI 78 32, 38 n. 64
VI 79 14, 32, 40, 40–41
VI 80 38, 41
VI 81ff. 38
VI 89 32
VI 158 159
VI 165–167 47
VII 54–55 n. 85
VII–XI 52, 53, 56, 142
VII 94–99 157
VII 102–131 157
VII 132ff. 157, 162 n. 141
VII 139ff. 24
VII 143 24
VII 146–147 78
VII 148–162 157
VII 162–210 55
VII 193ff. 24, 200
VII 203ff. 50 n. 76
VIII–XI 52
VIII 50–51 22 n. 21
VIII 59 26 n. 36, 70 n. 22
VIII 85ff. 24
VIII 87 24
VIII 90–91 78
IX 82
IX–X 168
IX 1–7 82
IX 9–18 170
X 153, 157, 169
X 4 70
X 5–16 86 n. 58
X 8–9 158, 170
X 13 170
X 15–22 85
X 40–45 158
X 40–52 86 n. 58
X 42–43 158, 170
X 58–60 94–96, 94 n. 4
X 135–137 94 n. 4
X 235–237 94 n. 4
X 319–322 80 n. 47
XI 4, 54, 75 n. 38, 123, 124, 152, 180
XI 1–7 137
XI 212 75 n. 38
XI 215 75 n. 38
XI 219 75 n. 38
XI 253 114–15
XI 253–261 83, 84 n. 53, 115
XI 259–261 84 n. 53
XI 262–267 62
XI 262–270 84 n. 53bis
XI 263 62 n. 6
XI 268–270 84 n. 53
XI 271–272 84, 84 n. 53
XI 273 75 n. 38
XI 273ff. 84 n. 53
XI 319–321 84, 84 n. 53
XI 322–328 84, 84 n. 53
XI 323–328 50, 134, 134 n. 7, 135
XI 323ff. 54
XII 4, 13, 51, 52, 54, 54 n. 84, 54–55 n. 85, 55–57, 122, 123, 124, 125, 128 n. 3, 131, 142, 142 n. 11, 180 n. 5
XII 27–30 50 n. 76
XII 47–50 50 n. 76
XII 51–54 50 n. 76
XII 59–62 50 n. 76
XII 67–70 50 n. 76
XII 89ff. 56

www.ingramcontent.com/pod-product-compliance
Lightning Source LLC
Chambersburg PA
CBHW030314080526
44584CB00012B/567
* 9 7 8 1 5 7 5 0 6 3 4 9 2 *